CANALETTO *in England*

Charles Beddington

with essays by Brian Allen and Francis Russell

CANALETTO *in England*

A Venetian Artist Abroad, 1746–1755

Yale Center for British Art
Dulwich Picture Gallery
Yale University Press, New Haven and London

This book was produced in association with the exhibition
Canaletto in England: A Venetian Artist Abroad, 1746–1755,
co-organized by the Yale Center for British Art and Dulwich Picture Gallery

Exhibition dates:
Yale Center for British Art, New Haven, CT, 19 October – 31 December 2006, and
Dulwich Picture Gallery, London, 24 January – 15 April 2007.

Exhibition curated by Charles Beddington.

Receiving curators:
Julia Marciari Alexander and Angus Trumble (Yale Center for British Art) and
Ian Dejardin (Dulwich Picture Gallery). Exhibition coordinated by Timothy Goodhue
(Yale Center for British Art) and Victoria Norton and Eloise Stewart (Dulwich Picture Gallery).

The exhibition at the Yale Center for British Art is generously supported by an indemnity
from the Federal Council on the Arts and Humanities.

At Dulwich Picture Gallery it is sponsored by the American Friends of Dulwich Picture
Gallery through the generosity of the Arthur and Holly Magill Foundation, the Edith Callam
Memorial Trust, the Elizabeth Cayzer Charitable Trust, the Italian Cultural Institute and an
anonymous donor; and The Friends of Dulwich Picture Gallery.

The indemnity of the exhibition at Dulwich Picture Gallery is provided by HM Government
through the UK Government Indemnity Scheme (administered by the MLA).

Honorary Patron at Dulwich Picture Gallery:
His Excellency Signor Giancarlo Aragona, KCVO,
Italian Ambassador to the United Kingdom

Designed by Derek Birdsall
Typeset by Elsa Birdsall / Omnific
Printed in Italy by Conti Tipocolor
Library of Congress Cataloging-in-Publication Data

Canaletto in England : a Venetian artist abroad, 1746/1755 /
by Charles Beddington.
    p. cm.
Issued in connection with an exhibition co-organized by the
Yale Center for British Art and Dulwich Picture Gallery.
 Includes bibliographical references and index.
 ISBN 0-300-11969-0 (alk. paper)
 1. Canaletto, 1697–1768—Exhibitions. 2. Art patronage—England—
History—18th century—Exhibitions. 3. England—In art—
Exhibitions. I. Canaletto, 1697–1768. II. Beddington, Charles. III. Yale
Center for British Art. IV. Dulwich Picture Gallery.
 ND623.C2A4 2006
 759.5—dc22
                2006017767

Cover illustration:
Westminster Bridge from the North with the Lord Mayor's Procession, 29 October 1746,
1746–47. Cat. no. 23 (detail).
Yale Center for British Art, New Haven, Paul Mellon Collection

Frontispiece: detail of Cat. no. 37

Contents

Directors' Foreword

The ten years that the great Venetian artist Giovanni Antonio Canal, known as Canaletto (1697–1768), spent in England have sometimes been passed over as an intriguing, if not overly significant, footnote to his illustrious career. But those ten years, from 1746, saw Canaletto at the height of his powers; and this exhibition amply demonstrates that the quality of the work he produced was in fact exceptionally high. This should not be a surprise, given that the artist had followed his most lucrative market to England. He had become the darling of the English aristocracy in Italy – no Grand Tour could be considered complete without the purchase of one of the famous Venetian's views – and when the political situation there made it difficult for the English to visit Venice, it cannot have been too difficult a decision for Canaletto to seek his patrons on their native soil. Canaletto lived, apparently quietly, in Silver Street (now called Beak Street), in the heart of what is now Soho. The presence of this giant in its midst seems to have attracted comparatively little notice from the artistic establishment, probably for the simple reason that he did not need to adver-tise to attract customers. Canaletto already had the right contacts, and the letters of recommendation from Venice's most famous British resident, Consul (Joseph) Smith, opened doors to a splendid array of patrons: the Duke of Richmond; the Duke of Norfolk; the Duke of Beaufort; and the future Duke of Northumberland and Earl of Warwick, among others. For these illustrious clients he painted views of their country houses and castles, and many of the works on show in this exhibition remain to this day in the stately homes for which they were commissioned; but he also continued his profitable line in Venetian views and *capricci* – the artist's studio remained for many a small corner of Venice in a foreign land.

Both the exhibition and publication are the result of a longstanding collaboration between two museums – the Yale Center for British Art and Dulwich Picture Gallery – and Charles Beddington, guest curator and author. That the Yale Center should join with Dulwich Picture Gallery to mount this exhibition is appropriate, since both institutions own different versions of Canaletto's view of Old Walton Bridge – classic 'British period' works, where an intensely British picturesque view is captured with the artist's characteristically Italian touch. Canaletto was far too subtle

and sensitive an artist simply to make Britain look Italian, but there was certainly no British artist who could have created quite the airy, light-filled atmosphere that suffuses his renditions of this subject.

Charles Beddington has made the study of Canaletto's English period one of his specialities. There is no-one better qualified to bring this neglected period of the artist's output to life. We are most grateful to him for all his hard and devoted work towards both the exhibition and the beautiful – and definitive – catalogue that accompanies it. He has been ably supported in this endeavour by Professor Brian Allen, and by Francis Russell, who have both con-tributed essays to the publication, complementing Charles's ground-breaking scholarship.

The catalogue has assumed its physical shape thanks to the hard work of a number of individuals. Julia Marciari Alexander, Associate Director of Exhibitions and Publications at the Center, coordinated the publication with Sally Salvesen at Yale University Press. We would like to extend our special thanks to Anna Magliaro, Publications Assistant at the Center, and to Catherine Bowe at Yale University Press, London, for their constant assistance on this project. We have been honoured to work with the award-winning book designer Derek Birdsall and his team at Omnific, who, in concert with Sally have created an impeccable and stunning publication.

At Yale, we would like to thank Julia Marciari Alexander and the Center's Curator of Paintings and Sculpture, Angus Trumble, who worked seamlessly with Charles Beddington and their counterparts at Dulwich Picture Gallery regarding all curatorial matters. Crawford Alexander Mann, doctoral candidate in the History of Art at Yale, and Eleanor Hughes, Postdoctoral Research Associate at the Center, provided crucial research and curatorial assistance. The exhibition has been expertly coordinated by the Center's Registrar, Timothy Goodhue, with assistance from the various members of staff in the Department of Exhibitions and Publications, especially Diane Bowman. Beth Miller, Associate Director for Development and External Affairs, provided critical assistance on contractual matters. As always, the installation and design team at the Center, led by Richard F. Johnson and Lyn Bell Rose, have set the stage at Yale for the work of this extraordinary artist to come alive once again for the twenty-first century visitor.

The exhibition at Yale has been generously supported by an indemnity from the Federal Council on the Arts and Humanities.

At Dulwich, the exhibition was organised in the first instance by the Head of Exhibitions, Victoria Norton; then Eloise Stewart as Acting Head of Exhibitions. Both were ably assisted by Mella Shaw, Acting Exhibitions Officer. The Gallery's previous Director, Desmond Shawe-Taylor, played an active and dynamic role in the early stages of the project.

The show at Dulwich has been made possible by the American Friends of Dulwich Picture Gallery through the generosity of the Arthur and Holly Magill Foundation, the Edith Callam Memorial Trust, the Elizabeth Cayzer Charitable Trust, the Italian Cultural Institute, and an anonymous donor. Once again, the Friends of Dulwich Picture Gallery have provided crucial support.

At Dulwich, we are very honoured that His Excellency Signor Giancarlo Aragona, the Italian Ambassador, should have agreed to stand as the exhibition's Honorary Patron. We thank him and Signora Aragona for their enthusiasm and support. We would also like to thank Anna Somers Cocks and her husband Umberto Allemandi for their tireless activity on our behalf.

An exhibition of this magnitude does not occur without a tremendous amount of back-of-house work in the years before the show opens. We would not have been able to mount *Canaletto in England: A Venetian Artist Abroad, 1746–1755* without the constant assistance of our curatorial colleagues at both the numerous institutions and the private collections that have so generously lent to the show. In particular, however, we must extend our immense gratitude to the private collectors who have parted for such extended lengths of time with those deeply valued objects with which they live. The fruits of the collaboration among all the participants in this ambitious project are themselves the legacy of the internationalism and cultural exchange that lie at the heart of this extraordinary artist's work.

Amy Meyers
Director, Yale Center for British Art

Ian Dejardin
Director, Dulwich Picture Gallery

Curator's acknowledgements

This exhibition stems directly from a month spent as a Fellow at the Yale Center for British Art in September 2000. I remain deeply grateful to all who made my stay in New Haven such an enjoyable one, but above all to Malcolm Warner, who was responsible for encouraging me to apply for a fellowship, and to Patrick McCaughey, both for supporting my application and for subsequently suggesting this exhibition. The idea was turned into reality by Amy Meyers, his successor as Director of the Yale Center for British Art, and by the successive Directors of the Dulwich Picture Gallery, Desmond Shawe-Taylor and Ian Dejardin, over a series of breakfast meetings at the Chesterfield Hotel in London. Near the site of Chesterfield House, the mansion which was the first home of the *capricci* kindly lent by Lord Brabourne (Cat. nos 58 and 59, among the works here exhibited publicly for the first time), the venue could hardly have been more appropriate. This book, and the exhibition it accompanies, should unquestionably be dedicated to Julia Marciari Alexander, the Associate Director of Exhibitions and Publications at the Yale Center for British Art, without whose tireless endeavours, well beyond the call of duty, neither would have seen the light of day.

William A. Coolidge, the last private owner of Cat. no. 69, once wrote 'I always feel that it is part of the obligation that goes with having pictures that they should be seen and appreciated as much as possible', and any undertaking of this kind owes a debt foremost to those who happily feel the same way, and have so generously agreed to be separated for months from their possessions. Crucial assistance in the securing of loans (and of comparative illustrations) has been provided by many friends and colleagues. In this respect the help provided by Henry Wyndham, Alex Bell and Arabella Chandos of Sotheby's, London, deserves a special mention, as does that received from (in alphabetical order) Dawson Carr, Hugo Chapman, Richard Day, Simon Dickinson, Everett Fahy, George Goldner, David Jaffé, David Ker, Alastair Laing, David Mason, James Miller, Hugo Nathan, and Otto Naumann. I am delighted to have met Götz Morgenstern, a true enthusiast, in time to discover that he was the only person outside Japan who knew the whereabouts of the Neave Roman *piazze* (Cat. nos 52, 53), which otherwise would not be in the exhibition. Viola Pemberton-Pigott kindly looked at the back of Cat. no. 50 for me.

My wife Amanda produced two wonderful sons during the preparation of the exhibition (the elder of whom, Freddie, learned the word 'picture' at a surprisingly early age) and should have received considerably more support than I was able to provide; she is owed a particular debt of thanks for her patience while I was absent in the eighteenth century.

Charles Beddington

CANALETTO IN ENGLAND

Charles Beddington

Figure 1
Venice: The Riva degli Schiavoni, looking West, c. 1736, oil on canvas, 49⅝ × 80½ in. (126.2 × 204.6 cm.).
Sir John Soane's Museum, London

Giovanni Antonio Canal, known as Canaletto (1697–1768), the greatest of the Italian eighteenth-century view painters, was not a keen traveller. In contrast with his contemporary and rival Antonio Joli (*c.* 1700–1777), who travelled extensively throughout Italy and Sicily, as well as visiting Spain, France, Germany and England, Canaletto seems to have left his native city on only three occasions. A visit to Rome in 1719–20, when he was in his early twenties, in order to assist his father in the production of stage sets for operas, was particularly significant, as it was there that he was first inspired to draw and paint his surroundings and consequently, in his own words, 'solemnly excommunicated the theatre', as we are informed by Antonio Maria Zanetti the younger.[1]

By the end of the 1720s Canaletto had established himself as the leading provider of Venetian views to foreign, mostly British, visitors to the city and indeed to a number of English patrons who never saw the city itself. In this he received considerable help from Joseph Smith (*c.* 1674–1770), an English merchant who had settled in Venice *c.* 1700 and was to serve as British Consul in the years 1744–60. Smith began in the early 1720s to form his unrivalled collection of Canaletto's paintings and drawings, which remains almost intact in the British Royal Collection following its sale to King George III in 1762. By the end of the 1720s Smith had adopted an equally significant role as the leading agent for the sale of the painter's work to British patrons.

Throughout the 1730s Canaletto was kept fully occupied satisfying the intense demand for Venetian views, many of them commissioned through Smith. That decade saw the production of the series of twenty-four views – two large and the remainder of a now standard small size – painted *c.* 1733–6 for the 4th Duke of Bedford and still owned by his descendant at Woburn Abbey, and a series of twenty small views painted immediately afterwards for the Duke's brother-in-law, the 3rd Duke of Marlborough, now scattered in private collections, as well as such masterpieces as *The Doge visiting the Church and Scuola di San Rocco* (London, National Gallery)[2] and *The Riva degli Schiavoni, looking West* (Fig. 1; London, Sir John Soane's Museum)[3], the most copied of all Canaletto's views.

By contrast, Canaletto's activity in the 1740s is far from predictable. In 1742 he again left Venice for the *terra firma*, apparently for only the second time. Accompanied by his nephew and most able pupil Bernardo Bellotto (1722–80),

he made drawings of Dolo and Padua, several of which would eventually be used for paintings. More immediately, some were used as the basis for etchings, a medium which held a brief but fruitful fascination for the artist in the first half of the 1740s but seems not to have concerned him at any other time. Bellotto's visit to Rome in 1742 inspired Canaletto to return to that city as the subject-matter for paintings for the first time since about 1720, notably in six large canvases in the British Royal Collection, a set of five upright views of 1742 and a horizontal view of the Colosseum of 1743.[4] Those were painted for Smith, as were thirteen *capriccio* overdoors, nine of which remain in the British Royal Collection and three are in private collections, which are his first *capricci* since the first half of the 1720s.[5] All the Roman views are signed and dated, as are seven Venetian views of 1743–4, and six of the overdoors; a further two of the overdoors are signed. Other than in the years 1742–4 Canaletto seems to have felt no need to sign his paintings between 1723 and 1754, and this may represent a response to the precocious talent of his nephew Bellotto.

All this diversification of subject-matter and adoption of new media demonstrate to what degree in the first half of the 1740s Canaletto felt the need for new challenges after two decades of concentrating on Venetian views. This may well have been one factor which determined his decision to transfer his studio to London for an extended period from May 1746. Another reason usually regarded as fundamental was the discouragement offered to potential travellers on the Continent by the War of the Austrian Succession (1740–8), which spread into Italy in 1742. It may also be noted that both Canaletto's view-painter nephews emigrated shortly after their uncle's departure for England, Bernardo Bellotto to Dresden in 1747 (taking up an invitation declined by Canaletto, according to Mariette)[6] and Pietro Bellotti[7] to Toulouse, probably in 1747/8. This might seem a curious decision, given that competition in the Venetian view-painting market was at an all-time low (Canaletto's most able rival, Michele Marieschi, had died prematurely in 1743), but would be explained by a paucity of clients. 'Of late few persons travel to Italy from hence during the wars', wrote George Vertue in his notebook in October 1746. If, however, the war was an important factor for Canaletto as is sometimes maintained, it remains to be established why he did not return home immediately on the signing of the Treaty of Aix-la-Chapelle in October 1748.

Vertue's notebooks are a prime source of information on the London art world in the period 1713–54, and the five paragraphs devoted to Canaletto provide by far the most important contemporary insights into his activity in England.[8] Vertue tells us that the artist was 'persuaded to it by Signor Amiconi History painter at his return to Venice coud best acquainted him with his success here, and also of the prospects he might make of Views of the Thames at London'. The figure painter Jacopo Amigoni had spent a decade in England 1729–39; Vertue informs us that when he left England, in August 1739, 'he was about publishing a Sett of prints of Views from pictures of Canalletti's [–] had ingravers in his house'.[9] Amigoni was but one of the more recent of a succession of prominent Venetian painters who had found visits to England profitable. Perhaps the most relevant precursor was the Modenese view painter Antonio Joli, who, having been in Venice in the 1730s, moved to London in 1744 and remained there until 1749. Amigoni's recommendation that Canaletto might make views of the Thames was particularly pertinent, to the point that one wonders if his arrival at a moment when Westminster Bridge was nearing completion was coincidental.

Canaletto arrived in England in May 1746. As Vertue informs us,

Latter end of May came to London from Venice the Famous Painter of Views Cannalletti … of Venice, the Multitude of his works done abroad for English noblemen & Gentlemen has procured him great reputation & his great merrit & excellence in that way, he is much esteemed and no doubt but what Views and works He doth here, will give the same satisfaction — though many persons already have so many of his paintings.

There he was to remain for nine years, except for an eight-month return to Venice in 1750–1. Here again our most helpful source is Vertue, who recorded in August or early September 1751 that the painter had recently 'made a Tour to his own country at Venice for some affairs there – in 8 months coming and going'. While we know that he attended a meeting in Venice on 8 March 1751, he was certainly back in London by 30 July and possibly by 24 May.

Vertue's implication that Canaletto's first English period lasted for four years is corroborated by another contemporary source, Stefano Orlandi, whose *Abecedario*, published in 1753, tells us that

Figure 2
Joseph Wilton, *Thomas Hollis*, c. 1762, marble,
height: 26 in. (66 cm). Private Collection, on loan to the
National Portrait Gallery, London (exhibited at Dulwich only)

*He made a voyage to London, where he remained for four years and
continually had opportunity from the gentlemen there to produce
new pieces from his industrious brush. He returned to his homeland
where he currently remains. He brought with him various sketches
of views and of the most notable sites of that large city, which it is
hoped that, at his convenience, he will want to consign to canvas.
Now he is newly returned to London.*[10]

That Canaletto interrupted his highly successful years in
London with a return to his native city is also recorded by
Zanetti[11] and, in almost identical words, by Mariette. The
only errant voice is that of Pietro Gradenigo, who noted on 28
July 1753 that 'Antonio Canaletto of Venice, the celebrated
view painter, [has] returned from England to his homeland',[12] for which the only satisfactory explanation is that the
news took nearly three years to reach Gradenigo.

It has long been presumed that Canaletto left England in
1755, shortly after completing his second view of *Old Walton
Bridge* and the drawing thereof (Cat. nos 38, 39; both Yale
Center for British Art), apparently signed and dated to that
year on the reverse, and thus the last record of the artist's
presence in England. Until recently there was, however, no
evidence of his renewed activity in Venice before 1760, the
date recently found on the reverse of *The Bucintoro returning to
the Molo on Ascension Day* (Dulwich Picture Gallery),[13] and
the first mention of him there was of 1761.[14] Such evidence
has recently been uncovered and published by Federico
Montecuccoli degli Erri in the form of three documents
establishing Canaletto's presence in Venice on 12 December
1755.[15]

Vertue may well not have been alone among his contemporaries in wondering how Canaletto would fare in England,
since 'many persons already have so many of his paintings'.
Such scepticism was, however, to prove misplaced, as the
painter must have been as busy in England as he ever was
in Venice. He attracted a number of highly useful new
clients, notably the 9th Duke of Norfolk,[16] the 4th Earl of
Chesterfield, the 5th Lord King and Thomas Hollis, all of
whom commissioned groups of three or more paintings.
Canaletto was fortunate to be on hand in London at the
moment when the newly completed Norfolk House and
Chesterfield House were in need of decoration (see Cat. nos
60–62 and 58, 59 respectively). The circumstances of King's
commission, the largest of the decorative schemes executed by
the painter in England (see Cat. nos 69–71), are unknown

and, despite the date 1754 on one of the canvases, only recently
has the 5th Lord King, rather than either of his elder brothers,
emerged as the probable patron. Thomas Hollis's set of six
views must have been the last substantial commission
executed by Canaletto in England; four of the paintings are
recorded as dated on the reverse 1754, and one 1755.
Comprising five English views and one of Rome (see Cat.
nos 4, 15, 33, 37; and Figs 10, 28.1), these are of two distinct
sizes, three measuring approximately 18¼ × 29½ inches and
three approximately 20½ × 24 inches; they vary strikingly in
style from the much larger but almost contemporary canvases
for Lord King, anticipating to some extent the usually small
and sombre paintings of the artist's later years. While a
not inconsiderable amount is known about Hollis and his
political and cultural enthusiasms, which included the commissioning of a bust of himself from Joseph Wilton, R.A.
(Fig. 2),[17] there is little to suggest any interest in the visual arts
other than in portraits of himself. Nor is there anything to
indicate why most of these particular subjects might have
been chosen, apart from the Roman view, which, showing
Hollis and his entourage in the foreground, was clearly
intended as a souvenir of his recent Grand Tour. That had, in
fact, been in two parts, a brief tour of Northern Italy in
1748–9 followed by a longer and more extensive visit from
1750 until his return to England on 4 June 1753.[18] What is
particularly interesting is that we know that while in Venice
Hollis befriended Joseph Smith, with whom he subsequently
corresponded, who is mentioned regularly in his surviving
diaries of 1759–70, and who was remembered in his will.
Furthermore, during the period of Hollis's stay in Venice,
8 December 1750–28 February 1751, Canaletto was also
there,[19] and it is tempting to suppose that patron and artist
may have been introduced by Smith, whose usefulness in
luring clients may thus have extended to the very end of
Canaletto's English years.

To those notable new clients should be added the patron
who acquired the group of ten paintings which remained
together in the possession of the Neave family until the late
nineteenth century (the majority until the late twentieth
century). This consisted of two pairs of views of Venice
and Rome datable to Canaletto's English period (*Venice:
The Churches of the Redentore and San Giacomo* and *The Prisons*
Figs 57.1 and 57.2;[20] *Rome: Piazza Navona* and *Piazza del
Quirinale*, Cat. nos 52, 53), a Venetian *capriccio* probably
painted in England (*Capriccio of the Scuola di San Marco from*

the *Loggia of the Palazzo Grifalconi-Loredan,* Fig. 3),[21] a larger view of Rome painted late in the English period or shortly after the artist's return to Venice (*The Piazza del Campidoglio and the Cordonata,* a large version of that painted for Hollis in 1755),[22] and two pairs of Venetian views certainly painted in Italy after 1755.[23] These form a coherent group, the two unpaired paintings, – the *capriccio* and the large Roman view – being of the same size as each other. The question of who might have been responsible for assembling it, between the late 1740s and the late 1750s, has, however, never been resolved, Constable merely stating that 'the group of paintings belonging to Sir Arundell Neave . . . were acquired by his forebears in the early nineteenth century'.[24] According to family tradition they were acquired by the founder of the family fortunes, Richard Neave (1731–1814), who was created a baronet in 1795.

Neave was a successful City merchant, heavily involved in the slave trade. He became Chairman of the Society of West Indian Merchants and was a director of the Bank of England for 48 years, becoming its Governor in 1783.[25] There is no question of his interest in the arts. He commissioned George Gibson to design offices in Broad Street, a town house, No. 6 Albemarle Street, and a country seat at Dagnam Park, Havering, Essex, an estate which he acquired in 1772.[26] Neave was a patron of Gainsborough, commissioning from him in the mid-1760s a life-size, full-length double portrait of himself and Lady Neave (d. 1830), in which he is depicted as a connoisseur, showing a drawing to his wife, whom he had married in 1761 (Fig. 4).[27] He is also thought to have commissioned from him a version of *The Market Cart* of 1786.[28] The family collection included a fine landscape by Canaletto's contemporary Francesco Zuccarelli, R.A. (1702–88), clearly painted in England and thus datable to the years 1752–62 or 1765–71. There is, however, no record that Neave

Figure 3
Capriccio of the Scuola di San Marco from the Loggia of the Palazzo Grifalconi-Loredan, probably early 1750s, oil on canvas, 34½ × 54 in. (87.7 × 137.2 cm.). Private Collection

Figure 4
Thomas Gainsborough, *Sir Richard and Lady Neave,* c. 1764/5, oil on canvas, 87 × 59 in. (221 × 150 cm.). Private Collection

visited Italy, and his known expenditure on the arts dates from later decades. In any case, the grouping of the paintings is of interest in showing Canaletto apparently continuing to supply paintings after his return to Venice to a client whom he had first encountered in England.

Canaletto was also successful during his English years in reviving the interest of several clients who had purchased Venetian views from him in previous decades, in several cases persuading them to be very much more useful than they had been before. While patterns in Canaletto patronage are the subject of Francis Russell's essay in this catalogue, this particular pattern deserves more emphasis in the present context. The 2nd Duke of Richmond, whom Canaletto lured back from the clutches of Antonio Joli,[29] painting for him the exceptional pair of London views *The Thames and the City from Richmond House* and *Whitehall and the Privy Garden from Richmond House* (Figs 25, 26), already owned a pair of Venetian views on copper of the late 1720s and at least one of the two even earlier *Allegorical Tombs of English Worthies*, painted by Canaletto in collaboration with other artists.[30] Sir Hugh Smithson, later Earl and Duke of Northumberland, who commissioned six important English views, had already acquired a pair of large and highly impressive Venetian views which was delivered by 31 June 1741, when it was mentioned in a letter by Frances, Countess of Hertford.[31] Lady Hertford also saw 'some views' of Venice owned by Francis Greville, Baron Brooke, later Earl of Warwick,[32] presumably including the large *Reception of an Ambassador at the Doge's Palace* of *c.* 1730, sold by the Earl of Warwick in 1974 and now in the Koetser Collection at the Kunsthaus, Zürich.[33] Brooke was to commission no fewer than five paintings and at least three drawings of Warwick (see Cat. nos 44–8).

Smithson and Brooke had both visited Italy on the Grand Tour, although in both cases at dates which do not correspond with those of their Venetian views by Canaletto: Smithson in 1733–4 and Brooke in 1739.[34] Smithson had dined in Rome on 12 November 1733 with Brooke's neighbour William Holbech, of Farnborough Hall, Warwickshire, whose commission of a pair of Venetian views datable on stylistic grounds to the early 1740s may have been inspired by Smithson's, especially as one of them is a horizontal variant of one of Smithson's.[35] By the time that Holbech came to redecorate Farnborough in 1750 his collection of Italian views had grown. The paintings by Canaletto had become a set of four and his view of *The Interior of the*

Pantheon by Giovanni Paolo Panini (1691–1765), dated 1734 (Private Collection, New York State), had been joined by three others, *The Interior of St Peter's, Rome* dated 1750 (Detroit Institute of Arts[36]), *The Piazza del Campidoglio and the Cordonata* and *The Piazza San Pietro* (both in a New York private collection). These were set into plaster framing by William Perritt for which payment was made in 1750.[37] According to a family tradition reported by Constable,[38] the two additional Venetian views by Canaletto, *The Bacino di San Marco from the Piazzetta* and *The Entrance to the Grand Canal, looking East*, were painted by the artist in England (see Cat. no. 55). A date towards 1750 would obviously be consistent with the second commission to Panini and with Perritt's framing and, as Constable points out,[39] is wholly acceptable on grounds of style, which differs markedly from the earlier pair (Figs 25, 26).

To these 'revived' patrons may be added another, although the evidence for his identity is circumstantial. At a London sale in 1895 a group of six paintings by Canaletto was dispersed,[40] all of which can be identified either with certainty or with an adequate degree of probability. They included four paintings datable to the early 1740s, in two pairs. One of these consisted of a large view of 'The Rialto' and a pendant 'Composition of Architecture with gondolas and figures', including, according to an annotation in ink in the auctioneers' copy of the catalogue, 'Palladio's proposed Theatre'. Judging from their unusual dimensions (38 × 50 in.), the first of these must be *The Rialto Bridge from the South,* first recorded in the Hanson Collection in the early twentieth century and now in an American private collection (Fig. 54.2), which has been interpreted as commemorating the visit to Venice of the paraplegic son of the Elector of Saxony, who spent some six months at the Palazzo Foscari from 21 December 1739.[41] Its pendant is likely to be the *Capriccio of the Grand Canal with Palladio's Design for the Rialto Bridge, the Basilica Palladiana and the Palazzo Chiericati*; a version of this of the appropriate size is first recorded in a New York sale in 1908 (said to have been previously in an English collection) and last recorded in a Bergamo private collection in 1973 (Fig. 54.3).[42] These were accompanied by a much smaller pair of Venetian views, *The Interior of the Basilica of San Marco* (Musée des Beaux-Arts, Montreal) and *The Courtyard of the Doge's Palace with the Giants' Staircase* (Private collection), the latter a small variant of one of the pair of paintings executed for Smithson in 1740–1.[43]

After a lacuna of a few years, two other paintings joined the group. *The Molo from the Bacino di San Marco on Ascension Day* (Cat. no. 54; Philadelphia Museum of Art) is its largest component;[44] it shows the Campanile after being damaged by lightning on 23 April 1745 and thus must have been painted shortly before or after Canaletto's arrival in England in May 1746.[45] This must have been followed closely by this patron's final – and most spectacular – acquisition from the painter, *Westminster Bridge from the North on Lord Mayor's Day, 29 October 1746* (Cat. no. 23; Yale Center for British Art). This is of the same unusual dimensions as the two earlier views of the Rialto Bridge, real and ideal, and would appear to have been designed to hang *en suite*. This would do much to explain the pronounced differences between the Yale painting's bright colour and gaiety and the sobriety of the Lobkowicz *City of Westminster from Lambeth* (Fig. 5), possibly the most 'naturalistic' of all the artist's depictions of the bridge, which is probably of quite similar date. The connection with the two Rialto views, which has hitherto been overlooked, provides a riposte to those critics who have used the Yale *Westminster Bridge* to demonstrate how Canaletto was unable to adapt his Venetian eyes to the very different character of his English subjects, the Thames being covered in waterborne craft like the Bacino di San Marco on Ascension Day, and London smog being replaced by Mediterranean sunshine. Indeed it provides highly significant support for recent theories that Canaletto's Whig patrons' display of his views of Venice – and of England made to resemble Italy – was intended in part to express their admiration for the political structure of the Venetian Republic. This painting has already been used to demonstrate this argument.[46]

The paintings were described in the 1895 sale catalogue as 'The Property of J. Carpenter Garnier, of Rookesbury Park, Fareham [Hampshire]', and there seems no reason whatsoever to doubt that their first owner was his forebear George Garnier (1703–63), also of Rookesbury, although he also had a London house in Jermyn Street. In 1735 Garnier was granted by the Duke of Cumberland, whom he served as physician, the highly profitable sinecure of Apothecary-General to the Army; he held this for life and was permitted to pass it to his son, who held it through the American War of Independence and is said to have made the enormous sum of £10,000 a year from it. Garnier's wealth must have been further augmented by his marriage in 1736 to a rich heiress, Frances Hopkins, who died in childbirth in 1739. Evidently

Figure 5
London: The Thames and the City of Westminster from Lambeth,
probably 1746, oil on canvas, 46½ × 93¾ in. (118 × 238 cm.).
Lobkowicz Collections, Nelahozeves Castle, Czech Republic

a highly cultivated man, his close friends included Hogarth, Garrick (a portrait of whom by Thomas Hudson was in J. Carpenter Garnier's second London sale in 1928),[47] Gibbon and David Hume. In this context it is particularly interesting that they also included Lord Chesterfield and Dr (later Sir) Edward Wilmot, Physician-General to the Army, both of whom were to acquire paintings from Canaletto during his English years (see Cat. nos 58, 59 and 16 respectively). Chesterfield addressed to Garnier a poem which begins with the words 'Garnier, my friend',[48] and a portrait of him in pastels by William Hoare of Bath was included in the 1895 sale,[49] while Wilmot, by a codicil to Garnier's will of 18 April 1760, was to receive ten guineas for a watch 'or what he pleased'.[50] Perhaps even more pertinent is the relationship of Garnier and of John Truesdale, husband of his younger sister Mary and like him a physician, with the family of the 2nd Duke of Richmond.[51] Garnier and Truesdale are referred to as the London doctors of Lady Caroline Holland, the Duke's eldest daughter, in December 1746, while Truesdale attended the Duke at Godalming in August 1750 and was (along with Wilmot) to attend Baroness Holland's son at Holland House in 1759.[52]

There is no documentary evidence of Garnier having any interest in paintings, or a particular interest in Westminster Bridge, but he was certainly an avid collector of porcelain; shortly before his death he presented to Captain Thomas Coram of the Foundling Hospital one of a pair of important Chelsea Gold-Anchor vases, which were later reunited and are known (coincidentally) as the Chesterfield Vases (Victoria and Albert Museum, London). Moreover he is recorded in Venice between December 1744 and May 1745, when he was given a doctorate by the University of Padua,[53] and it is quite likely that he had visited Venice on other, earlier, occasions, as, according to family tradition, John and Mary Truesdale were resident there for a time.[54]

There is reason to believe that Canaletto's activity in England brought him financial rewards beyond those he enjoyed at any other time in his long and industrious career. The painter was surprisingly poor at the time of his death in 1768; indeed, given Joseph Smith's wealth, one is bound to wonder if Canaletto was not one of the first artists to be exploited to the point of abuse by their dealers. He is known, however, to have made investments on two occasions in his long and industrious career, the first during his brief return to Venice from London in 1750–1, the second following his

final return to Venice from London in 1755. The documents which establish Canaletto's presence in Venice on 8 March 1751 and on 12 December 1755 all relate to investments, the first of 2,150 ducats invested with the Arte dei Luganegheri, the later three of 2,200 ducats invested with the Pio Ospedale degli Incurabili.[55]

Of Canaletto's forty-eight views of English subjects, thirty-five are of London, five being of considerable size (all approximately 46 × 93 in.). As mentioned above, once the painter's career had got underway in the 1720s, he had tended to use relatively small canvases (or, in the late 1720s, copper-plates) for his Venetian views, no doubt in large part due to the impracticality of shipping large canvases abroad. Only when local patrons presented themselves were larger canvases employed with enthusiasm, as for *The Riva degli Schiavoni, looking West*, painted for a Venetian resident, Marshal von der Schulenburg (Fig. 1). During the painter's years in England such restrictions clearly did not apply, and his eagerness to work on a large scale is immediately apparent, even if the clientele for the results was not. The pair of paintings of *The Thames and the City from Richmond House* and *Whitehall and the Privy Garden from Richmond House* (Figs 25, 26),[56] generally regarded as the masterpieces of Canaletto's English period, was presumably painted on commission for the 2nd Duke of Richmond. Topographical details have been taken to indicate that they were painted in the summer of 1747.[57] Two surviving drawings (see Fig. 9; Cat. no. 21) suggest that they were originally conceived as panoramic views, and it would seem that the reason for curtailing the sizes of the canvases was in order to fit them into the overmantel spaces at Goodwood which they still occupy.

Canaletto's first depictions of London on the largest scale were thus the views of *The Thames and the City of Westminster from Lambeth* and *The Thames and the City on Lord Mayor's Day* in the Lobkowicz Collection (Figs 5, 6).[58] They were acquired for the collection by Ferdinand Philip, 6th Prince Lobkowicz (1724–84), who was something of a play-boy and otherwise demonstrated little interest in the visual arts.[59] A note of 15 July 1752 from the prince to his steward at Roudnice Castle indicates that only then was the arrival of the two paintings he had bought in England anticipated. The view of Westminster must have been painted several years earlier. It shows the bridge as it appeared in the summer of 1746, before September of that year, and thus only a few months after Canaletto's arrival in England.[60] Rather more

conclusive, given the unreliability of the state of the bridge as evidence for dating depictions of it,[61] is the existence of two paintings by Antonio Joli which are clearly based on the Lobkowicz *Westminster*.[62] While these both show the bridge complete, and the larger of the two shows Lambeth Palace from a different viewpoint (in the smaller the composition is curtailed on both sides), both are substantially copied, with considerable attention to detail, from Canaletto's prototype. In this respect they are unique in Joli's œuvre and must indicate that Canaletto allowed him access to his painting before Joli's departure from London in 1749. While the Lobkowicz paintings are always described as a pair, they are markedly different in character, the festivity of the City view contrasting with the placidity of that of Westminster (a contrast heightened today by the neglected state of the latter). Such differences between pendants are highly unusual in Canaletto's work, but not unique, another instance being the pair of views of *The Grand Canal looking North-East from the Palazzo Balbi* and *The Bacino di San Marco on Ascension Day with the Bucintoro returning to the Molo,* which were in the collection of Sir Robert Walpole by 1736.[63] Possibly the Westminster view was a speculation and Lobkowicz commissioned the City view to serve as its pendant several years later. Given the success of both Lobkowicz compositions, it is perhaps surprising that Canaletto never painted another version of either.

The other three London views of the largest format seem even more likely to have been speculative ventures. On 25 July 1749 the painter placed the following announcement in the *Daily Advertizer*:

> *Signor Canaleto hereby invites any Gentleman that will be pleased to come to his House, to see a Picture done by him, being* A View of St James's Park, *which he hopes may in some Measure deserve their Approbation. The said View may be seen from Nine in the Morning till Three in the Afternoon, and from Four till Seven in the Evening, for the Space of fifteen Days from the Publication of this Advertizement. He lodges at* M[r]. *Richard Wiggan's, Cabinet-Maker, in Silver-Street, Golden Square.*

This was duly recorded by Vertue.[64] The painting must be the view of *The Old Horse Guards from St James's Park* now in the collection of the Sir Andrew Lloyd Webber Art Foundation (Cat. no. 17). Elizabeth Einberg has suggested that Canaletto may have hoped that it would catch the eye of Sir Watkin Williams Wynn (1692–1749), Member of

Figure 6
London: The Thames and the City on Lord Mayor's Day,
before 1752, oil on canvas, 46⅝ × 93½ in. (118.5 × 237.5 cm.).
Lobkowicz Collections, Nelahozeves Castle, Czech Republic

Parliament for Denbighshire and one of the richest Tory landowners in the country, whose London house, No. 1 Downing Street, is shown on the right, being prepared for occupation for the London season. If so, the artist's hopes were dashed by Sir Watkin's death on 26 September as the result of a fall from his horse while out hunting.[65] He did, however, find a less obvious client for the painting in the 4th Earl of Radnor, who paid 80 guineas for it.[66] The advertisement is also the first evidence of the location of Canaletto's London lodgings. Silver Street, which is now called Beak Street, is just to the north of Golden Square. Canaletto lived at the present No. 41, on the north side almost opposite the end of Upper John Street (and the Canaletto café) (Fig. 7). It bears a blue plaque.[67] Finberg records that 'there was until recently an old studio, or workshop with a skylight, in the garden at the back of this house'.[68] Interestingly, it has

recently been found that Amigoni, who is said to have encouraged Canaletto to visit England, had a house in the same street during the years 1732–4, and it seems to have been the centre of the Italian, especially Venetian, community in London.[69]

In 1751, presumably encouraged by his previous success with advertising, Canaletto posted a second announcement in the *Daily Advertiser*:

> *Signior Canaletto | Gives notice that he has painted the Representation of Chelsea College, Ranelagh House, and the River Thames, which if any Gentleman and others are pleas'd to favour him with seeing the same, he will attend at his Lodgings, at Mr. Viggan's, in Silver-Street, Golden Square, for fifteen Days from this Day, the 31st of July, from Eight o'Clock in the Morning to One in the Afternoon, and from Three in the Afternoon to Six at Night, each Day.*

This event was again recorded by Vertue, who added some interesting comments on the painting: '... being a work lately done to shew his skill – this valud at 60. or 70 pounds ... it is tho[t] that this View is not so well as some works of Canaletti formerly brought into England. nor does it appear to be better than some painters in England can do.'[70] That opinion would seem to have been shared by Canaletto's clientele, as the painting remained unsold and was subsequently cut up, presumably in the view that the parts would be easier to sell than the whole. These, now in the Museo de Bellas Artes, Havana, and at Blickling Hall (Cat. no. 34; National Trust), together make up the whole width of the painting, and show it to have been as large as the largest of Canaletto's English views. Despite the high quality of execution, Vertue's unenthusiastic response to this painting was also shared in the following centuries; the Blickling section was attributed to Samuel Scott from the nineteenth century until as late as 1955.

In the equally large *Whitehall and the Privy Garden looking North* (Fig. 8)[71] Canaletto carried through one of the intended panoramic views which he had not been permitted to execute for the Duke of Richmond. The viewpoint is, however, moved to the left of those employed for the related drawing of 1747 (Fig. 9) or the painting at Goodwood (Fig. 25), being a house belonging to the Earl of Loudoun rather than the adjacent Richmond House. The focus is thus far more on Parliament Street, the important new road driven through the slums to link Whitehall with the Palace of Westminster and Westminster Bridge, work on which began

Figure 7
Detail of John Rocque's *A Plan of the Cities of London and Westminster, and Borough of Southwark* (1 map on 24 sheets). London: John Pine and John Tinney, 1746. Beinecke Rare Book and Manuscript Library, Yale University

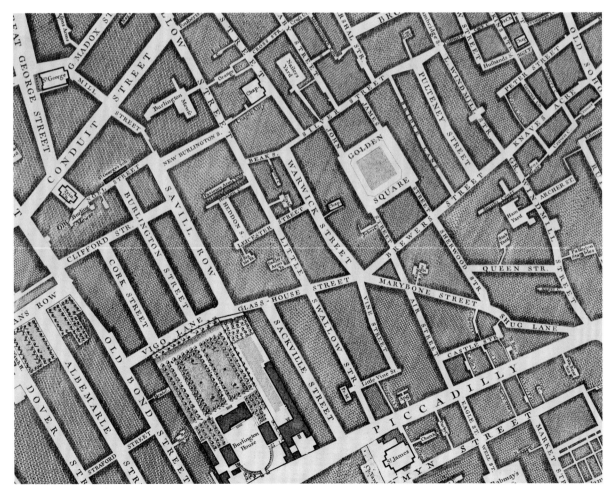

Figure 8
London: Whitehall and the Privy Garden looking North, probably 1751,
oil on canvas, 46½ × 93 in. (118 × 236.2 cm.).
His Grace the Duke of Buccleuch and Queensberry, KT, Bowhill

Figure 9
*London: Whitehall, the Privy Garden, Montagu House and the Thames from
Richmond House*, 1747, pen and brown ink with grey wash, 14½ × 29⅜ in.
(36.8 × 74.7 cm.). Whereabouts unknown

in 1746 and was concluded in 1756, and which is still today the widest street in London. This is shown at a significantly more advanced stage than in the drawing, indicating a date in 1751 or 1752, probably the summer of 1751.[72] Again there has been speculation as to who the artist may have thought would be tempted by it; Hayes suggested the Earl of Loudoun,[73] Finberg the 2nd Duke of Montagu, although his death on 5 July 1749 clearly rules him out in the light of the correct dating. Montagu House is undeniably prominent, however, and Francis Russell proposes the Duke's son-in-law and daughter, Lord and Lady Cardigan, as possible targets.[74] In the event the painting did not find a buyer until its purchase in Venice by John Crewe in 1761; this is the only one of Canaletto's large speculations that he was obliged to take back with him to Italy.

While the earlier of Canaletto's two views of *The Royal Naval Hospital, Greenwich* (Cat. no. 2) would seem to demonstrate his ability to imbue a considerable degree of conviction into a scene which at that time he only knew from a print (Fig. 2.1), the pair of canvases showing *The City from the Terrace of Somerset House* and *The City of Westminster from the Terrace of Somerset House* (Cat. nos 7, 8) shows how ably he could recapture the atmosphere of a place at some distance from it, geographically and, on numerous other occasions, temporally as well. For, as Finberg already recognized, the provenance of these from the collection of Joseph Smith itself strongly suggests that they were painted in Canaletto's native city.[75] They were the last paintings by the artist acquired by Smith, and the only English views, presumably providing him with poignant reminders of home. On stylistic grounds they are unlikely to date from after 1755, and there is every reason to believe that they may have been among the 'affairs' which Vertue mentions as the reason for the painter making 'a Tour to his own country at Venice' in 1750–1.[76] There is also technical evidence that they were painted in Italy, as they are on a Venetian type of canvas, coarser than that customarily employed by Canaletto in England, and the ground is russet as in the painter's work in his native city, rather than light grey as in much of his English production.[77]

This use of a lighter ground gives most of Canaletto's English paintings a tonality quite distinct from his Italian production, both before and after. In other respects the artist's work in England shows a development of tendencies already apparent in his Venetian paintings of the first half of the 1740s, which were to develop further after 1755. Notable among these is his abbreviation of motifs, such as the way that shades of dark green are brushed, often with a relatively large brush, over khaki in the foregrounds of such paintings as the large view of *The Old Horse Guards from St James's Park* (Cat. no. 16) and *The Grand Walk of the new Spring Garden, Vauxhall* (Cat. no. 31), creating almost abstract patterns. Similarly there is an increasing tendency for background figures to be composed of calligraphic squiggles and dots, a mannerism which becomes distinctly more widespread after Canaletto's return to Venice. Inevitably, he was happy to bathe his English scenes in afternoon sunshine more characteristic of Italian summers than of England's more northern climate, as he had, indeed, almost all his paintings since the

Figure 10
Rome: The Piazza del Campidoglio and the Cordonata, 1755, oil on canvas, 20½ × 24¼ in. (52 × 61.5 cm.).
Private Collection

1720s (although the light is wintry in many paintings of *c.* 1738–42). At this stage in his development there are often rosy tints in the sky. In particular, there is rarely a hint of the infamous palls of smog with which London was beset from the sixteenth century until December 1962. From their high chromatic key the vast majority of the paintings done by Canaletto in England, including *capricci* and Italian views, are immediately recognizable as such. To this writer's eye, there are only a few borderline cases, notably the *Capriccio of the Scuola di San Marco from the Loggia of the Palazzo Grifalconi-Loredan*[78] and *The Piazza del Campidoglio and the Cordonata, Rome*,[79] both of the same size and both, as mentioned above, from the Neave group.[80]

Dating Canaletto's work within the English period on stylistic grounds, however, is often far from straight forward. Even Constable, not one to concern himself unduly over dating, expresses surprise at finding that the Duke of Northumberland's *The City seen through an Arch of Westminster Bridge* (Cat. no. 24) was engraved as early as 1747, since, although it is one of the artist's most striking composi-tions, its execution includes the sort of short-cuts which one expects to see only in work of several years later.[81] Constable directly, and somewhat illogically, suggests a later date for the *Westminster Bridge under Construction, from the South-East* (Cat. no. 25), which there is every reason to presume is its pendant and of similar date.[82] The six paintings of the Hollis group of 1754–5 (Cat. nos 4, 15, 33, 37; Figs 10, 28.1), in particular, are in a style which contrasts notably with the set of seven for Lord King which are almost contemporary. As Constable points out in the case of the Hollis *Piazza del Campidoglio and the Cordonata, Rome* (Fig. 10), if nothing were known of its history one would presume that it was painted some time after Canaletto's return to Venice.[83] The colouring of the Hollis paintings is sombre rather than ebullient and the atmosphere moody, especially in the superbly stormy *Old Walton Bridge* of 1754 (Cat. no. 37; Dulwich Picture Gallery). Very similar in style is the view of *Dolo on the Brenta* (Fig. 11), based on an etching by the artist himself datable to the early 1740s, itself derived from drawings made on the spot. This is, in fact, pre-cisely contemporary with it, an inscription on a label on the stretcher giving the date '1754', indicating that it was origi-nally inscribed on the reverse in exactly the same way as the paintings of the Hollis group and the Dicker view of *Old Walton Bridge* (Cat. no. 38).

It has become customary to denigrate Canaletto's English work, often taking as a starting point an entry made by Vertue in his notebook in June 1749:

Signor Cannelletti from Venice haveing now been in England some time, has painted Several Views about London of the new bridge at Westminster. & London bridge. & about whitehall, also for the Duke of Richmond – and in the Country for the Duke of Beaufort, Views of Badmington - &c. on the whole of him something is obscure or strange. he dos not produce works so well done as those of Venice or other parts of Italy. which are in Collections here. and done by him there. especially his figures in his works done here, are apparently much inferior to those done abroad. which are surprizeingly well done & with great freedom & variety – his water & his skys at no time excellent or with natural freedom. & what he has done here his prospects of Trees woods or handling or pencilling of that part not various nor so skillful as might be expected. above all he is remarkable for reservedness & shyness in being seen at work, at any Time, or anywhere. which has much strengthened a conjecture that he is not the veritable Cannelleti of Venice. whose works there have been bought at great prices. or that privately there, he has some unknown assistant in makeing or filling up his p. . . . of works with figures [84]

Vertue wrote this the month before Canaletto began to exhibit individual paintings in his studio, as discussed above, and there are, of course, explanations for much (if not all) of this criticism. Vertue himself offers clarification of some of it in an entry for the following month. After stating that 'at last after some time I heard how that dificulty, was spread about. that this man was not the person so famd in Italy at Venice',[85] he explains how the confusion was due to Bellotto's persistent use of his uncle's surname.[86] Much of it may well be due to the jealousy directed by native painters towards foreign artists, an issue at the time and one which Vertue turns to in the paragraph immediately following the June entry cited above; this begins 'it has been an old observation in England – that yᵉ Arts of painting & sculpture wants encouragement – and that none but foreianers have excelld in any branch of those polite Arts'.[87]

As Constable points out, support for this explanation is found in the writings of the watercolourist Edward Dayes, although these are of rather later date (he was born in 1763):

The picture dealing tribe carried their assurance so far, as to deny that Cannaletti was the person who painted his pictures at Venice, that is, on his arrival at London and when, by the provocation, he was tempted to sit down and produce some to convince the public, they still persisted that the pieces now produced were not in the same style; an assertion which materially injured him for a time and made him almost frantic. By this scheme they hoped to drive him from the country, and thereby to prevent him detecting the copies they had made from his works, which were in great repute.[88]

Vertue's suggestion that Canaletto may have had an assistant in his London studio is particularly intriguing, not least because discussion of the idea is notably absent from all other literature on the subject to this day. While such an assistant is unlikely to have been delegated the execution of figures, it seems highly likely that one was employed, given the painter's considerable workload and what is known of his practices in Venice. Canaletto's characteristic exercise of quality control has resulted in the contributions of such an assistant being usually indiscernible, but possibly not always so.

Vertue's note of June 1749 was used as late as 1899 by H. P. Horne to denigrate the *Interior of the Rotunda at Ranelagh*, which had been recently purchased by the National Gallery (Cat. no. 33), along with the *Eton College*, which had been bequeathed to the collection in 1876 (Cat. no. 40), and the *Alnwick Castle* (Fig. 12).[89] Even Constable is surprisingly scathing about the quality of Canaletto's English work, especially as he himself warns of the dangers of using as comparisons the Venetian views executed at the height of his powers in the 1730s.[90] In this writer's view, the painter should be commended for continuing to seek new problems for which to find new solutions at a fairly advanced stage in his career. It must also be recognized that, uneven though Canaletto's work in England may be, it is still qualitatively superior to that of any English and almost any other Italian view painter active at that date, the one obvious exception being Bellotto, then painting the masterpieces of his first Dresden period. Another, more debatable, exception is Francesco Guardi (1712–93), then at the outset of his career

Figure 12
Alnwick Castle, c. 1752, oil on canvas,
44¾ × 55 in. (113.7 × 139.7 cm.).
Collection of the Duke of Northumberland

as a view painter. It should also be noted that several of the masterpieces of Canaletto's years in England remain in fairly inaccessible private collections and that a considerable proportion of the Italian views and *capricci* painted in England have not hitherto been recognized as such.[91]

Most of Canaletto's London views are inevitably on a less grand scale than the paintings mentioned above. Somerset House, situated on a bend in the Thames, afforded the best views of both the City and Westminster, and it is hardly surprising that other, smaller versions of the pendants done for Smith are known. The pair in the Yale Center for British Art (Cat. nos 5, 6) has the distinction of being earlier in date; very probably they are Canaletto's first depictions of these important subjects, since engravings of both of them were published in London on 1 August 1750. A later, small version of *The City of Westminster from the Terrace of Somerset House*, first recorded in the collection of the Dukes of Hamilton and Brandon, who are thought to have acquired it in the early twentieth century, was de-accessioned by the Yale Center for British Art in 1988 and is now again in an English private collection (Fig. 7.2).[92] While that painting has no known pendant, a later, small version of *The Thames from the Terrace of Somerset House, looking towards the City* is paired with a view of Westminster Bridge.[93]

Another successful composition shows *The City of Westminster from near the York Water Gate*, with the York Buildings Water Tower on the right. Two painted versions of this are known, the larger of which, at Penrhyn Castle, was recently acquired by the National Trust (Fig. 13.1);[94] a drawing of it at Yale is one of the finest of Canaletto's drawings of London (Cat. no. 13). The composition is also known in three versions painted by Samuel Scott (*c*. 1702–1772), a rare instance of a close connection between Canaletto and his most talented English competitor.

Westminster Bridge is the subject depicted by far the most often throughout the painter's English years. The engineering phenomenon of the age, it is shown in numerous stages of construction in a series of paintings and drawings dating from between 1746 and 1754. It is characteristic of Canaletto's *modus operandi* that the sequence of depictions does not always correspond with the state of construction of the bridge. Six of these are of the same composition, taken from the Surrey bank looking south, with the corner of a building on the far left. They consist of three paintings – two of which, both in British private collections (one is Cat.

no. 27),[95] show three similar barges in fairly similar positions – and three drawings, in the Royal Collection,[96] the British Museum (Cat. no. 28) and at Stourhead (The National Trust),[97] in which the boats and figures are carefully differentiated. The latest version, that painted for Hollis in 1754, is the only one where the bridge is not complete but is shown during the repairs of June–July 1750, hardly the proudest moment in the history of its construction (Fig. 28.1).[98] The only logical explanation for this variation is that the artist felt that it would justify his signed statement on the back of the canvas that the composition was painted for Hollis 'for the first and last time'.[99] All the versions of the composition except the Windsor drawing show the balustrade with too many domed alcoves, one of the not infrequent indications of the artist's lack of concern for topographical accuracy.[100]

Many of Canaletto's views show buildings which were either newly completed or refurbished, or alternatively about to be demolished or irrevocably altered. Prominent among the former are the Royal Naval Hospital at Greenwich (Cat. nos 1–2), Northumberland House (Cat. no. 14), Hawksmoor's Gothic West towers of Westminster Abbey (Cat. no. 19), the Rotunda at Ranelagh (Cat. nos 32, 33), and Old Walton Bridge (Cat. nos 37–38); among the latter are Old Somerset House (Cat. no. 11), Alnwick Castle (Fig. 12) and the Holbein Gate shown in several paintings (Figs 8, 26 and Cat. no. 15).[101] The Old Horse Guards, mentioned above, were depicted shortly before their demolition in the winter of 1749–50 (Cat. nos 16–18), and the New Horse Guards were shown under construction, from the same viewpoint, probably between November 1752 and November 1753 (Fig. 18.1).[102] This last is one of Canaletto's three known paintings on panel, all of which date from his London years, the others being *Old Somerset House* (Cat. no. 11) and *The Interior of Henry VII's Chapel, Westminster Abbey* (Fig. 20.1; Museum of London).[103] His lodgings being above a cabinet maker's may well have a relevance here, but it must also demonstrate his interest in experimenting with supports other than canvas, as he had with copper plates for a brief period in the late 1720s. In general, Canaletto approached London as a subject in much the same way as he had Venice in the 1720s, covering all the obvious attractions and never straying further from the River Thames than St Paul's Cathedral (Cat. no. 4). Only occasionally did he delve behind the ornamental façade, although, as in the

masterpiece of the mid-1720s popularly known as *The Stonemason's Yard* (London, National Gallery), this tended to produce the most brilliant results, notably the Buccleuch and Goodwood views of Parliament Street (Figs 8 and 25).

Canaletto's English views are by no means confined to London, although he clearly felt no need to venture far from the capital. Even the two subjects of paintings which are further than a day trip away from London, and which he certainly visited, Warwick and Badminton, are no more than some sixty miles apart (see Cat. nos 44–8, and 42, 43 respectively). Warwick is the subject of five paintings and five drawings, thus receiving significantly more of the artist's attention than any other English subject except the Thames at Westminster. Like Westminster Bridge, Warwick Castle is shown at various stages of 'improvement' in the five paintings and three of the drawings; payments from Lord Brooke for these are documented on 19 July 1748, 28 July 1748, 3 March 1749,[104] 24 March 1752 and 27 July 1752, indicating two distinct campaigns of work (see Cat. nos 44–8). Two other drawings of the town, of uncertain early provenance, show *St Mary's Church and Church Street* (Cat. no. 49) and *The Town and Castle of Warwick from the Gardens of the Priory* (Yale Center for British Art).[105]

Canaletto's views of *Badminton House from the Park* and *Badminton Park from the House* (Cat. nos 42, 43) are first mentioned by Vertue in his note of June 1749 transcribed above. The trees are shown fully out, which suggests that they may have been painted the previous summer, possibly immediately after the first views of Warwick Castle. The house is shown with the pediment and twin cupolas added *c*. 1745 by William Kent, who also designed Worcester Lodge and several garden buildings. The view of the park, unique in Canaletto's *œuvre* in being almost entirely without buildings, the composition 'reduced to a few geometric shapes of gravel, grass, and trees set against a low horizon',[106] is a good example of an offbeat subject eliciting a particularly inspired response from the artist.

Canaletto's only view of a subject in Northern England, or indeed of anywhere north of Warwick, is *Alnwick Castle* (Fig. 12).[107] Although of striking composition, this is distinctly less vibrant in execution than the other components of the group of paintings by the artist now housed in the castle itself. Its shortcomings, which are reflected in the fact that, as mentioned above, this was one of the paintings of which Canaletto's authorship was questioned by H. P. Horne in

1899, might suggest that the painter was following an earlier model. While no graphic source for the composition has been identified, two other paintings of it are known. One of these, of similar size, also owned by the Duke of Northumberland and currently at Albury Park, was considered autograph by Constable but has since been attributed to William Marlow (1740–1813), who is known to have worked for the Duchess of Northumberland, and whom Horace Walpole records as having been working on copies of Canaletto in 1771.[108] Marlow's birth date clearly rules out his version as the prototype. The other, significantly smaller, version, last seen at auction in 1982,[109] is generally accepted as the work of Samuel Scott, by whom it was apparently formerly signed and dated 1752.[110] Its early provenance is not known,

although the 1st Duke of Northumberland certainly owned a pair of marines by Scott, possibly purchased in 1765 (and certainly before 1770) and still in the collection.[111] Scott's painting is considered by Constable and Kingzett a copy (with slight variations) of Canaletto's. The possibility should be entertained, however, that the relationship was in fact the reverse and that Scott was the originator.

It is perhaps surprising that Canaletto executed no *capricci* of London buildings which might have anticipated William Marlow's remarkable *Capriccio of St Paul's Cathedral on the Grand Canal* of *c.* 1797 (London, Tate). The only Canaletto painting of London which has been described as a *capriccio*, that of *The Banqueting House, Whitehall* made for Hollis (Cat. no. 15), is imaginary only in that Hubert Le Sueur's

Figure 13
Capriccio of Roman Ruins with a Classical Church and the Colleoni Monument, probably 1754, oil on canvas, 59¼ × 53⅛ in. (150.5 × 135 cm.). Private Collection, Monte Carlo

Figure 14
Capriccio of a Renaissance Palace with a large Gateway, probably 1754, oil on canvas, 59¼ × 53⅛ in. (150.5 × 135 cm.). Private Collection, Monte Carlo

equestrian statue of King Charles I, erected in 1675 near Northumberland House (see Cat. no. 14), has been moved down Whitehall to a point adjacent to that of the King's execution, a conceit which must have held a strong appeal for the fiercely republican patron. *Capricci* were more esteemed than view paintings by the more intellectual of Canaletto's fellow countrymen, both on account of the powers of imagination which they demanded and because, naturally enough, Venetians rarely felt a need for a record of a view which they could enjoy on a daily basis with a minimal amount of footwork.

It should also be remembered that, in the same way, many of the painter's views of English country seats were probably painted for London houses, and that some of his London views must have originally adorned country houses. While *capricci* must have held less appeal for many British patrons, they were clearly not without their admirers, to judge from the not inconsiderable number executed by Canaletto during his English years. The most important are the three groups of which the patrons and all the components are known, those painted for Norfolk House, Chesterfield House, and the 5th Lord King (see Cat. nos 60–62; 58, 59; 69–71 respectively). The three executed for the 9th Duke of Norfolk for Norfolk House in St James's Square, where they were hanging among nineteen portraits in the Large Drawing Room on the ground floor by 1756, are unquestionably the artist's masterpieces in this genre of the English years (Cat. nos 60–62). The complexity of the compositions, incorporating a frothy mixture of Renaissance palaces and porticoes, a Gothic church façade, the Arch of Titus and the Pyramid of Caius Cestius, shows Canaletto's imagination at its most fertile and was never to be attempted again. Nor are any of the compositions reflected in his later creations, perhaps surprisingly, since most of his other English-period *capricci* are known in more than one variant.

The majority of the artist's other painted *capricci* can be categorized as either 'Renaissance buildings by or near the Venetian Lagoon' or 'Ruins of Roman fora with neoclassical porticoed churches'. All three components of the group executed for the 4th Earl of Chesterfield for his wife's 'Dressing or Sitting Room' and for the Music Room at Chesterfield House in Great Stanhope Street are of the first type (Cat. nos 58, 59; Fig. 58.2). While they must be close in date to the group for Norfolk House, only one of them is a unique composition (Cat. no. 58), each of the other two being known in several versions.

The composition in the oval canvas showing *A Renaissance Pavilion flanked by two ruined classical Arches over a Waterway by the Venetian Lagoon* (Fig. 58.2) went through a particularly large number of permutations. An almost square version with different boats was sold from the estate of Sir Michael Sobell in 1995.[112] That corresponds, with minor variations, with a drawing sold in 1984,[113] which was probably preceded by another drawing, last seen at auction in 1971, in which the two arches pass behind the pavilion and there are other differences, giving it the character of a preparatory study.[114] Another almost square painting, in the Baltimore Museum of Art, shows a simplified version of the composition, with only one arch.[115] There are also two small painted variants in which the composition is extended to the left to include a ruined Corinthian temple, of which the prime version was sold from the estate of Helen E. Abell of Kentucky in 1998.[116] A painting offered for sale in 1991 from the estate of Lydia Morrison would seem to be an exact studio copy of the Abell version, despite having been apparently signed and dated 1754 on the reverse, providing of course that one accepts that Canaletto had studio assistance at this time.[117]

The Chesterfield *capriccio* showing *A Renaissance Palace with a large Gateway* (Cat. no. 59) is similarly known in other variants, two painted and one drawn. One of the paintings

(Fig. 14) formed part of the important decorative scheme for the 5th Lord King, in which it was paired with a *capriccio* of the 'Ruins of Roman fora with neoclassical porticoed churches' type (Fig. 13). A signed canvas of almost exactly half the size, probably owned by William Beckford of Fonthill and possibly painted for his father, repeats this last composition with unusual fidelity, although in reverse (Fig. 15). A neoclassical church is also seen through a ruined archway in the splendid *capriccio* in an English private collection which has never before been reproduced (Cat. no. 64).

Some of Canaletto's works of the imagination, however, do not fit into either of these categories. Particularly inspired are the two imaginary landscapes from the King group (Cat. nos 70, 71). Along with the *Capriccio of a ruined Gothic Chapel by a Sluice Gate* (Cat. no. 69), these recall, in a highly idealized manner and with some wholly extraneous elements, the character of the landscape around Ockham Park, the patron's country seat. Several of the components of the set of thirteen

Figure 15
Capriccio of Roman Ruins with a Classical Church and the Colleoni Monument, c. 1754, signed, oil on canvas, 28 × 53 in. (71 × 135 cm.). Private Collection, England (exhibited at Dulwich only)

overdoors executed for Joseph Smith and now in the Royal Collection, five of which are dated 1744,[118] are of a distinct type, being fundamentally view paintings deliberately transformed into *capricci* by the introduction of subsidiary elements which do not belong there; that showing the Piazzetta with the bronze Horses of San Marco set on pedestals along its central axis is a good example.[119] The same mentality is seen in a *capriccio* of the Rialto Bridge with the Lagoon beyond which was recently rediscovered in a private collection (Fig. 16).[120] This is 'signed' with the coat-of-arms of the Canal family (over the archway on the right).[121] Extensive *pentimenti* show that this was originally intended as a view, but it seems never to have been completed as such. Its grey ground (and, to some extent, its English provenance) suggests that it is a unique example of this type of Venetian *capriccio* executed in England. Similar thought processes are seen in a drawing in the British Museum (Cat. no. 68) depicting the church of San Giorgio Maggiore very much as in Canaletto's painted view of the subject (Cat. no. 56), but with an English Perpendicular bell-tower. The finished *capriccio* drawings which can be associated with his English period differ notably in type from most of the paintings. In the majority of these, elements of patently English inspiration are introduced into compositions of otherwise thoroughly Italian character, as in the sheet in the Metropolitan Museum of Art, New York, where an English Gothic church tower is set amongst classical ruins, which include a Roman triumphal arch inspired by the still-extant Arch of the Sergi at Pula (Pola) in Istria, clearly derived from a print (Cat. no. 66). In another drawing, in the Detroit Institute of Arts, which was to be used for a painting after Canaletto's return to Venice, an English Perpendicular chapel is given an incongruous classical portico and is again set near a ruined Roman triumphal arch, this time next to the Venetian Lagoon (Cat. no. 67).

Canaletto's ability to conjure up from drawings highly competent paintings of scenes he had not seen for many years is already well demonstrated by the six large Roman views of 1742–3 executed for Smith, mentioned above, which very successfully disguise the fact that he had not seen the subject-matter for more than two decades. There can be no question that when he came to England he brought with him old drawings, impressions of his own engravings, and prints by other artists which he thought might be useful for this purpose. This is already suggested by the presence of two sketches of buildings adjacent to the Horse Guards building (Figs 16.1, 16.2) and a hasty sketch of what must surely be St Paul's Cathedral (Fig. 4.1) in a sketchbook which otherwise seems to consist entirely of Italian subject-matter.[122] Moreover many of the paintings certainly executed in England testify to this practice. In the King group of paintings the five pure *capricci* were accompanied by a depiction of buildings on the Isola di San Michele (now the Venetian cemetery island) of which several drawings are known, and also by the most monumental of all Canaletto's depictions of *The Bacino di San Marco on Ascension Day*, the most glamorous of all Venetian subjects (Fig. 17),[123] for which the artist probably used a drawing which passed from Joseph Smith to the Royal Collection in 1763.[124] A particularly surprising detail is the figure clearly dressed as a 'Chinaman' in a gondola in the right foreground; the rowers of the brightly coloured barge in the distance to the left also appear to be in oriental costume. 'Chinamen' in exotic barges also feature in one of the King *Imaginary Landscapes* (Cat. no. 70) and in the ex-Sobell version of the *Renaissance Pavilion flanked by two ruined classical Arches over a Waterway by the Venetian Lagoon*. It surely cannot be coincidental that, as *The*

Figure 16
Capriccio of the Rialto Bridge with the Lagoon beyond, c. 1746, oil on canvas, 17 × 27½ in. (43.2 × 69.8 cm.). Private Collection, United Kingdom

Figure 17
Venice: The Bacino di San Marco on Ascension Day, probably 1754, oil on canvas, 59⅞ × 54⅛ in. (152 × 137.5 cm.), in the original English frame.
Private Collection

Gentleman's Magazine informs us, on 25 May 1749, 'Being the birth day of his R[oyal] H[ighness] Pr[ince] George, who then enter'd into his 12th year, … Their R. H. the Pr. and Princess of *Wales*, with the nobility, were rowed in their barge a head of the wager men, followed by Prince George, the young Princesses, &c., in a magnificent new built barge, after the *Venitian* manner, and the watermen in *Chinese* habits …'125 There is another reference to this barge, now no longer considered Venetian, on 1 August of the same year, when, after the boat race which 'started at *Greenwich* for the Prince of *Wales*'s cup, to go to the *Nore*, and back again … The Pr. of Wales, with 6 or 7 attendants, in his *Chinese* barge, and the rowers in *Chinese* habits, drove gently before, for some time …'126 Such figures are not found in Canaletto's work done in Italy, and it has been suggested that, like the presence of views of Venice – and above all of the Bacino on Ascension Day – in English collections, the inclusion of 'Chinamen' may have been intended to convey a political message.127

Other Venetian views certainly painted in England include *The Bacino di San Marco and the Dogana from the Piazzetta* (Cat. no. 55) and *The Entrance to the Grand Canal, looking East* (Fig. 55.1) painted for William Holbech for Farnborough Hall, probably in 1749–50, and mentioned above. The house is some twelve miles from Warwick, and if Canaletto visited it at some stage in his execution of the commission, which is quite likely, he could easily have done so while working for Lord Brooke.

Other views of Venice almost certainly painted in England include a group of five 'portraits' of the Venetian churches of San Giorgio Maggiore and the Redentore, and one of the Prisons, all measuring approximately 18 × 30 in. These were all originally in pairs, only one of which, *The Redentore* and *The Prisons*, formerly in the Neave collection, remains together, the only components of the group with an early provenance (Figs 57.1, 57.2).128 One of the two pairs of *San Giorgio Maggiore* and *The Redentore* is here exhibited together for the first time (Cat. nos 56, 57). Of the other, *The Redentore* is in a private collection and the *San Giorgio Maggiore*, the only component of the group not to have been seen on the art market in recent years, remains untraced (Fig. 56.1).129 The idea of pairing depictions of Palladio's most famous Venetian churches was not a new one. A rather larger pair, acquired by the Manchester City Art Gallery in 1984, is of similar type but different character, with bulkier figures suggesting a date in the 1730s.130 Intermediary in style and

probably painted in Venice before 1746 is a version of the *Redentore* composition of similar size to the Manchester pair.131 This is said to have been acquired by Peter Baker shortly after 1781, when he became a Member of Parliament, married, purchased the estate of Ranston in Dorset, and commissioned a full-length portrait of his wife from Thomas Gainsborough (New York, Frick Collection). This view was accompanied (until 1960) by a depiction of San Giorgio Maggiore, of identical size and similar date.132 That is, however, of a composition entirely different from the other paintings of the church, and the differences in scale and horizon level from the Baker *Redentore* make them unlikely pendants.

A similarly unexpected discrepancy between two pendants is seen in the pair of paintings in the collection of the A. G. Leventis Trust, which was probably executed in England. One of these shows the Piazzetta, looking north, with the Campanile under repair after being struck by lightning on 23 April 1745; the other, a *capriccio* of Renaissance buildings including the Ponte Santa Trinità, Florence, differs markedly in scale and horizon level.133

Several other Venetian views datable to the English period have come to light in recent years. Two paintings (apparently from a set of four, the other two being untraced), showing *The Piazza San Marco, looking East, with a Procession* and *The Entrance to the Grand Canal, looking East,* were sold at auction in 1997.134 Of these the view of the Piazza San Marco, which is notably weaker in execution than the pendant, was enlarged by the artist at top and bottom in order to conform in size. Its original dimensions were similar to those of the only other known depiction of the subject from Canaletto's English years, that first recorded in the collection of the Earls of Durham and now in a Belgian private collection;135 these are thus the latest in date of all Canaletto's representations of this popular composition. A pair of Venetian views painted on grey grounds and datable with certainty to the English years shows *The Church of Santi Giovanni e Paolo* and *The Entrance to the Grand Canal from the Piazzetta*.136 These are of oval format, highly unusual in Canaletto's œuvre but also used for one of the three Chesterfield *capricci* (Fig. 58.2). They are presumed to have been commissioned by Sir William St Quentin, 4th Bt (1700–1770), also a patron of Gainsborough, possibly for his house in Bruton Street (a short walk from Canaletto's studio, as well as from Chesterfield House) rather than for his country seat of Scampston.

Not surprisingly, there was also a demand for views of

Rome from Canaletto's English clientele, which he was similarly able to fulfil by basing paintings on the drawings he had made there in his youth (1719–20) and on prints by other artists. *The Piazza del Campidoglio and the Cordonata* painted for Hollis in 1755 has already been mentioned (Fig. 10), as have the *Piazza Navona* and *Piazza del Quirinale* from the Neave group (Cat. nos 52, 53). Particularly impressive are the signed *Arch of Constantine* (Cat. no. 51) and *The Roman Forum with the Basilica of Maxentius and the Church of Santa Francesca Romana* (Cat. no. 50), which must originally have formed parts of decorative schemes yet to be identified, possibly indeed the same scheme. This writer is inclined to regard as works of late in the English period a small version of the latter and a pendant *Colosseum* in the Galleria Borghese, Rome, for which they were acquired in England in 1908.137

Several paintings have been incorrectly attributed to Canaletto as works of his English period, some of which can be established as the work of different artists. The second of the two views of Alnwick Castle in the collection of the Duke of Northumberland, also accepted by Constable but more recently attributed to William Marlow, has already been mentioned.138 A small portrait on panel showing an artist in front of a distant view of St Paul's Cathedral similar to that in the background of the Goodwood *Thames and the City from Richmond House* has a contemporary inscription identifying the subject as Canaletto (Anglesey Abbey, National Trust). This was sold at auction in 1830 and 1895 described as a self-portrait and was published as such by Francis Watson in 1956. There is regrettably no comparable image to confirm that it does indeed record Canaletto's features, the only certain likeness of the artist being Antonio Visentini's engraving after Giambattista Piazzetta for the frontispiece of his *Prospectus Magni Canalis Venetiarum*, published in 1735. The attribution to Canaletto was doubted by Constable,139 justifiably so, since it has recently been found to be signed with the initials 'EG'.140 Other incorrect attributions include a view of the New Horse Guards after completion, formerly – but apparently no longer – in the Drury-Lowe Collection at Locko Park, which was accepted by Constable,141 but exhibited in 1982 as the work of an imitator.142 A view of *The Interior of King's College Chapel, Cambridge*, of which versions given to Canaletto are recorded in the collections of Horace Walpole in 1842, Samuel Dickenson in 1775 and John Hawkins in 1824 (these last two possibly the same painting), has recently been bequeathed to the Virginia Museum of

Fine Arts, Richmond, Virginia. That was considered 'not wholly convincing' by Constable in 1962,[143] but he voiced no such doubts when he included the work in his monographic exhibition of 1964–5.[144] It is in poor condition, but the present writer was not inclined to accept it as Canaletto's work when he saw it in a private collection in Richmond in 1996.[145] It must, however, record a Canaletto original, and may, for instance, be the Dickenson-Hawkins painting copied from Walpole's original, which remains untraced. A large, but otherwise close, version of the smaller of Canaletto's two views of *The Old Horse Guards from St James's Park* (Cat. no. 16) was offered from the Fermor-Hesketh Collection at auction in 1988 as a second autograph rendition;[146] this idea failed to convince anyone at the time, but it raises yet again the issue of whether the painter could have had an assistant or worked with other, local artists during his London years.

The question of Canaletto's influence on British topographical and landscape painting is beyond the scope of this exhibition, but it is to be hoped that this largest ever gathering of the painter's English work will provide a fitting testimony to an artist who has recently, finally, been granted an entry in the *Oxford Dictionary of National Biography*.[147]

Notes

1. A. M. Zanetti, *Della pittura veneziana e delle opere pubbliche dei veneziani maestri*, Venice, 1771, p. 462: 'Ciò fu circa l'anno 1719, in cui comunicò, così dicea egli, solennemente il teatro'.
2. Constable no. 331.
3. Constable no. 122.
4. Constable nos 378, 382, 384, 386, 390 and 387.
5. Constable nos 374, 451–7, 460, 462 and 476; Constable/Links 1989, II, no. 459*** (in error for 459**), and Links 1998, p. 43, no. 459**.
6. 'Le Roi de Pologne, Electeur de Saxe, n'ayant pu avoir l'oncle, a fait venir à Dresde le neveu' (P.-J. Mariette, *Abécédario*, ed. P. de Chenevières and A. de Montaiglon, in *Archives de l'Art Français*, Paris, I, 1851, p. 114).
7. Bernardo and his descendants in Poland seem to have been the only members of the family to spell their surname with a final 'o'.
8. Vertue's notebooks in the British Library have been published in full by the Walpole Society in six volumes. The references to Canaletto are in Add. MSS. 23079 and 23074, published in *The Walpole Society*, XXII, Vertue *Note Books*, III.
9. Vertue *Note Books*, III, p. 94.
10. 'Fece un viaggio in Londra dove fermatosi Quattro anni, ebbe continuamente occasione da quei Signori di produrre nuovi parti del suo industrioso pennello. Ritornato in patria dove presentemente trattiensi. porto con se varj abbozzi delle vedute e dei siti più riguardovoli de quell'ampia Città, i quali con suo comodo è da sperare, ch'ei vorrà consignare alle tele. Ora nuovamente è ritornato in Londra'.
11. 'Passò due volte in Londra dove dimorò e dipinse per molti anni; e acquistò gloria e danari' ('He went twice to London where he lived and painted for many years, acquiring glory and money').
12. 'Antonio Canaletto Veneziano celebre Pittore da Vedute ritorna da Inghilterra in Patria'. See *Notizie d'arte tratte dei notatori e degli annali del N. H. Pietro Gradenigo*, ed. L. Livan, Venice, 1942, p. 10.
13. Constable no. 339.
14. Russell, *op. cit.*, 1999, p. 181.
15. F. Montecuccoli degli Erri, *Canaletto incisore*, Venice, 2002, pp. 6–7.
16. The Dukes of Norfolk are also recorded as having owned a view of *The Molo, Venice, from the Bacino di San Marco* (Constable no. 104), which appears from photographs to date from the 1730s, but it is not known when it was acquired.
17. See D. Wilson, 'A bust of Thomas Hollis by Joseph Wilton RA: Sitter and artist revisited', *The British Art Journal*, V, No. 3, Winter 2004, pp. 4–26.
18. J. Ingamells, *A Dictionary of British and Irish Travellers in Italy 1701–1800 compiled from the Brinsley Ford Archive*, New Haven and London, 1997, pp. 512–13.
19. *Pace* Constable, who states (I, p. 40) that he was not.
20. Constable nos 84 and 318.
21. Constable no. 467.
22. Constable no. 397.
23. Constable nos 71 and 176; 46 and 74.
24. Constable I, p. 137.
25. A fellow director was Sir Humphrey Morice (1723–85), who owned a fine pair of Venetian views on copper dating from the late 1720s and a studio view of the Bacino di San Marco (Constable nos 89, 117 and 140).
26. His country home had previously been at nearby Havering-atte-Bower. Dagnam was demolished in the 1950s.
27. E. Waterhouse, *Gainsborough*, London, 1958, p. 83, no. 513; currently on the London market.
28. According to the catalogue of the sale at Christie's, London, 27 June 1885, lot 27, from which withdrawn by Sheffield H. M. Neave; re-entered, 15 May 1886, lot 85, unsold, and sold 2 April 1887, lot 113; Waterhouse, *op. cit.*, p. 122, no. 1003.
29. See p. 41.
30. Constable nos 232 and 235; 516–17.
31. Constable nos 36 and 80; exhibited Rome 2005, nos 56–7; *Correspondence between Frances, Countess of Hartford (afterwards Duchess Somerset) and Henrietta Louisa, Countess of Pomfret, between the years 1738 and 1741*, London, 1805, III, p. 343.
32. *Ibid.*
33. Constable, under no. 356; C. Klemm, *Die Gemälde der Stiftung Betty und David M. Koetser*, Zürich, 1988, pp. 143–5, no. 62, illustrated in colour. Also formerly at Warwick Castle was a studio copy of a small variant of Smithson's *Courtyard of the Doge's Palace with the Giants' Staircase* of 1740–1; for both see Constable, under no. 80.
34. Smithson's paintings, which are first recorded at Stanwick, the house he inherited from his grandfather in 1733, do, however, correspond in date with his marriage in 1740; Brooke's Reception painting was presumably an ambassadorial commission which had been left on the painter's hands.
35. Constable nos 38 and 45; the absence in the former of Antonio Gai's gates to the Loggetta of the Campanile, erected in 1742, suggests that these paintings were executed immediately after those for Smithson. Here again the date of the paintings does not correspond with that of the patron's Grand Tour.
36. A. Derstine in R. Ward Bissell *et al.*, *Masters of Italian Baroque Painting: Detroit Institute of Arts*, Detroit and London, 2005, pp. 140–1, no. 46, illustrated in colour.

37. For photographs of copies of several of the paintings in the original framing, see J. Cornforth, 'Farnborough Hall, Warwickshire', I, *Country Life*, CXC, No. 28, 11 July 1996, p. 55, fig. 8, and *ibidem*, II, *Country Life*, CXC, No. 29, 18 July 1996, pp. 50–2, figs. 1–2 and 7. Coincidentally, Perritt had in 1741–2 decorated the interior of the Rotunda at Ranelagh (see Cat. nos 32, 33).

38. Constable I, p. 148, and II, under no. 38.

39. Constable I, p. 148.

40. Christie's, London, 13 July 1895, lots 23–8.

41. Links 1998, pp. 23–4, no. 228*; the reasons for this identification have never been clear to the present writer.

42. Constable no. 458(b); exhibited Bergamo, 1969, colour pl. XVIII; exhibited Vicenza, 1973, no. 7, as from a Bergamo private collection.

43. Constable nos 79 and 81; exhibited Rome 2005, nos 65–6.

44. Constable no. 344.

45. A drawing of the damage to the Campanile is at Windsor (Constable no. 552). The possibility that the painting was executed in England is supported by Parker's observation that a replica of that drawing in the British Museum (Constable no. 553) is on paper with a watermark of the 'Strasbourg Lily' type, 'never met with among Canaletto's drawings made in Italy [but occurring] repeatedly in those of his English period' (Parker 1948, p. 40, under no. 55). It should also be noted that a painting showing the Campanile under repair (Constable/Links 1976, no. 67*) was almost certainly painted in England, since its pendant is a *capriccio* which includes elements closely related in type to those in other *capricci* of the English period (Constable/Links 1976, no. 472*). The size of the Philadelphia painting gives further support to this suggestion.

46. Redford 1996, p. 78.

47. Christie's, London, 27 July 1928, lot 143.

48. In Dodsley's Collection of Poems; see A. E. Garnier, *The Chronicles of the Garniers of Hampshire*, Norwich and London, 1900, p. 22.

49. See note 39; lot 21.

50. I am indebted to his descendant Richard Garnier for this information.

51. Garnier was clearly close to his brother-in-law, who, by his will of 1760, was to be his heir in the event of the death of his own son.

52. S. Tillyard, *Aristocrats: Caroline, Emily, Louisa and Sarah Lennox 1740–1832*, London, 1995, pp. 39, 41, 80 and 109.

53. Ingamells 1997, p. 391.

54. See Garnier, *op. cit.* in note 49, pp. 18 and 21, footnote. The implication is that Truesdale was based there at the time of their marriage; they had evidently returned to England by 1746.

55. All these investments were interest-bearing, nearly two-thirds of Canaletto's investments in 1755 being in favour of his two younger sisters, who relied upon him for financial support. The total is paltry compared with the 10,000 ducats which the figure painter Francesco Fontebasso had in the bank at the time of his death the year after Canaletto's. For all these details I am indebted to Montecuccoli degli Erri, *loc. cit.* under note 16.

56. Constable nos 424 and 438; exhibited New York 1989–90, nos 65–6, and Birmingham 1993–4, nos 9 and 12.

57. Hayes 1958, p. 345.

58. Constable nos 425–6. Only the latter has ever been exhibited outside the Czech Republic, and only on one occasion, in *The Glory of Venice*, London and Washington, 1994–5, no. 133.

59. See p. 42.

60. Walker 1979, pp. 237–8.

61. See below and Fig. 28.1.

62. The larger of these was sold at Christie's, London, 9 July 1993, lot 47; the smaller (long attributed to Canaletto, see Constable, under no. 426) is in the collection of the Bank of England; see M. Manzelli, *Antonio Joli: opera pittorica*, Venice, 1999, pp. 108–9, nos L.11–12, fig. 81 and colour pl. XLIII.

63. Constable nos 216(a) and 216(b) and 340; the former was sold at Sotheby's, London, 7 July 2005; the whereabouts of the latter have been unknown since its sale by Ader Tajan, Paris, 15 December 1993, lot 13.

64. Vertue *Note Books*, III, p. 151.

65. Einberg 1992.

66. See p. 45.

67. There is no justification for the presence of another blue plaque on Canaletto House, 10 Howley Place, Little Venice, stating that Canaletto 'worked from a studio on this site 1746–1755'. I am grateful to Monique Kornell for bringing this to my attention and to Emily Cole and Catherine Benson for confirming that it was not authorised by the London County Council.

68. Finberg 1921, p. 35, note 1.

69. M. Manfredi, 'Jacopo Amigoni: a Venetian painter in Georgian London', *The Burlington Magazine*, CXLVII, No. 1231, October 2005, pp. 676 and 677, note 12.

70. Vertue *Note Books*, III, p. 158.

71. Constable no. 439.

72. Hayes 1958, p. 346.

73. Hayes 1958, p. 346, note 31.

74. See p. 41.

75. Finberg 1921, p. 38; Constable I, p. 143.

76. Presumably also at this time he updated his view of *The Grand Canal looking North from near the Rialto Bridge* in Smith's collection (now in the Royal Collection; Constable no. 233) by adding the brand new façade of Smith's own house, the Palazzo Mangilli-Valmarana.

77. I am grateful to Viola Pemberton-Pigott for bringing this to my attention.

78. Constable no. 467.

79. Constable I, pp. 145–6, and no. 397, described as earlier than the Hollis version, in which case an English origin would be almost certain.

80. Constable nos 467 and 397.

81. Constable no. 412.

82. Constable no. 434.

83. Constable I, p. 147.

84. Vertue *Note Books*, III, p. 149.

85. Vertue *Note Books*, III, p. 151.

86. This confusion indeed persists to this day in German-speaking countries, where the name 'Canaletto' is used primarily to refer to the younger artist.

87. Vertue *Note Books*, III, p. 150.

88. E. W. Bradley, *The Works of the late Edward Dayes*, 1805, p. 322; quoted by Constable I, pp. 35–6.

89. H. P. Horne, *Magazine of Art*, 1899, pp. 243ff.; quoted by Constable I, pp. 36 and 144.

90. Constable I, pp. 139–45.

91. 'At this period in Canaletto's life it is sometimes difficult to say whether a painting or drawing was made in England or Venice …' (Constable I, p. 147); 'Most of the imaginary views seem to have been produced after 1740 and little more can be attempted than to separate those of the pre-England period from those which came after the return to Venice. There are few who would claim to be able to identify those executed *in* England or even to say whether these account for a large or small proportion of the whole' (Links 1994, p. 202).

92. Constable no. 430; last sold at Christie's, London, 17 November 1989, lot 3.

93. Constable nos 428(a) and 436(a); both in an English private collection.

94. Constable nos 427 and 427(a).

95. The other is Constable no. 436(a).

96. Constable no. 749.

97. Constable no. 746(b).

98. Constable no. 437(b) as untraced; Links 1998, p. 41, pl. 236.

99. 'per la prima ed ultima volta'.

100. Walker 1979, p. 241. This might suggest that the Windsor drawing is the only one which postdates the completion of the bridge in 1750.

101. Canaletto also depicted in drawings the newly erected Hampton Court Bridge (Cat. no. 36) and Old London Bridge only a few years before the removal of the houses on it (Cat. no. 3). Vertue's note of June 1749 suggests that there may also have been a painting of the latter subject, which may be that last recorded in a sale in 1801 (see Constable, under no. 738).

102. Constable no. 417; last seen at Christie's, London, 6 July 1984, lot 87 (sold after the sale and now in a European private collection).

103. Constable no. 433(a), incorrectly described as on canvas and as a doubtful attribution.

104. New style. Until 1751 the year ended on 25 March so this payment was recorded as of 3 March 1748.

105. Constable no. 756; not included in the exhibition because of its delicate condition.

106. V. Pemberton-Pigott in New York 1989–90, p. 61.

107. Constable no. 408.

108. Constable, under no. 408; Constable records the Marlow version as at Alnwick and the Canaletto version as at Albury Park, but the locations are now reversed.

109. It was offered at Christie's, London, 20 November 1981 (lot 59), and again on 5 March 1982 (lot 35).

110. Constable, under no. 408; Kingzett 1982, p. 77.

111. Kingzett, 1982, pp. 20–1, Marines M and N.

112. Constable no. 511; Christie's, London, 8 December 1995, lot 76; subsequently with P. & D. Colnaghi & Co. Ltd.

113. Christie's, London, 4 July 1984, lot 82; Links 1998, p. 53, no. 825*, pl. 240.

114. Constable no. 823; this appears to be signed lower left.

115. Constable no. 511(c). This has been thought to be a fragment, unnecessarily in the opinion of this writer. It is not as obviously of the English period as the other variants.

116. Constable, under no. 512; Christie's, New York, 29 January 1998, lot 95.

117. Constable no. 512; offered unsuccessfully at Sotheby's, New York, 30 May 1991, lot 64.

118. See note 5.

119. Constable no. 451.

120. I am grateful to Arabella Chandos of Sotheby's for showing this to me.

121. This form of 'signature' is also seen in Cat. no. 61.

122. Constable I, p. 142, and II, nos 735–6.

123. Constable no. 343; hidden in the Portuguese Champalimaud collection since 1973, this briefly became accessible when it was sold at Christie's, London, 6 July 2005, lot 20.

124. Constable no. 643. This drawing had earlier been used by Bernardo Bellotto as the basis for his painting of the subject at Castle Howard.

125. *The Gentleman's Magazine*, 19, May 1749, p. 235. This and the following reference are quoted by Picard 2000, pp. 34 and 305, notes 55–6.

126. *The Gentleman's Magazine*, 19, August 1749, p. 377.

127. I am grateful to Emile Debruijn for this suggestion.

128. Constable nos 84 and 318. Offered at Christie's, New York, 25 January 2002, lot 78, and on the London art market in 2004.

129. Constable nos 317 and 301.

130. Links 1998, pp. 30 and 32, nos 301* and 318**, pls 235–6.

131. Constable no. 318*. Sold at Christie's, London, 11 April 1986, lot 54, and since in a London private collection.

132. Constable no. 124*. Sold from the Estate of Alice Tully at Christie's, New York, 11 January 1995, lot 38.

133. Constable nos 67* and 472*.

134. Links 1998, pp. 5 and 18, nos 8* and 171*, pls 277–8. Sold at Sotheby's, London, 3 July 1997, lot 94.

135. Constable no. 8. Offered at Christie's, New York, 12 January 1996, lot 38, and sold after the sale.

136. Links, 1998, pp. 16 and 31, nos 146* and 308*, pls 249 and 265. Offered at Sotheby's, London, 7 December 1994, lot 72, and sold after the sale.

137. Constable, under no. 380 and no. 388.

138. Constable, under no. 408.

139. Constable no. 519, as 'Attributed to Canaletto'.

140. An attribution to the Irish view painter Edmund Garvey, who exhibited in London from 1767 and settled there in 1778, may be considered.

141. Constable no. 418.

142. Nottingham University Art Gallery, *Locko Park and the Drury-Lowes: A Derbyshire Family and its Art Treasures*, 1982, no. 20, as 'Circle of Canaletto'. This is known to the present writer only from a photograph.

143. Constable no. 411, as 'Attributed to Canaletto'.

144. Exhibited Canada 1964–5, p. 128, no. 105, illustrated.

145. It was restored and laid down on aluminium in 1984.

146. Christie's, London, 8 July 1988, lot 130.

147. C. Beddington in the *Oxford Dictionary of National Biography*, Oxford, 2004, 9, pp. 885–7.

THE LONDON ART WORLD
OF THE MID-EIGHTEENTH CENTURY

Brian Allen

Figure 18
Marco Ricci, *Rehearsal of an opera, c.* 1709, oil on canvas,
19 × 22 in. (48.3 × 55.9 cm.). Yale Center for British Art,
Paul Mellon Collection

It has long been accepted that the prime reason for Canaletto's move to England in late May 1746 was the sharp falling away of his clientele in Venice as a result of the difficulties of travel in mainland Europe during the War of the Austrian Succession (1740–8). Canaletto was in his forty-ninth year when he arrived in London and had long enjoyed fame throughout Europe. For the unmarried Canaletto the decision to move abroad must have been somewhat easier than for those with heavy domestic commitments, but leaving the relative calm of the Venetian lagoon, which was isolated from most of the major skirmishes of the mid-eighteenth century, must still have been a momentous decision. The fact that so many British travellers had acquired paintings by him during their stay in Venice must have given him confidence that England would remain a buoyant market for his work, if not solely for views of Venice, then for views of the Thames and its splendid and soon to be completed new bridge at Westminster.[1]

Many of Canaletto's compatriots – artists, musicians, architects and poets – could be found at work across the courts of Europe in the mid-eighteenth century, not least because they possessed a variety of skills and a versatility that could not be easily matched elsewhere.[2] Over the four decades prior to Canaletto's arrival in 1746 a number of his fellow countrymen had already tried their hand in England, with varying degrees of success and mostly as decorative history painters. Antonio Pellegrini (1675–1741), Sebastiano Ricci (1659–1734) and his nephew Marco Ricci (1676–1730; Fig. 18), and another adopted Venetian, Antonio Bellucci (1654–1726), had all been active in the first two decades of the century, and we are told that Sebastiano Ricci earned so much money in England that he was obliged to pay a special tax before he could export it when he returned to Venice in 1716.[3]

That first wave of Venetian painters was followed by Giuseppe Grisoni (1699–1769), who arrived *c.* 1720 and, like Bellucci, worked at that great lost house Cannons for the Duke of Chandos, one of a group of powerful arbiters of taste in England who gave considerable support to these émigré Italians.[4] Grisoni, who also painted portraits, eventually returned to Italy in 1728 with his young English pupil William Hoare (1707–92) in tow.

More sustained success was enjoyed by Jacopo Amigoni (*c.* 1682–1752), who was trained in Venice and worked in England for ten years between 1729 and 1739. Although primarily a decorative history painter, Amigoni struggled to find sufficient patronage in that increasingly redundant genre and found it necessary to turn to portrait painting, in which he enjoyed considerable success as a result of patronage from Queen Caroline and other members of the Royal family.[5] Late in his sojourn in London, Amigoni was joined by his former pupil, the itinerant Italian-Swiss portrait painter Cavaliere Rusca (1696?–1769), who enjoyed brief success in London as a portraitist in 1738–9 before finally settling in Milan in 1740. Other Italian painters who made their mark in England just before Canaletto's arrival include the extravagant Florentine portraitist and history painter Andrea Soldi (c. 1703–1771), who arrived in 1735 and enjoyed considerable success before his bankruptcy in 1744, and the versatile Andrea Casali (c. 1700–1784), who stayed for twenty-five years after his arrival in 1741.[6]

To a considerable extent, the decade prior to Canaletto's arrival in London had been dominated by foreign-born painters; and to the Italians already mentioned we can add Philip Mercier (1689?–1760), German-born but of French Huguenot origin, who came to England in 1716 and stayed for the rest of his life, and Jean-Baptiste Van Loo (1684–1745), whose prolific five-year stint as a fashionable portrait painter in London from 1737 was cut short only by ill-health. Still active too was the Swede Michael Dahl (1659–1743), who had settled in London as early as 1689, and who only retired, as a result of old age, c. 1740, as well as his fellow countryman and former pupil Hans Hysing (1678–1753).[7]

The foreign domination of the London market for portraiture was, however, stubbornly contested by the native-born painters such as Jonathan Richardson (1665–1745), John Vanderbank (1694–1739), and indeed Canaletto's exact contemporary William Hogarth (1697–1764), who actively applied himself to portrait painting for a few brief years from about 1740. Still in the early part of their careers at that date were (to name but a few) Richardson's son-in-law and former pupil Thomas Hudson (1701–1779), who in 1740 returned from a kind of exile in Devon to establish a very fashionable practice, and Vanderbank's pupil Arthur Pond (1701–1758). The talented young Scot Allan Ramsay (1714–1784), who, having returned from the first of four trips to Italy in 1738, had also made his mark and could boast in April 1740 that he had 'put all your Vanlois [Van Loo] and Soldis and Roscos [Rusca] to flight and now play the first fiddle myself'.[8] Significantly, Ramsay did not even bother to mention his English rivals.

By the early and mid-1740s anti-French sentiment in particular and the fear of Jacobitism were to some extent to put a dampener on the pronounced continental tastes that had developed in London over the previous few years, and we should remember that Canaletto's arrival at the end of May 1746 came at a highly sensitive moment, only a matter of weeks after the defeat of the Jacobite rebels at the Battle of Culloden on 16 April.

George Vertue, who chronicled the London art world of the first half of the eighteenth century in such detail, remarked significantly in 1743, that is to say just after the fall of Walpole's government, on the rise of native talent: 'since Mr. Vanlo, painter left England the most promising young Painters make most advances possible to be distinguisht in the first class – of those that make the best figure Hymore [.] Hudson Pond Knapton Ramsey Dandridge Hussey Hogarth Wills'.[9] Whereas in the year of Kneller's death (1723) Vertue had only been able to compile a list of twenty-three 'painters of Note in London', most of them foreign, by 1748 an article entitled 'The Art of Painting' published in the *Universal Magazine* listed fifty-six names, most of them English.[10] The absence of Canaletto from this list is particularly striking and may confirm a suspicion that after two years in London he remained a largely invisible figure, except to a small coterie of aristocratic patrons.

Those rising artists mentioned by Vertue in 1743, all of them portrait painters, were of course not rivals for Canaletto, and, indeed, in the 1730s and 1740s landscape painting was still only beginning to establish itself as an economically viable genre for an artist. Many of those landowners who were spending fortunes improving their houses and estates wanted some kind of pictorial record of their considerable investments, and this demand, coupled with a buoyant market for pastiches of the Arcadian landscapes of Claude Lorrain, Nicolas Poussin and Gaspard Dughet, provided employment for painters like John Wootton (c. 1683–1764) and George Lambert (1700–65). Canaletto's speciality, view painting, also had a very modest tradition in London before 1746 and was largely the preserve of foreign painters, usually of Dutch or Flemish extraction, such as Jan Siberechts (1627–1703?; Fig. 19), Leonard Knyff (1650–1722) and Peter Tillemans (c. 1684–1734). By the 1740s, the early paintings of Richard Wilson (1713?–1782) and works by the little-known Joseph Nickolls (active 1726–1755) and John Griffier (active 1738–1773) suggest that view painting

was beginning to gain in popularity.

Canaletto would have known nothing of these artists before his arrival, but he might have been more concerned by the presence in London of his compatriot Antonio Joli (c. 1700–1777), who probably arrived in 1744, having travelled from Venice via Dresden. Joli was employed primarily as a scene painter at the King's Theatre in the Haymarket from 1744 to 1748 but eventually left for Madrid in 1750.[11]

Figure 19
Jan Siberechts, *Wollaton Hall and Park, Nottinghamshire*, 1697, oil on canvas, 75½ × 54½ in. (191.8 × 138.4 cm.). Yale Center for British Art, Paul Mellon Collection

Figure 20
Edward Haytley, *Chelsea Hospital*, c. 1746,
oil on canvas, diameter: 22 in. (56 cm.).
The Foundling Museum, London

Neither is it clear if Canaletto had any inkling that his works were being copied in London long before his arrival, although he must have been alarmed by what he was to discover in London. One such copyist whom we can identify is Joseph Baudin, who, Vertue tells us, 'so much imitated Canaletti'.[12] A visitor to Baudin's studio in about 1740 recorded that his pictures and prints 'had so good an effect that I almost imagined myself to be once more taking a turn about Venice, which I left but three months ago'.[13] In 1745 Vertue also mentions that Francis Harding (active c. 1730–c. 1766) was 'continually immitating paintings of Canaletti of Venice Views &c. & also paintings of Paulo Panini with good success' and that they were 'hard to distinguish … from the originals'.

Rather interestingly, Vertue also noted in 1745 that some 'pieces of Landskip in Rounds' were presented to the Foundling Hospital in London by Francis Harding, but these seem to have disappeared.[14] Curiously, in 1751, Vertue recorded (surely erroneously) that there were twelve roundel landscapes on view at the Hospital, 'all done by different painters', although only eight, listed precisely by title in a different source from the same year, have survived.[15] This group of eight small landscape roundels in gilded, oak-leaf cluster frames decorated the Governors' Court Room at the Hospital, alongside the four large history paintings by Hogarth, Hayman, Highmore and Wills.[16] It is tempting to suppose that these Canaletto-like landscapes of the other charitable hospital foundations in London, painted by Edward Haytley (active 1740–1761; Fig. 20), Samuel Wale (1721–1786), Richard Wilson (c. 1713–1782) and the young Thomas Gainsborough (1727–1788; Fig. 21), were a concerted response to Canaletto's presence in London.[17] The three by Wale and the Gainsborough were certainly in place by 11 May 1748, and the others must have been installed soon after.[18]

What would Canaletto have made of the native painters in London? One wonders if he might have shared the views of the French Abbé le Blanc, whose *Letters on the English and French Nations*, translated and published in Dublin in 1747, not long after his arrival, must have touched a very raw nerve among English artists. In Letter XXIII, entitled 'On the State of Painting and Sculpture in England', the Abbé argued that, whilst English connoisseurs were buying many of Europe's greatest art treasures, 'England had not hitherto bred one painter'.[19]

Many of Canaletto's English contemporaries saw the lack of a formal state-run academy in London as the overwhelming impediment to advancing the visual arts in Britain; agitation for the establishment of such a body had been fermenting for some time before the 1740s. That very complex story cannot be related fully here but it is worth noting the views of some contemporary commentators on the subject. Comparing England with Italy, Robert Campbell, in his interesting book *The London Tradesman*, essentially a guide for parents planning to apprentice their sons, and, incidentally, also published in 1747, wrote:

> The several Academies for Painting [in Italy], Not only produce Painters, but give a general Taste for Painting to the whole Body of the People. The respect that is paid to Men eminent In this Profession, is another Encouragement for Parents to breed their Children in that Way ... Were the lovers of Painting among our nobility to contribute to the erecting and maintaining Academies for Painting, as is done in other Nations, we should in a few Years boast of as Eminent as any in Italy.[20]

This was a theme pursued by others, including William Hogarth's friend Dr James Parsons, who in his treatise on physiognomy replied to the Abbé le Blanc's criticisms of the state of art in England by drawing attention to the achievements of English artists such as Sir James Thornhill (1675/6–1734) at St Paul's Cathedral and Greenwich, Hogarth at St Bartholomew's Hospital, and the important collection of contemporary art just put on view at the still incomplete Foundling Hospital in Bloomsbury. If English artists 'were bless'd with the same academical Endowments that other Nations can boast of', wrote Parsons, 'we should undoubtedly have as great Proficients in the Arts of Painting and Sculpture as any other Nation: For it is notorious, that our Youth have made as good a Figure in foreign Academies as any that were educated at them; and we have had some, who, by dint of Genius, have born away Prizes from those of every other Nation'.[21]

The architect John Gwynn (1713–1786) voiced a similarly commercial argument in an essay published in 1749 designed to elicit support for an academy:

> shall we ever be obliged to foreign Workmen for all that is beautiful and masterly in our Churches and Palaces ? ... there may be great Pecuniary Advantages, such as ought to engage the Attention of the mere Merchant, obtained from our Improvements in the Art

Figure 21
Thomas Gainsborough, *The Charterhouse, London*, c. 1748, oil on canvas, diameter: 22 in. (56 cm.).
The Foundling Museum, London

When Canaletto returned permanently to Venice in 1755
the debate over the establishment of a more formal academy
was still raging: in that year yet another plan emerged, drawn
up by a select committee of twenty-six artists from the existing
rather informal St Martin's Lane Academy. Disagreement
with their potential partners, the Society of Dilettanti, over
the proposed governance of such a body led to abandonment
of this scheme; but the Society of Artists was eventually
formed at the end of 1759. The Royal Academy was finally
established only in 1768, the year of Canaletto's death, some
thirteen years after he had returned to Venice.[23]

It has been suggested that Canaletto's main reasons for
travelling to London were essentially commercial. It was
Vertue who first noted that Canaletto came to England 'to
putt [his fortune] into the Stocks here for better security. or
better interest than abroad',[24] and it is certainly true that in the
mid-eighteenth century London was, perhaps more than any
other city in Europe, emerging not only as a cultural
centre but as the fastest growing commercial environment in
Europe. Jacopo Amigoni, so Vertue tells us, had been a
wealthy man in 1739, when he left England after ten years,
taking £4,000 or £5,000 with him on his return to Italy,
and, if Vertue is to be believed, it was Amigoni who was
eventually instrumental in persuading Canaletto to make the
journey to London.

Amigoni, however, might also have cautioned Canaletto
about the attitudes of some of the native painters in London.
Twelve years earlier he had himself been a victim of an
orchestrated, though ultimately rather absurd, campaign that
exposed the overtly xenophobic insecurities of the Hogarth
circle. On 4 May 1734, ironically the day that Amigoni's
English rival Sir James Thornhill died, James Ralph
(1705?–1752), the editor of a pro-ministerial newspaper, the
Weekly Register, launched a vitriolic attack on Amigoni and
those British patrons who preferred the work of foreigners.

According to Ralph, Amigoni's paintings were 'only calculated to please at a Glance by the artful Mixture of a Variety
of gay Colours, but have no solidity in them'. This was part of
Ralph's defence of English painters such as William
Hogarth and Francis Hayman (1708–1776), who were
desperate for opportunities to establish their credentials as
history painters. It is entirely likely, however, that there was a
personal element in Hogarth's position in this debate, since
his father-in-law, Sir James Thornhill, had recently been
humiliated by Amigoni, whose work had been brought in to
replace Thornhill's at Moor Park, Sir Benjamin Styles's opu-
lent Palladian house in Hertfordshire (Fig. 22).[25] Hogarth
had also discovered, just a few months earlier, that Amigoni
was negotiating with the governors of St Bartholomew's
Hospital in London (where Hogarth was himself a governor) to undertake the decoration of the new building's staircase. Hogarth moved quickly to pre-empt him by offering to
decorate the staircase walls free of charge, thereby throwing
down the gauntlet to the foreign history painters. The resulting paintings, *The Pool of Bethesda* and *The Good Samaritan*,
both complete in 1737, represent an extraordinary leap in
scale and ambition for Hogarth, who had hitherto worked
only on a small scale, and they were the clearest statement of
his future aspirations as a history painter.[26] Significantly, the
attacks on Amigoni in the *Weekly Register* abruptly ceased
after the governors accepted Hogarth's offer.

The xenophobic attitudes so prevalent in England in the
1740s may also explain, at least in part, why Canaletto seems
to have maintained such a low profile while he was in
London. Apart from a few remarks in Vertue's notebooks,
his years there are marked by an apparently pronounced lack
of contact with his fellow artists, if we are to judge by the lack
of any substantial accounts of him discovered in any written
sources. This is in contrast to other foreigners at work in
London in the 1740s, such as the French draughtsman
Hubert Gravelot (1699–1773), who was active as a teacher of
drawing at his own drawing school in Exeter Street off the
Strand and at the St Martin's Lane Academy, or the Swiss-
born Carl Marcus Tuscher (1705–51) and his compatriot,
the goldchaser George Michael Moser (1706–83), who both
played a very active role in the politics of the London art
world in the 1740s.[27] Canaletto seems to have remained aloof
from the pressing issues of local concern, particularly the
need to establish a more formal academy, that preoccupied the
artists of Hogarth's circle in the informal environment of the

Figure 22
Sir James Thornhill and Jacopo Amigoni,
Interior of the Hall, Moor Park, Hertfordshire

St Martin's Lane Academy. With his accomplished Venetian training and his network of European contacts Canaletto no doubt felt rather more secure in his exalted status, albeit in the lesser genre of view painting, than his London counterparts, whose prime concern was to liberate themselves from the constraints of the hopelessly inadequate system of patronage that so limited their professional opportunities in London. It remains remarkable, nevertheless, that the presence in London of so celebrated an artist should elicit so few comments about his activities. One suspects that had Canaletto been a history painter we might have heard a great deal more about him.

During Canaletto's time in London there was also a notable shift in attitude away from contemporary Italian art, at least in more *avant-garde* quarters on both sides of the English Channel – a development that cannot have been to Canaletto's advantage. Whilst the glories of the Italian Renaissance were still enthusiastically extolled, it was deemed by many informed commentators that Italian art had been more or less in steady decline ever since. In an essay in Samuel Johnson's *The Idler*, written in 1759, Joshua Reynolds (1723–92), whose dismissive attitude towards contemporary Italian art first manifested itself the moment he arrived in Italy in 1749, wrote that 'The Italians seem to have been continually declining … from the time of Michel Angelo to that of Carlo Maratti, and from thence to the insipidity to which they are now sunk'.[28] In the second of his *Discourses*, delivered to the students at the newly established Royal Academy in London on 11 December 1769, Reynolds warned his students not to be too impressed by contemporary Italian art:

> To a young man just arrived in Italy, many of the present painters of that country are ready enough to obtrude their precepts, and to offer their own performances as examples of that perfection which they affect to recommend. The Modern, however, who recommends himself as a standard, may justly be suspected as ignorant of the true end, and unacquainted with the proper object, of the art which he professes. To follow such a guide, will not only retard the Student, but mislead him.[29]

Before Reynolds left for Italy, it had even been suggested to him, by Lord Edgcumbe, that he should study with his Italian contemporary Pompeo Batoni (1708–1787), but Reynolds replied that he had nothing to learn from him.[30]

By the mid-1740s it might also be argued that a British audience was becoming increasingly discriminating in its attitude towards art, and especially towards landscape painting. Good-quality landscapes by the great Rome-based painters of the seventeenth century such as Claude Lorrain, Nicolas Poussin, Gaspard Dughet and Salvator Rosa were arriving in England in increasing quantities, and so, too, were outstanding examples by the great Dutch landscape painters of the period like Ruisdael, Hobbema and Cuyp.[31] This more sophisticated taste encouraged the relegation of the kind of topographical landscape practised by Canaletto, no matter how accomplished, into the ranks of those works that Jonathan Richardson described in his essay *The Connoisseur* of 1719 as being unable to 'Improve the Mind' or 'excite Noble Sentiment'.[32] For a painter like Canaletto who, as his eccentric early patron Owen MacSwinny put it in 1727, excelled at 'painting things which fall immediately under his eye' the tide was evidently turning against him.[33]

Richardson's view was still essentially that professed forty years later by Joshua Reynolds, in that same *Idler* essay, published in 1759, where he criticized those painters who merely 'imitated' nature which resulted in painting 'no longer being considered as a liberal art, and sister to Poetry; this imitation being merely mechanical, in which the slowest intellect is always sure to succeed best; for the Painter of genius cannot stoop to drudgery … the Grand Style of Painting requires this minute attention to be carefully avoided'.[34] Art like Canaletto's was, in Reynolds's mind, consistent with the values of the Dutch school. He writes

> The Italian attends only to the invariable, the great and general ideas which are fixed and inherent in universal Nature; the Dutch, on the contrary, to literal truth and a minute exactness in the details, I may say, of Nature, modified by accident. The attention to these petty peculiarities is the very cause of this naturalness so admired in the Dutch, which if we suppose it to be a beauty is certainly of a lesser order, that ought to give place to a beauty of a superior kind, since one cannot be obtained without departing from the other.

Significantly, in the same essay, Reynolds referred to the Venetian school as a whole as 'the Dutch part of Italian genius'.[35]

This debate was fuelled by others, including Giuseppe Baretti (1719–1789), a compatriot of Canaletto's from Turin, who arrived in London in 1751 with a minor literary reputation and quickly became a part of the Johnson circle. Baretti was very robust in his defence of the art of his native land when he wrote in a letter to his brothers in 1760 that 'The Arts in England are more perfect than in other modern countries. Except for painting, sculpture, architecture and music, in which the English cannot come near us, no matter how hard they try, in the rest they defeat us and all others'.[36] Baretti was later to write, in response to Samuel Sharp's overtly Protestant rant against contemporary Italian life, *Letters from Italy* (1767), that Italian artists 'will allow very freely, that Italy cannot boast of so enchanting a pencil as Reynolds's … they praise the landscapes of Barret and Wilson, and the horses of Stubbs' and he then goes on at length to point out the superiority of contemporary Italian art and its popularity abroad.[37]

Some of Canaletto's British contemporaries, such as the portrait painter John Astley (1724–1787) and the young Scots Cosmo Alexander (1724–1772) and Gavin Hamilton (1723–98), who, like Reynolds, were all back in London in 1753 after periods of study in Rome, were, as the cautious and astute Reynolds noted in a letter to Joseph Wilton, over-stretching themselves financially by renting or purchasing expensive studio space. Canaletto, by contrast, seems to have lived comparatively modestly.[38] Although on his arrival in London he seems to have taken lodgings in Whitehall, near the house of his first patron, the Duke of Richmond, he is later listed by Vertue in 1749 as lodging in the house of the cabinet maker Richard Wiggans in Silver Street, Golden Square, Soho (see Fig. 7).[39] Silver Street, Golden Square, no longer exists under that name, since its name was changed to Beak Street in 1883. It ran to the north of Golden Square, between Warwick Street and the junction of Cambridge and Little Windmill Streets (now Lexington Street). Richard Wiggan's house was situated on the north side of Silver Street, opposite Upper James Street.[40] Silver Street consisted of single-fronted four-storey houses with rooftop garrets, 'being intended for tradesmen and lower middle class occupation'.[41] Presumably as a single man Canaletto did not require an entire house, but was his placing of himself at a distance from the artists' quarter of Covent Garden a conscious act of isolation? Perhaps, too, he felt that he would be more at ease in Soho with its large, cosmopolitan community of foreign, predominantly Huguenot, artists and craftsmen. Silver Street was in fact the centre of the Italian – especially Venetian – community in London. Amigoni had resided in Silver Street between 1732 and 1734, as had the Bolognese artist Gaetano Brunetti, who specialized in trompe-l'oeil effects, during those same years.[42]

Vertue noted that Canaletto initially seems to have had a 'shyness of showing his works' but that eventually he resorted to 'advertisement in the publick news papers'.[43] On 26 July 1749 Canaletto placed an advertisement in *The Daily Advertiser* inviting any Gentleman

that will be pleased to come to his House, to see a Picture done by him, being A View of St James's Park, *which he hopes may in some Measure deserve their Approbation. The said View may be seen from Nine in the Morning till Three in the Afternoon, and from Four till Seven in the Evening, for the Space of fifteen Days from the Publication of this Advertizement.*

The picture referred to is almost certainly that now in the collection of the Sir Andrew Lloyd Webber Art Foundation (see Cat. no. 17), for which Canaletto wanted £60 or £70.[44] Two years later, on 30 July 1751, a similar advertisement appeared, again in *The Daily Advertiser*, giving notice that Canaletto's view of 'Chelsea College, Ranelagh House, and the River Thames' (Cat. no. 34) was available for viewing. English artists, led by Hogarth, had only recently begun to realize the potential of this kind of direct marketing of their work, but the Italians seemed rather more adept at infiltrating this new more commercial system. From the moment of his arrival in London Canaletto seems to have been aware of the potential of the print market and, for instance, it was probably before his temporary return to Venice in 1750 that he produced the four drawings of Vauxhall Gardens which were engraved by J. S. Müller and Edward Rooker and published by Robert Sayer in December 1751 (see Fig. 31.1).[45]

Canaletto's time in London undoubtedly elicited a mixed response; those picture dealers and copyists who traded falsely on his name, for instance, must have been especially hostile to his presence, and they may have helped spread the scurrilous rumours, repeated by Vertue in June 1749, that the artist in London was not the genuine Canaletto. Vertue later realized his mistake, having learned that there had been confusion between the identities of Canaletto and his talented nephew Bernardo Bellotto (1722–80), and clarified the matter.[46] Horace Walpole, who took up the chronicler's pen after Vertue's death, was also completely indifferent to Canaletto's presence, even to the point of later suggesting, somewhat absurdly, that both Samuel Scott (*c.* 1702–1772; Fig. 23) and William Marlow (1740–1813) 'were better painters than the Venetian'.[47]

The xenophobic mood of the 1740s seems to have slowly mellowed in the years following Canaletto's departure in 1755 as a new wave of foreign artists settled in London. It is an interesting fact that twenty per cent of the founding members of the Royal Academy, established in 1768, were foreign.[48] Johan Zoffany (1733–1810) came from Germany in 1760; Angelika Kauffman (1741–1807) came from Switzerland; Dominic Serres (1722–93) came from France as a prisoner of war *c.* 1758, and Benjamin West (1738–1820) arrived via Italy from America in 1763. Four of Canaletto's compatriots made up the Academy's numbers: Giovanni Battista Cipriani (1727–1785) was brought to England by William Chambers in 1755; his fellow Florentine, the engraver Francesco Bartolozzi (1728–1815), followed nine years later; Francesco Zuccarelli (1702–1788), who had first settled in London for a decade from 1752, returned for a further six years in 1765. Like their compatriot Agostino Carlini (d. 1790), all enjoyed successful careers in an increasingly cosmopolitan metropolis.

Figure 23
Samuel Scott, *Westminster Bridge under Construction*, c. 1742–5, oil on canvas, 27 × 47 in. (68.6 × 119.4 cm.).
Yale Center for British Art, Paul Mellon Collection

Notes

1. Walker 1979.
2. For a study of this phenomenon see *Italian Culture in Northern Europe in the Eighteenth Century*, ed. Shearer West, Cambridge, 1999, pp. 10, 13.
3. Lione Pascoli, *Vite de' Pittori, Scultori ed Architetti Moderni; vita di Bastiano Ricci*, 2 vols. (Rome, 1730 and 1736), II, p. 381, quoted by Jeffrey Daniels, *Sebastiano Ricci* (Hove, 1976), pp. xiv–xv. For decorative painting in general see Edward Croft-Murray, *Decorative Painting in England 1537–1837*, 2 vols. (London, 1962, 1970), and also Brian Allen, in Birmingham 1993–4, pp. 30–7.
4. C. H. Collins Baker and M. I. Baker, *The Life and Circumstances of James Brydges, First Duke of Chandos, Patron of the Liberal Arts*, Oxford, 1949; Susan Jenkins, 'The Patronage and Collecting of James Brydges, first Duke of Chandos 1674–1744', unpublished DPhil thesis (University of Bristol, 2002), and also Susan Jenkins, 'An Inventory of His Grace the Duke of Chandos's Seat at Cannons taken June 19th 1725 by John Gilbert', *The Walpole Society*, LXVII (2005), pp. 93–192.
5. See John Woodward, 'Amigoni as a Portrait Painter in England', *Burlington Magazine*, XCIX (1957), pp. 21–3.
6. For Soldi see John Ingamells, 'Andrea Soldi – I', *Connoisseur*, Vol. 185 (March 1974), pp. 192–200, and 'Andrea Soldi – II', *Connoisseur*, vol. 186 (July 1974), pp. 178–85; for Casali see Croft-Murray, *op. cit.*, II, pp. 181–3.
7. For Mercier see John Ingamells and Robert Raines, 'A Catalogue of the Paintings, Drawings and Etchings of Philip Mercier', *Walpole Society*, XLVI (1976–78), pp. 1–70; for Van Loo see Fiona Wilson, 'Jean-Baptiste Van Loo in England', unpublished MA thesis (Courtauld Institute of Art, University of London, 1993); for Dahl and Hysing see Wilhelm Nisser, *Michael Dahl and the Contemporary Swedish School of Painting in England*, Uppsala, 1927.
8. Allan Ramsay to Alexander Cunyingham, 10 April 1740 (Scottish Record Office, GD 331/5/20); see also Alastair Smart, *Allan Ramsay: Painter, Essayist and Man of the Enlightenment*, New Haven and London, 1992, p. 74.
9. Vertue *Note Books*, III, p. 117.
10. For the 1723 list see Vertue *Note Books*, III, pp. 12–13, and for the full list of names in the 1748 list see W. T. Whitley, *Artists and their Friends in England 1700–1799*, 2 vols. (London, 1928), I, p. 104.
11. Croft-Murray, *op. cit.*, I, p. 225; for Joli see also Mario Manzanelli, *Antonio Joli opera pittorica* (Studio LT2, 1900).
12. Vertue *Note Books*, IV, p. 30.
13. Hilda F. Finberg, 'Joseph Baudin, imitator of Canaletto', *Burlington Magazine*, LX (April 1932), p. 204.
14. Vertue *Note Books*, III, pp. 126–7.

15. Vertue *Note Books*, III, p. 157, and Whitley, *op. cit.*, I, p. 164.
16. They are now on view at the Foundling Museum, where the Hospital's art treasures are preserved.
17. First suggested by Michael Liversidge (Birmingham 1993–4, p. 110). All eight roundels are illustrated in colour in *Manners & Morals. Hogarth and British Painting 1700–1760* (London: Tate Gallery, 1987), nos 163–170.
18. See Benedict Nicolson, *The Treasures of the Foundling Hospital*, Oxford, 1972, p. 25.
19. Le Blanc, *Letters on the English and French Nations*, 2 vols., Dublin, 1747, I, pp. 156–9.
20. Robert Campbell, *The London Tradesman ... etc ... being a Compendium of all the Trades, Professions, Art ... now practised in the Cities of London and Westminster*, London, 1747, pp. 95–8.
21. James Parsons, *Human Physiognomy Explained*, London, 1747, pp. iv–v.
22. John Gwynn, *Essay on Design: Including Proposals for Erecting a Public Academy to be Supported by Voluntary Subscription (Till a Royal Foundation can be Obtain'd) For Educating the British Youth in Drawing*, London, 1749, pp. 42–3, 45.
23. For a full discussion see Ilaria Bignamini, 'The Accompaniment to Patronage. A Study of the Origins, Rise and Development of an Institutional System of the Arts in Britain, 1692–1768', unpublished PhD thesis (Courtauld Institute of Art, University of London, 1988), and the same author's 'George Vertue, Art Historian and Art Institutions in London, 1689–1768: A Study of Clubs and Academies', *The Walpole Society*, LIV (1988), pp. 19–148.
24. Vertue *Note Books*, III, p. 132.
25. See John B. Shipley, 'Ralph, Ellis, Hogarth, and Fielding', *Eighteenth Century Studies*, I, no. 4 (1968), pp. 313–31. For more on Amigoni see Leslie Hennessey, 'Jacopo Amigoni (c. 1685–1752). An Artistic Biography with a Catalogue of his Venetian Paintings', unpublished PhD dissertation (University of Kansas, 1983), pp. 33–58.
26. Ronald Paulson, *Hogarth, His Life, Art and Times*, 2 vols., New Haven and London, 1971, I, pp. 382–8.
27. For Gravelot see Hanns Hammelmann (edited and completed by T. S. R. Boase), *Book Illustrators in Eighteenth-Century England*, New Haven and London, 1975, pp. 38–42. For Tuscher see Brian Allen, 'Carl Marcus Tuscher: A German Artist in London', *Apollo*, vol. 122 (July 1985), 32–5. For Moser, who eventually became the first Keeper of the Royal Academy, see Richard Edgcumbe, *The Art of the Goldchaser in Eighteenth-Century London*, Oxford, 2000, p. 88.
28. [Joshua Reynolds], 'To the Idler', no. 79 (Saturday 20 October 1759), reprinted in *The Literary Works of Sir Joshua Reynolds*, 3 vols., London, 1819, II, p. 233.
29. *Discourses on Art. Sir Joshua Reynolds*, ed. Robert R. Wark, New Haven and London, 1997, p. 28.

30. See C. R. Leslie and T. Taylor, *The Life and Times of Sir Joshua Reynolds with Notices of Some of His Contemporaries*, 2 vols., London, 1865, I, p. 48.
31. See Elizabeth Manwaring, *Italian Landscape in Eighteenth Century England. A Study Chiefly of the Influence of Claude Lorrain and Salvator Rosa on English Taste 1700–1800*, London, 1925, and Frank Simpson, 'Dutch Painting in England before 1760', *Burlington Magazine*, XCV (February 1953) 39–42.
32. Jonathan Richardson, *The Connoisseur* (London, 1719), pp. 44–5.
33. Quoted by Finberg 1920, p. 23.
34. Reynolds, *loc. cit.*, p. 230.
35. *ibid.*, pp. 231, 234.
36. Giuseppe Baretti, *Lettere familiari di Giuseppe Baretti a suoi tre fratelli Filippo, Giovanni e Amadeo* (Venice, 1763), quoted by Shearer West in 'Xenophobia and Xenomania: Italians and the English Royal Academy' in West, *op. cit.* (note 2), p. 131. West points out that the 'other arts' to which Baretti referred were the arts of modern manufacture, as opposed to the 'fine' arts.
37. Giuseppe Baretti, *An Account of the Manners and Customs of Italy*, 2 vols., London, 1769, I, pp. 264–5.
38. First published by Martin Postle, 'An early unpublished letter by Sir Joshua Reynolds', *Apollo*, CXLI (June 1995), pp. 11–18, and *The Letters of Sir Joshua Reynolds*, ed. John Ingamells and John Edgcumbe, New Haven and London, 2000, pp. 13–16.
39. Vertue *Note Books*, III, p. 151, and Finberg 1921, pp. 34–5, 46.
40. For a schematic map showing the location of Canaletto's lodgings see Hugh Phillips, *Mid Georgian London. A Topographical and Social Survey of Central and Western London about 1750*, London, 1964, p. 236.
41. See F. H. W. Sheppard, *Survey of London*, XXXI, Part 2: *The Parish of St James's Westminster*, London, 1963, p. 174.
42. See Martina Manfredi, 'Jacopo Amigoni: a Venetian painter in Georgian London', *Burlington Magazine*, CXLVII (October 2005), pp. 676–8.
43. Finberg, *loc.cit.*, p. 32, Vertue *Note Books*, III, p. 151.
44. See Einberg 1992, and London, Royal Academy, *Pre-Raphaelite and Other Masters. The Andrew Lloyd Webber Collection* (2003) no. 283.
45. Constable / Links 1989, II, p. 576, no. 748.
46. Vertue *Note Books*, III, pp. 149, 151.
47. See Walpole *Correspondence*, vol.33 (1967) p. 299.
48. See Shearer West, *loc.cit.* pp.120–1.

PATTERNS OF PATRONAGE

Francis Russell

Figure 24
The Venetian Room at Castle Howard photographed in the 1920s

Canales, alias Canaletti, is come over with a letter of recommendation from our old acquaintance the Consul of Venice to Mac in order to his introduction to your Grace, as a patron of the politer parts, or what the Italians understand by the name of virtù. I told him the best service I thought you could do him w.ᵈ be to let him draw a view of the river from yr Dining-room, which in my opinion would give him as much reputation as any of his Venetian prospects.[1]

Thomas Hill's letter of 20 May 1746 to Charles Lennox, 2nd Duke of Richmond and Lennox (1701–50), is the natural departure point for any examination of the complex webs of family, geography and political interest that linked most of the patrons of Canaletto's English years.

The Duke, grandson of King Charles II by his politically acute French mistress, Louise de Kérouaille, Duchess of Portsmouth, had, as it happened, been one of the earliest, if not the first, of the painter's English customers. In November 1727 he had been sent by Owen MacSwinny – the 'Mac' of Hill's letter – one of the remarkable pairs of small views of Venice on copper that have a key place in Canaletto's early development. Yet earlier, in 1726, the Duke had been tempted to buy ten of the celebrated series of Monuments to the Remembrance of a Set of British Worthies, which MacSwinny had commissioned from a consortium of Venetian and other Italian painters, including Canaletto. MacSwinny had been astute enough to gauge the political temperature of the time and to sense that there would be a market for such celebrations of the Whig Revolution of 1688. In view of the Duke's Stuart descent and continuing owner-ship of his grandmother's estate of Aubigny in France, the ten canvases placed in the Dining Room at Goodwood should be understood both as substitutes for mural schemes of the type so fashionable in the previous generation and as clear statements of the Duke's allegiance to the House of Hanover.

MacSwinny was the first English agent to employ Canaletto. Yet more crucial to the artist's career was his long relationship with Joseph Smith, the 'consul of Venice', a merchant who for several decades was the central figure of the English community at Venice. Smith himself became Canaletto's most important patron, but he was equally, if not more, significant as the intermediary in commissions for others. Documents of 27 February 1733, 7 January 1735 and 27 April 1736, which the late Mairi Draper enabled this writer to publish in 1988,[2] establish that the payments for the great series of vedute originally at Bedford House and now at

Woburn were made through Smith's brother John, who evidently acted for him in London. The patron was John Russell, 4th Duke of Bedford (1710–71), who had visited Venice on the Grand Tour but is unlikely to have been able to place an order of such magnitude before he succeeded his elder brother in October 1732.

The Bedford family was very conscious of its contribution to the Revolution of 1688 and indeed owed its Dukedom to this. As was suggested by the writer in 1985,[3] and has been argued in considerable detail by Professor Eglin,[4] there was a correlation between the long-standing English interest in the Venetian constitution and the demand among certain Whig families for views of Venice. Both as a state, albeit a republic, in which the position of the sovereign was effectively balanced by that of a patrician oligarchy, and as a maritime trading power, the Serenissima could be compared with England; and although the parallels were remarked upon much less in the eighteenth century than earlier there is some evidence that the relevance of the Venetian example was not forgotten. Indeed the Duke of Bedford's heir, Lord Tavistock, would in a letter of 1763 tease his friend and neighbour Lord Upper Ossory: 'I had forgot to desire you to study a little the constitution of the republic of Venice, in order to inspire you to a proper dread of aristocracy; I am sure it is very useful for an Englishman.'[5]

It is clear that a number of the Duke's relations by marriage were also significant patrons of Canaletto. The 4th Duke of Bedford – like the elder brother he succeeded, Wriothesley, 3rd Duke of Bedford – married a granddaughter of John Churchill, 1st Duke of Marlborough. His wife, Lady Diana Spencer, daughter of Charles Spencer, 3rd Earl of Sunderland (himself a distinguished collector), was to die in 1735, but the enduring connections of the family are implied by the marriage in 1762 of Caroline, his daughter by his second wife, to Sunderland's grandson, George, 4th Duke of Marlborough. Some years ago I argued that the only series of Canaletto vedute that is fully comparable to Bedford's set, the twenty pictures formerly at Langley Park, Buckinghamshire, were painted for his brother-in-law, Charles, successively 5th Earl of Sunderland and 3rd Duke of Marlborough (1706–58), who rebuilt the house, and were sold with it by the 4th Duke to Sir Robert Harvey in 1788. John Harris's recent discovery of an undated late nineteenth-century guide to Langley confirms this hypothesis.[6]

The Duke of Bedford was not the only brother-in-law with whom the Duke of Marlborough shared an interest in Venetian vedute. For the latter's elder sister, Lady Anne Spencer, had in 1720 married William, 1st Viscount Bateman (c. 1695–1744), who, presumably when in Venice in 1718, had secured a significant group of views by Carlevarijs and was later to obtain two studio versions of components of the Woburn series of Canalettos.[7] Yet another of their brothers-in-law also collected Venetian views: the Duke's elder half-sister, Lady Frances Spencer, had in 1717 married Henry Howard, Viscount Morpeth (1694–1758), who succeeded as 4th Earl of Carlisle in 1738. His collection of vedute included not only what is one of Canaletto's absolute masterpieces, the Bacino, now at Boston, as well as other works by the artist, but also major groups of pictures by the young Bellotto and Marieschi. It was evidently Carlisle's inheritance of his father's great mansion, Castle Howard, and the resources that had funded this that stimulated his patronage of vedutiste. But he was no doubt aware of the example of his wife's half-brother and brother-in-law when he determined to collect views of Venice. Until its contents began to be scattered in the late nineteenth century, the Venetian Room at Castle Howard was the locus classicus of Venetian topographical painting in England (Fig. 24). Unlike the Dukes of Marlborough and Bedford, Carlisle patronized Canaletto's rivals, but like them he was clearly more interested in Canaletto's Venetian subjects than his painting per se: none of the three, significantly, employed Canaletto in his English years.

A prominent Canaletto buyer of the 1730s was Thomas Osborne, 4th Duke of Leeds (1713–89), who was in Venice in 1734. In 1740 he married another granddaughter of the Marlboroughs, Mary, daughter of Francis, 2nd Earl of Godolphin, by Henrietta, Duchess of Marlborough, jure sua. Godolphin's eponymous cousin and heir, the 2nd Baron Godolphin, married in 1743 Anne, daughter of another prominent Whig plutocrat, John, 2nd Earl Fitzwilliam, and brother of William, 3rd Earl Fitzwilliam, who commissioned the notable series of eight canvases by Canaletto which remains in his descendant's possession.

The closely interconnected world of the great Whig families is attested by a further dynastic link. The Duke of Leeds' father, Peregrine, 3rd Duke of Leeds, had married, as his second wife, Lady Anne Seymour, sister of Algernon, Earl of Hertford, who in 1748 succeeded their father as 7th Duke of Somerset. The latter's wife, Frances, elder daughter

and co-heiress of Henry Thynne, was a formidable personality, as can be sensed in the celebrated correspondence with her friend, Henrietta, Countess of Pomfret, whose mother-in-law, Lady Leominster (or Lempster), was a daughter of Thomas Osborne, 1st Duke of Leeds, the 3rd Duke's grandfather. On 20 June 1741, when Lady Pomfret was in Venice, Lady Hertford made it clear that she needed no description of the place:

I have (in imagination) attended you to the doge's palace at Venice, the front of which I am acquainted and charmed with, from a large picture [The Ducal Palace; the Scala dei Giganti, Constable no. 80] *that Sir Hugh Smithson has of it, painted by Canaletti. Lord Brooke has also some views of that city* [presumably Constable, under nos 80 and 356], *painted by the same master.*[8]

Lady Hertford's son-in-law, Sir Hugh Smithson, 4th Bt (1715–86), who would succeed her husband in 1750 as 2nd Earl of Northumberland of the 1749 creation and was in 1766 elevated as Duke, had been in Venice in 1733, and it is conceivable that he ordered his pair of impressive large Canalettos then. More probably he did so later in the decade, as their scale may imply that they were intended for specific positions at Stanwick Park, Yorkshire, which was rebuilt, c. 1739–40, with the assistance of Daniel Garrett. The son of Lady Hertford's sister Mary, Francis, 8th Baron and, from 1746, 1st Earl Brooke (1719–1753), for whom the earldom of Warwick was to be revived in 1759, had gone on the Grand Tour in 1739. Both Smithson and Brooke were of impeccable Whig allegiance – as their elevation attests – and both were to be notable patrons of Canaletto in his English years.

The survival of Hill's letter to the Duke of Richmond establishes the importance that Joseph Smith placed on the Duke. There were obvious reasons for this. The Duke was one of the great figures of the time. He had held the office of Lord High Constable of England at the Coronation of King George II in 1727 and was appointed Master of the Horse in 1734/5, serving as one of the Lords Justices of England in the King's absence on the Continent in 1740 and on three subsequent occasions. The Duke was on the closest of terms with Thomas Pelham-Holles, 1st Duke of Newcastle, who, with his younger brother Henry Pelham, Prime Minister in 1743–54, had been a key figure in the Walpole administration and was, with brief intervals, to be in effective control of the machinery of government and the most power-

Figure 25
London: The Thames and the City from Richmond House, probably 1747,
oil on canvas, 41¾ × 46¼ in. (106 × 117.4 cm.).
The Trustees of the Goodwood Collection

ful champion of the Whig interest until the death of King George II in 1760. The voluminous correspondence between the Dukes establishes that in August 1738 the Duke of Richmond secured from the Duke of Newcastle a promise of the reversion of the consulship at Venice for Smith.[9] Two years later, after the death of the incumbent Consul, Neil Brown, the Minister received an application for the post from Sir John Willes, the Lord Chief Justice. But a letter of 16 July from Richmond House made it clear that the Duke of Richmond would not agree 'to relinquish that promis'.[10] The following June the Duke returned to the issue: 'I beg you would be so good as to appoint Smith Consul'.[11] And Smith was duly appointed. He must have been well aware how much he owed to the Duke of Richmond's intervention.

Smith's connection with Canaletto is too well known to call for recapitulation here. But he was not of course the only intermediary involved in the sale of Venetian views to English patrons. Carlisle, as is now well known, used the services of Antonio Maria Zanetti, who coyly refrained from naming the young painter – almost certainly Marieschi – whom he recommended in preference to Canaletto in a letter of 3 June 1740. In this context it is interesting that James Harris, M. P. (1709–1780), in an addition of 1743 to his 'Account' of his pictures, records his acquisition of four canvases:

> *Four Views of Venice – the two larger by Marieschi, representing, one of them, St Marks place on a public day; the other, the Entrance of the Grand Canal – the two lesser by Antonio Bellotti, one representing the Custom house, the other, the Rialto. The two first cost 20 guineas, ye two last ten. They were painted all at Venice & imported at my Request by M^r. W^m. Hayter of London, Merc.^{t} 1743.*[12]

These would appear to be the earliest references to either artist in an English source. The confusion of Bellotto's christian name with that of his uncle and the fact that Hayter bought a further Marieschi which he believed to be by Canaletto, bequeathing it on his death to Harris – who clearly thought it was by the painter not of his two Marieschis but of the Old House Guards which he was left by another friend – show that even a quite sophisticated collector found it impossible to distinguish the authorship of such works; and this in turn explains the rumours as to Canaletto's own identity which circulated when he was in England.

In this context, the Duke of Richmond's support could clearly be crucial. The Duke, as Hill would have known, had commissioned three large topographical canvases for Richmond House from Antonio Joli, who worked in London between 1744 and 1749: Hill may well have sensed that the Duke would warm to the suggestion in his letter. The two views from Richmond House are indeed among the signal achievements of Canaletto's English period. These have been persuasively dated to the summer of 1747 and were preceded by two drawings, both of panoramic format. The compositional changes between the drawings and the pictures were clearly determined by the selection of a narrower format for the latter, and it is logical to suppose that this in turn was dictated by their intended function. For the pictures are first recorded – in 1822 – above the two chimneypieces in the Great Hall, now the Long Hall, at Goodwood.[13] The two still hang in these positions, and there is every reason to suppose that they were ordered for them, since the canvases correspond closely in width with the openings of the chimneypieces.

Never a man to neglect a promising idea, Canaletto made a masterly reprise of the composition of the study for the Whitehall and the Privy Garden from Richmond House. The viewpoint is moved to the left, to avoid giving disproportionate prominence to the Richmond House stables and to show the west front of the adjacent Montagu House, the London residence of John Montagu, 2nd Duke of Montagu (1690–1749), the Master General of the Ordnance. The Duke, who had married Mary, youngest daughter of John Churchill, 1st Duke of Marlborough, was a close political ally of the Dukes of Richmond and of Newcastle. His intimacy with the Richmond family is suggested by a charming letter of 1744, protesting about the smell of Lord George Lennox's pet fox, which pervaded his 'new Room'.[14] And he was a close friend of MacSwinny and Hill, both of whom visited him at Boughton in the summer of 1747, as the former had also done in 1744. In 1748 the Duke in turn was a visitor at Goodwood. Finberg's suggestion that the celebrated *Whitehall and the Privy Garden looking North* (Fig. 8) was painted with the Duke of Montagu in mind is understandable: if Constable's dating of 1751–2 is correct, Canaletto may, alternatively, have hoped to tempt the Duke's son-in-law and daughter, Lord and Lady Cardigan, subsequently Duke and Duchess of Montagu of the second creation, both of whom collected pictures. In any case the picture gives an idea of the panoramic terms in which Canaletto originally conceived the Richmond commission.[15]

Figure 26
London: Whitehall and the Privy Garden from Richmond House, probably 1747, oil on canvas, 42 × 46 in. (106.7 × 116. 8 cm.).
The Trustees of the Goodwood Collection

41

Canaletto seems to have secured his first London commission from Sir Hugh Smithson even before the Richmond House views were undertaken. For the centrings of the arch shown in the *The City seen through an Arch of Westminster Bridge* (Cat. no. 24) were presumably removed soon after it was keyed in July 1746, and the composition was engraved in the following year. Smithson, like the Dukes of Richmond and Bedford, had been one of the numerous commissioners responsible for the project to build Westminster Bridge, which was unquestionably the greatest engineering-cum-architectural undertaking of the time in London. He had assiduously attended meetings of the commission.

The composition is among Canaletto's most arresting. It has no obvious precedent in his earlier work, and it is therefore tempting to suppose that it may have been suggested by the painting by Antonio Joli showing an 'arched piece of building through which the view of St George's church and the Custom House in Venice are seen', which was in the Hall at Richmond House,[16] or by that painter's view of London through an arched structure, which exists in a number of versions. Whatever the genesis of Canaletto's composition, the picture clearly satisfied Sir Hugh and his wife, Lady Elizabeth. Smithson's patronage was to provide Canaletto with some of the more challenging subjects of his English career: the wonderful oblique view of Westminster Bridge (Cat. no. 25), and a prospect of Alnwick (Fig. 12), one of the two great houses that formed part of Lady Elizabeth's Percy inheritance.

Smithson did not need the Duke of Richmond's encouragement to turn to Canaletto, and was indeed to be the most loyal patron of his English years. But the Duke's commission was surely the catalyst that led to two of the great masterpieces of the artist's career, the panoramas supplied to Prince Ferdinand Philip, 6th Prince Lobkowicz (1724–1784; Figs 5, 6), who visited London in 1745. John, 20th Earl of Crawford (1702–1749), the general who lived for many years in Flanders, wrote a letter of introduction for him to the Duke at Brussels on 12 January.[17] Lobkowicz is known to have visited Goodwood and was rumoured to be in love with the Duke's daughter, Lady Emily Lennox, as she informed her confidante, Lady Anne Hamilton, in a letter of 3 December 1745:

The truth of the matter is that he is vastly fashionable, and as I happen to speak French and to know most of his acquaintances in Holland, he takes it into his head to talk a good deal to me . . .[18]

Lobkowicz also maintained a very public flirtation with the wife of the Venetian ambassador, and so there is an engaging irony in his securing two masterpieces by a Venetian, whose work he would have seen as a guest of the Richmonds. Many years later the supposed subject of his attentions, long since Duchess of Leinster, would hear from her son, the Marquis of Kildare, then on the Grand Tour, that the Prince whom she had described as a 'giddy, good-natured, wild young man' had 'turned bigot'.[19]

Whether Lord Brooke called in Canaletto in 1747 or 1748 remains to be established. Like Smithson, his cousin by marriage, Brooke, as has been seen, already owned works thought to be by Canaletto; if these are to be identified with pictures that remained at Warwick, one of them was a version of Smithson's *Scala dei Giganti*.[20] His ancestor Fulke Greville, 1st Baron Brooke, had received a grant of Warwick Castle in 1604 and proceeded to modernize it. Brooke was understandably proud of his inheritance: his earldom of 1746 was in the name of Brooke of Warwick Castle, but, just over two months after the extinction in 1759 of the Warwick earldom held by the Rich family, he was created Earl of Warwick, and he subsequently tried to secure for this second earldom the precedence of his earlier creation. Canaletto's sequence of views of Warwick Castle attest thus as much to its owner's sense of pride as to the artist's probing visual analysis. Payments of 1748, 1749 and 1752 suggest that he visited Warwick early in 1748 and again in 1752 (see Cat. nos 44–8).

When at Warwick, Canaletto was no more than fourteen miles from a house where another former patron had embarked on a programme of remodelling. William Holbech (*c.* 1699–1771) of Farnborough Hall had visited Venice on the Grand Tour in the spring of 1734 and secured two pictures by Canaletto at that time. He moved in a rather different world from that of Canaletto's great Whig patrons, though in the scientist Martin Folkes he had a mutual acquaintance with the Duke of Richmond. In the later 1740s Holbech determined to remodel his house, calling for advice on his friend and neighbour Sanderson Miller, squire of nearby Radway. The climax of the decoration of the 'new' house was the Saloon (now the Dining Room), and the stuccadore William Perritt was paid on 14 November 1750 for work in that room.[21] This establishes a *terminus ante quem* for the commission of two further pictures by Canaletto (Cat. no. 55; Fig. 55.1), which with the original pair and Panini's *Campidoglio* made the room a quintessential statement of

Figure 27
Detail of Fig. 5

Grand Tour taste. A tradition that Canaletto selected the craftsmen who supplied the plaster frames is not plausible, but it is certainly conceivable that he was consulted about the project at the time of his first visit to Warwick. The two additional canvases were, like the earlier pair, of Venetian subjects and are unlikely to have been the only Venetian views Canaletto supplied during his first half decade in London.

By 1749 Canaletto had succeeded in extending the range of his patrons. In June of that year Vertue recorded that he had worked 'in the country for the Duke of Beaufort'.[22] Charles Somerset, 4th Duke of Beaufort (c. 1709–56), was a patron of a very different stamp from the Duke of Richmond. A Tory, he was keenly aware of his Plantagenet descent, and had found the perfect wife in Elizabeth, sister and heiress of Norbonne, Lord Botetourt, of whom a contemporary wrote: 'She had in her veins the blood of Berkeley and of Botetourt, in her demarche the greatness of the Queen of Sheba.'[23] The wonderful way the park fans out in front of Badminton in the view from the house (Cat. no. 43) is intriguingly reminiscent of earlier treatments of the Bacino. Yet the choice of subject was surely not the artist's, but reflected a Tory, even Jacobite, view of the role of a territorial aristocracy.

The impending demolition of the Old Horse Guards in 1749 no doubt prompted Canaletto to paint his great panorama of that building seen from St James's Park (Cat. no. 17). This was acquired, for 80 guineas, by John Robarts, 4th Earl of Radnor,[24] on whose death in 1757 it was bequeathed, with a huge Hobbema and a legacy of 100 guineas, to his friend James Harris (see p. 38 above), who described it as 'a large morning view of ye Parade in St James's Park & Old Horse Guards'. Lord Radnor's place among Canaletto's London patrons is difficult to explain, but the history of the smaller *Old Horse Guards from St James's Park* (Cat. no. 16), datable to the autumn of 1749, is suggestive. This was sold in 1975 by Sir Arthur Wilmot, 8th Bt, whose ancestor Dr Edward Wilmot (1693–1786), elevated in 1759 as a baronet, was the son-in-law of the celebrated doctor and connoisseur Dr Richard Mead. It might be supposed that Mead acquired the picture; but Wilmot himself is the more plausible candidate. Already high in the royal favour, he saw Richmond's heir, Lord March, through a serious illness in 1743, and when the King himself was sick later that year at Biberach the Duke regretted that Wilmot was not in attendance.[25] By 1750 he was the Duke's personal physician.[26]

Like his father-in-law, and like the physicians of Bath whom Gainsborough painted with such distinction, Wilmot may have seen owning pictures as a way of confirming the status of his profession, and since he was Physician-General to the Army, the Horse Guards was a subject of particular relevance to him.

Lady Emily Lennox's reference to the Dutch friends she shared with Prince Lobkowicz is not surprising, for the Duke of Richmond's connection with Holland was of long standing. His mother-in-law was Dutch: he had been married at The Hague in 1719 and was there with surprising regularity in later years. Dutch acquaintances are likely to have been among several links between the Duke of Richmond and another patron in whose favour Canaletto would supplant Joli, Lord Chesterfield, and also with the Hon. Thomas King, later 5th Lord King, who evidently commissioned the last major series of decorative canvases the artist undertook in England (See Cat. nos 69–71; Figs 13, 14, 17).

Philip Stanhope Dormer, 4th Earl of Chesterfield (1694–1773), served as Ambassador at The Hague in 1728–32 and returned there in 1745. Although Chesterfield was not an intimate of the Duke of Richmond, he had asked him to find a French chef in 1725 and had also known his father; when the Earl was in office the two were colleagues, and in Solomon Dayrolles, Chesterfield's godson, they had a close mutual friend.

Chesterfield was widely recognized as one of the most cultivated of his contemporaries. His picture collection was not substantial, and his attributions were not necessarily reliable, for a version of Joos van Cleve's *Madonna of the Cherries* that surfaced recently can be identified as his 'Leonardo'.[27] The only conventional vedute he owned were five Venetian views, given to Marieschi, which were sold from the Ranger's House at Blackheath in 1782. Chesterfield House, on which work began in 1746, was the most sophisticated London mansion of its date, celebrated for the finesse of its interior. On the ground floor of this was the Ante Room, for which Joli supplied five decorative capricci. The upstairs rooms were evidently fitted up somewhat later, and Chesterfield commissioned from Canaletto two overdoors for the Countess's Sitting Room (Cat. nos 58, 59) and an overmantel for the Music Room (Fig. 58.2). The three architectural *capricci* were integral elements of sophisticated rococo decorative schemes carefully calculated to be seen from a low viewpoint. They must have been supplied before mid-February

Figure 28
Detail of Cat. no. 44

45

1752, when the Chesterfields held a great assembly to celebrate the opening of the house, but could of course have been commissioned somewhat earlier, either before Canaletto's return to Venice late in 1750 or after he was back in London in or before the following July.

Chesterfield House had been designed by Isaac Ware, one of the more thoughtful Palladian architects of his generation. Closely contemporary, and yet more ambitious in scale, was Norfolk House, St James's Square, built in 1748–52 for Edward Howard, 9th Duke of Norfolk (1686–1773). The architect was Matthew Brettingham, whose first undertaking had been as executant architect at Holkham – where a view by Canaletto was used in the overmantel of the Lady Leicester's Sitting Room. He had enlarged and altered Richmond House in 1744 and was also employed at Goodwood and may well, therefore, have been concerned with the decoration of the Hall there, for which Canaletto's two Richmond House views had almost certainly been intended. The Duke of Norfolk's Sussex estates almost marched with those of the Duke of Richmond, so it is hardly surprising that he, or his determined wife, also acquired pictures from Canaletto. It would be tempting to suppose that these were intended for a specific interior – and the Music Room now in the Victoria and Albert Museum shows how ambitious the interiors of Norfolk House were – but there is no evidence for this. And in the event the three pictures (Cat. nos 60–62), still happily in their original frames by John Cuenot en suite with so many others supplied for the house, were ranged with dozens of portraits and other canvases in the Drawing Room on the ground floor, as the 1777 inventory attests.[28]

There is no incontrovertible evidence as to the original destination of the remarkable series of pictures formerly in the possession of the Earls of Lovelace at Ockham in Surrey. Four brothers succeeded at Ockham in close succession: John, 2nd Lord King (d. 1740), Peter, 3rd Lord King (d. 1754), William, 4th Lord King (d. 1767), and their brother, Thomas, 5th Lord King (1712–1779). The fourth brother had married at Delft 17 August 1734 Wilhelmina Catherine, daughter and heiress of Johan Troye, a member of the sovereign council of Brabant. Her inheritance seems to have made possible the largest decorative commission of Canaletto's English years. One of the series, the *Capriccio with a ruined Gothic Chapel*, now at Boston (Cat. no. 69), clearly had a particularly prominent place, for its dimensions suggest that

it was intended as an overmantel and it alone is dated, 1754. Two upright *capricci* at Washington (Cat. nos 70, 71), both with references to England, and specifically to Box Hill in Surrey, some eight miles from Ockham, must have been intended for the same room.[29] For another, perhaps very marginally larger, Canaletto supplied a wider overmantel with the church of San Michele and presumably his two large upright Italian *capricci*.[30] *The Bacino di San Marco on Ascension Day* (Fig. 17)[31] is of the same size and date as the latter pair, but it would not have hung altogether happily with these and so may have been in a third room.[32] Whether intended for Ockham or for a London House the King pictures constitute the most substantial achievement of Canaletto's last years in London.

One of the large *capricci* from the Ockham series[33] is related in composition – and perhaps in date – to a very much smaller horizontal canvas in the Cadogan collection, which in turn has a pendant. While it has been suggested that the two – with other pictures by Canaletto – were obtained by Charles, 3rd Baron and 1st Earl Cadogan, the claims of his father, Charles, 2nd Baron Cadogan (1685–1776), son-in-law of the celebrated collector Sir Hans Sloane, might also be considered. He was the younger brother of Marlborough's trusted ally, William, 1st Earl Cadogan – an outstanding collector of old masters – whose elder daughter, Sarah, was the Duke of Richmond's wife. The destruction of the Cadogan archives means that the question cannot be resolved.

Of Canaletto's patrons in London, none was more individual than Thomas Hollis (1720–1776; Fig. 2), who had inherited Corscombe in west Dorset in 1738 and was unusual in being an avowed republican, although this did not prevent him from association with Whigs of a more moderate stamp such as Chesterfield's protégé, the courtier Francis, 10th Earl of Huntingdon (1729–1819). On his first visit to Italy, in 1748–9 – when Canaletto of course was in London – Hollis had been accompanied by his life-long friend and eventual heir, Thomas Brand (1719–1804), elder son of Timothy Brand of the Hyde, Ingatestone, and first cousin of the slightly older Thomas Brand (c. 1717–1770) of the Hoo, who was evidently in Venice in the autumn of 1738 and had secured a distinguished group of four *vedute* by Canaletto. Hollis returned to Venice in the winter of 1750–1 – when Canaletto was briefly back from London – and subsequently commissioned the six views supplied in 1754–5 (Cat. nos 4, 15, 33, 37; Figs 10, 27.1).

The most original of Hollis's compositions was surely the *Old Walton Bridge* now at Dulwich (Cat. no. 37), a second version of which was supplied in 1755 to Samuel Dicker, M.P. (d. 1760), who had built the bridge at a cost of £10,000 (Cat. no. 38). A successful Jamaica merchant, Dicker returned to England and acquired an estate at Walton-on-Thames, where the Duke of Newcastle's nephew and heir, Lord Lincoln, was the other major proprietor. The location of his property may have aroused the interest in building bridges for which Dicker was to become widely known: Grosley would write that 'by that means [he] became Pontifex Maximus'.[34] In July 1750 the Duke of Richmond and Henry Pelham were to have visited Dicker, whose support was needed for an ecclesiastical appointment, but were both prevented from doing so on health grounds by Dr Wilmot.[35] It was, however, with Pelham's support that Dicker was elected as Member of Parliament for Plymouth in 1754, although he was soon to be recognized as an adherent of the Duke of Bedford. He was an associate of at least one other probable patron of Canaletto, William Beckford (1709–1770), greatest of Jamaica plutocrats, with whom Dicker was consulted about West Indian affairs by the Board of Trade.[36] Dicker had a relatively insignificant place among Canaletto's patrons in his London years. He, however, clearly sought to ingratiate himself with the great Whig noblemen of the day, and while this may not have dictated the pattern of his artistic patronage it is fascinating to see how he, a relative outsider on the London political scene, had links with others who employed the artist. Even before he reached London, Canaletto must have been aware how small and closely interlocked was the world of his potential patrons. MacSwinny and Hill – with Consul Smith inevitably in the background – may have done the painter a better service than any of those concerned anticipated when the former canvassed the Duke of Richmond on his behalf.[37]

Notes

1. Richmond Papers, Sussex Records Office, slightly misquoted by the Earl of March, *A Duke and his Friends. The Life and Letters of the Second Duke of Richmond*, II, London, 1911, p. 602.

2. Francis Russell, 'The Pictures of John, Fourth Duke of Bedford', *Apollo*, June 1988, p. 406.

3. Francis Russell, in Gervase Jackson-Stops, ed., *The Treasure Houses of Britain*, Washington, 1985, p. 250 under no. 169.

4. Eglin, 2001.

5. J. H. Wiffen, *Historical Memoirs of the House of Russell from the Time of the Norman Conquest*, II, London, 1833, p. 521.

6. Francis Russell, review, *Burlington Magazine*, CXLI, March 1999, p. 181.

7. For the views of Venice by Carlevarijs, see Charles Beddington, *Luca Carlevarijs* (exhibition catalogue, San Diego, 2001), pp. 21–3.

8. Correspondence between Frances, Countess of Hertford and the Countess of Pomfret, 1738–44, London, 1806, p. 112.

9. Timothy J. McCann, ed., *The Correspondence of the Dukes of Richmond and Newcastle 1724–1750*, Sussex Record Society, 73 (1984), p. 36.

10. *Idem*.

11. *Ibid.*, p. 63.

12. 'An Account of my Pictures. 1739', Malmesbury Ms.

13. D. Jacques, *Visit to Goodwood, the Seat of His Grace the Duke of Richmond, Near Chichester*, 1822, p. 62. I am indebted to Rosemary Baird for this reference.

14. Earl of March, *op. cit.*, II, p. 431.

15. Finberg 1921, pp. 75–6. Further evidence that Canaletto hoped to work for the Duke of Montagu or his successors is suggested by the drawing *Richmond House Terrace and the West End of Westminster Bridge* (Cat. no. 22) which is extensively annotated with details of colour. The fact that the design – already not altogether accurate – was successively developed in a series of drawings (Constable/Links 1989, nos 780 and 786 a–b) suggests that when the anticipated commission failed to materialize, Canaletto revised this as the basis of drawn *capricci* that present obvious parallels with his painted *capricci* of the 1750s.

16. Edward Croft-Murray, *Decorative Painting in England, 1537–1837*, II, London, 1970, p. 226.

17. The letter is to be published by Rosemary Baird. I am indebted to John Somerville for pointing out that the Lobkowicz in question was not his cousin, Prince Joseph Lobkowicz, as Fitzgerald believed.

18. Brian Fitzgerald, *Emily, Duchess of Leinster 1731–1814: A Study of her Life and Times*, London and New York, 1949, p. 15.

19. *Ibid.*, p. 213. It is possible that he referred to another member of the Lobkowicz family.

20. Constable/Links 1989, under no. 80.

21. [Gervase Jackson-Stops], *Farnborough Hall*, London, 1984, p. 7.

22. Vertue *Note Books*, III, p. 149.

23. The Complete Peerage.

24. This price is specified in James Harris's 'Account'; see note 12.

25. McCann, *op. cit.*, pp. 111 and 117.

26. *Ibid.*, p. 304.

27. Russell 1988, pp. 627–30. The version of the *Madonna of the Cherries* is now owned by Hester Diamond, New York (John O. Hand, *Joos van Cleve* (New Haven and London, 2004), no. 122–2).

28. I am indebted to John Martin Robinson for this information.

29. Constable nos 475, 473 and 474

30. Constable nos 367, 478 and 504

31. Constable no. 343.

32. For a further account of the commission see the entry for the picture, Christie's, London, 6 July 2005, lot 20.

33. Constable no. 504.

34. Quoted in *The History of Parliament, The House of Commons, 1754–90*, ed. Lewis Namier and John Brooke, London, 1964, pp. 304–5.

35. McCann, *op. cit.*, p. 117.

36. The possibility that Alderman Beckford was a patron, albeit indirectly, of Canaletto is suggested by a reference to a *capriccio* quoted by S. Blackmore in Derek E. Ostergard, ed., *William Beckford, 1760–1844: An Eye for the Magnificent*, New Haven and London, 2001, p. 270.

37. In addition to those mentioned in previous notes I am indebted for information to Viscount Chelsea, the Earl of Chichester, Everett Fahy, John Harris, Bozena Kowalczyk, the Countess of Malmesbury, and not least to Charles Beddington.

Figure 29
Detail of Cat. no. 41

I

Greenwich: The Royal Naval Hospital

Before 1750?
Oil on canvas
26 × 41¼ in. (66 × 104.8 cm.)

The National Maritime Museum, London

Provenance:
Colonel B.P.R. Thomson, Windsor.
A.M. Thomson, Windsor, by 1926.
Miss Beatrix Thomson, Windsor.
With Spink & Son, London, from whom acquired by
Sir James Caird in March 1939 for £550 and presented to
    the National Maritime Museum on 12 April 1939
    (Acc. no. 1939/1766).

Selected Exhibitions:
London 1977, no. 14.
New York 1989–90, no. 74.
Birmingham 1993–4, no. 30.
Turin, Montreal, Washington and Marseille 1999–2000,
    no. 421 (exhibited Turin and Montreal only).

Selected Literature:
Constable 1927, pp. 17 and 18.
Constable I, pl. 75; II, no. 414.
Puppi 1968, no. 275 A, illustrated.
Dacey 1981, pp. 485–7, fig. 36.
Links 1981, no. 224, illustrated.
Links 1982, p. 173, pl. 168.
Corboz 1985, I, pp. 74 and 215, figs. 255 and 257
    (colour detail); II, p. 730, no. P 449, illustrated.
Constable / Links 1989, I, pp. lxxiv–lxxv, pl. 75;
    II, no. 414.
Links 1994, p. 191, pl. 173 (colour).

The grandest secular building in Greater London, the Royal Naval Hospital is one of the masterpieces of English Baroque architecture, and one with which all three of its leading exponents were involved. Sir Christopher Wren, the principal architect of the hospital, first visited the site in 1694 in the company of Samuel Pepys and acted as Surveyor 1696–1716, giving his services free of charge. Nicholas Hawksmoor, as Wren's personal assistant from 1696 and Clerk of the Works 1698–1735, was responsible for the daily running of the project, and Sir John Vanbrugh, a member of the board of directors from 1703, succeeded Wren as Surveyor in 1716.

The hospital owed its foundation to the enthusiastic support of Queen Mary, who shared the throne with her husband King William III. The sight of wounded sailors returning from the defeat of the French off Cape Barfleur in 1692 had inspired her to urge the Treasury 'to hasten … the grant of Greenwich as a hospital for Seamen' to parallel the Chelsea Hospital for military pensioners completed in 1692 (see Fig. 34.). In 1694 almost the entire site of the Tudor Palace of Placentia – the birthplace of three Tudor monarchs, Henry VIII, Mary and Elizabeth – was granted to the project; after the sudden death of the Queen in December of that year, the King instigated what had been 'the darling object of her life', issuing a charter to found a hospital 'for the reliefe and support of Seamen serving on board the Shipps and Vessells belonging to the Navy Royall'. Although building was to take more than half a century, progress was initially rapid, the first forty-two pensioners being accommodated in 1705; there were 350 by December 1708 and 1,550 by 1755. The hospital closed in 1869, the buildings being occupied by the Royal Naval College in 1873 and today by the National Maritime Museum, the University of Greenwich and the Trinity College of Music.

The plan, of four blocks symmetrical across a central axis, was dictated by Queen Mary's insistence that the hospital must not obscure the river view from the Queen's House shown at the centre of Canaletto's composition. The celebrated villa was begun in 1616 by Inigo Jones for Anne of Denmark, wife of King James I, and was completed in 1638 for Henrietta Maria, wife of King Charles I. The only viewpoint which affords a satisfactory frontal view of the whole complex is thus from the River Thames or, as here, from the Isle of Dogs. One of the few details of the ensemble shown in this painting which differs from its appearance today is what appears to be a pediment crowning the central bays of the Queen's House. This was, in fact, a gable, only six or seven feet high and substantially hidden by the balustrade; it was probably removed during a re-roofing in 1822 (Bold 2000, p. 85). It was, however, depicted as a pediment in a number of engravings of the time, including one in Wren's *Parentalia* (London, 1750, facing p. 328). The elevated viewpoint and other details indicate the use of another additional engraving, that by Jacques Rigaud also employed for Canaletto's other depiction of the subject (Fig. 2.1). The morning sunshine and the numerous watercraft milling about on the tranquil waters, giving the scene an Italianate air, are constant elements in Canaletto's idealisation of his English subjects.

Professor W. G. Constable, publishing the painting for the first time in 1927, considered it to 'belong to the years before Canaletto's temporary return to Venice in the autumn of 1750, when he retained something of the breadth in conception and treatment which mark his best Venetian work'. Links initially (1981) followed that dating, but subsequently (1982 and 1994) dated the painting to *c.* 1753. The year 1752, the supposed date of completion of Queen Mary's Block, is taken as a *terminus post quem* for its execution in the catalogues of the 1989–90 and 1993–4 exhibitions. It now seems, however, that 'by 1751 the Hospital was structurally complete' (Bold 2000, p. 167), and in any case it would be rash to presume that the painting could not date from several years earlier. Regrettably, no assistance is provided by its history, of which nothing is known before the last century unless it could be the *Greenwich Hospital* sold with the Peel Heirlooms in 1900 (Robinson and Fisher, London, 10 May 1900, lot 205; 105 guineas to Leggatt), which was described as measuring 27 × 45 in.; otherwise unrecorded, that is given a separate entry by Constable (Constable no. 414(a)).

2

Greenwich: The Royal Naval Hospital

Before 1746
Oil on canvas
23½ × 37 in. (59.7 × 94 cm.)

Private Collection, on loan to Tate Britain

Provenance:
Acquired in Italy in 1871 by Sir James Hudson for John
Samuel of London (much of whose collection was
bequeathed to the National Gallery, London by his
nieces the Misses Cohen in 1906, including paintings
by Francesco Guardi, Marieschi, Sebastiano Ricci,
Giandomenico Tiepolo, Zais and Zuccarelli).
Prince George, 2nd and last Duke of Cambridge of the
fourth creation, KG, KT, KP, Gloucester House,
Piccadilly, London; his posthumous sale, Christie's,
London, 11 June 1904, lot 15 (220 guineas to Agnew).
With Agnew's, London, 1924.
Walter Spencer Morgan Burns (d. 1929), North Mymms
Park, near Hatfield, Hertfordshire.
His widow, Mrs. Walter Burns, the sister of J. Pierpont
Morgan (who owned no. 15 in this catalogue).
Their son, Major-General Sir George Burns, KCVO,
CB, DSO, OBE, MC, North Mymms Park; his sale,
Christie's, London, 29 June 1979, lot 48 (the sale was
subsequently cancelled and the painting returned to
the vendor).

Selected Exhibitions:
Turin, Montreal, Washington and Marseille 1999–2000,
no. 422.

Selected Literature:
Finberg 1921, p. 56.
Constable II, no. 414(b).
Puppi 1968, no. 275 B.
Dacey 1981, pp. 485–7, fig. 35.
Links 1981, under no. 224.
Links 1982, p. 173.
Constable / Links 1989, I, pp. lxxiv–lxxv; II, no. 414(b).
Links 1994, p. 191.

Although this painting was regarded by Links as contemporary with Canaletto's other depiction of the subject
(Cat. no. 1), it differs markedly from it in its topographical
inaccuracies, as Jane Dacey has pointed out. Although
topographical precision was never one of the painter's prime
concerns, the divergences here are surprising. Beyond the
twin domes, the colonnades fronting the Queen Mary Block
on the left and the King William Block on the right are
incorrectly shown with an upper order with pediments
over the end bays. The proportions of the domes and their
supporting drums appear somewhat stunted and the square
bases of the drums are missing, while the domes have only
one rather than two rows of oval lunettes. The plinths of the
colonnades on the river sides of the Queen Mary and King
William Blocks extend well into the central court area, and
the Royal Arms are shown in all four of the pediments of
the Queen Anne and King Charles Blocks facing the river,
whereas they actually only appear in the second from the
right. In the distance, the Queen's House is depicted with a
recessed rather than a projecting centre, while the character
of the Royal Observatory on the hill beyond has been
completely misunderstood, resulting in it resembling more
closely an Italianate fortress. Finally, the colouration of the
Union Jacks is incorrect.

None of these errors is apparent in the other version
(Cat. no. 1). As Dacey has pointed out, all are due to the
painting's derivation from an etching inscribed in the plate
'Rigaud fecit 1736', the author of which has been identified
as the French draughtsman Jacques Rigaud by whom
drawings of Stowe, Hampton Court and St James's Park
are also known (Fig. 2.1). While Canaletto frequently based
his paintings on prints by other artists (see, for instance,
Cat. nos 51–3; Fig. 10), this would seem to be the only
instance of him copying fairly precisely the ships, boats and
figures as well as the topography. Dacey concludes that this
painting is the earlier of the two versions and that its style
'could just conceivably place it in the pre-English period of
1740–46'. This is surely correct, the darker tonality and less
fluid application of the paint being characteristic of that
period in the artist's development and without parallel in the
work of his English years, or indeed in any of his work after
1746. The suggestion is further reinforced by the fact that the
painting appears to have remained in Italy until 1871, which
would seem to indicate that it was never delivered to the
patron.

Figure 2.1
Jacques Rigaud, '*Prospect of Greenwich Hospital from the River*', 1736,
engraving, sheet 14⅞ × 28⅜ in. (37.8 × 72.1 cm.).
National Maritime Museum, London

A hitherto unpublished painting of this view in an
English private collection (Fig. 2.2) is the only known
English view by Francesco Guardi; it is, indeed, the only
known view by him of anywhere outside the Veneto except
for the *Castel Sant'Angelo, Rome* in the National Gallery
of Art, Washington, D.C. Since Guardi visited neither
Rome nor England, both paintings were by necessity based
on prints, the Greenwich view on an engraving by J. June
published by Bakewell and Parker and datable to *c.* 1750
(information from E.H.H. Archibald, private communication, 1993). Like Canaletto, Guardi has painted the
ensigns the wrong colours. Thus, had Canaletto never
made the journey to England in 1746, his and Guardi's only
English views would both be of Greenwich. The subject
must have held a particular appeal for British naval officers
who found themselves in Venice and were able to provide
the local painters with prints to copy.

Figure 2.2
Francesco Guardi, *Greenwich: The Royal Naval Hospital*, 1780s,
oil on canvas, 24¼ × 33¼ in. (61.6 × 84.5 cm.). Private Collection

3

Old London Bridge

Probably 1746–50
Pen and brown ink with grey wash
12 × 21¼ in. (30.6 × 54 cm.)

Lent by The Trustees of the British Museum
Exhibited at Yale only

Provenance:
(Probably) Sale, 1766 (sold for 3 guineas).
J.C. Blofeld, from whom purchased in 1909
  (Acc. no. 1909·4·6·4).

Selected Exhibitions:
Venice 1982, no. 53.
Birmingham 1993–4, no. 32.
London 2003, no. 2.25.

Selected Literature:
Finberg 1921, p. 59, pl. XVII.
Finberg 1922, p. 77, no. 2.
Constable I, pl. 137; II, no. 738.
Corboz 1985, II, p. 733, no. D 111, illustrated.

Old London Bridge was not only the most picturesque of London bridges but also, until the construction of Fulham Bridge in 1729 and Westminster Bridge in 1738–50 (see Cat. nos 23–30), the only bridge across the Thames below Kingston, twelve miles upstream. A bridge has stood on the site since the Roman occupation. After the destruction of wooden bridges by a storm in 1091 and a fire in 1136, the first stone bridge was begun in 1176. Supported by nineteen piers, this was to survive for six hundred and fifty years, although five arches were swept away during a great frost in 1282 and half the structure was destroyed by fire in 1633. It was always a hive of activity – its gatehouse was the preferred location for the display of traitors' severed heads between 1305 and the Restoration, that of William Wallace being followed by those of Jack Cade, Thomas More, Bishop Fisher and Thomas Cromwell. An old proverb said that the bridge was made for wise men to go over and fools to go under, but both routes were highly problematical. By 1201 there were already houses on it and the roadway was unfeasibly narrow, the arch of the gatehouse forming a bottleneck eighteen feet wide. Three thousand people are said to have been killed when a fire broke out in 1212/13, and nine in 1396 in the crush to see the infant French bride of Richard II. By the eighteenth century the traffic jams were insupportable. Of equal concern was the current under the bridge. Resulting from the piers and their starlings taking up eighty percent of the width of the riverbed, this was treacherous and often deadly, boats only being able to pass through at high tide. *The Gentleman's Magazine* stated in 1753 that 'shooting the bridge is almost universally dreaded as the risque of life' (quoted by Picard 2000, p. 19). The current was, however, of great benefit to the waterworks of Pieter Moritz, a German, which from 1582 supplied water to the city. Initially consisting of one waterwheel under the first arch, by 1737 there were four. The water was pumped 'to a bason on the top of a high tower of wood which stands on the sterling of the first arch on the north west end of the Bridge. By which means the water is raised to any part of the city' (J. Entick, *A New and Accurate History and Survey of London, Westminster and Southwark*, London, 1766; quoted by Picard 2000, p. 23). The water tower is clearly seen in this drawing, which shows the bridge from the West, as are the Fishmongers' Hall, the Monument and the tower of the church of St Magnus Martyr.

By Canaletto's day, the bridge was in a perilous state, and the matter was referred to a committee in 1746; this view is the last before the removal of the houses in 1758–62, when the width of the roadway was increased to forty-six feet and the two central arches were replaced by a single span. It was demolished in 1830, a new bridge of five arches being constructed slightly upstream in 1823–31, which was to remain until its sale and removal to Lake Havasu City, Arizona in the 1960s. Canaletto may well have been aware that the bridge's days were numbered, and this is a finished drawing, presumably intended for sale or as the basis for a print. Finberg (1922) points out that F.P. Seguier (*Dictionary of the Works of Painters*, 1870) records the sale at auction in 1766 of four drawings 'in Indian ink' by Canaletto of London views. One of these, which fetched the respectable sum of three guineas, showed Old London Bridge and, since no other drawing by Canaletto of the subject is known, it seems highly probable that this is it. The other drawings showed *The Old Horse Guards, St James's Park* (probably Cat. no. 18), *Westminster Abbey from York Buildings* (possibly Cat. no. 13) and *London from the Centre Arch of Westminster Bridge* (possibly the earlier version of Cat. no. 29). Presuming that these were all in the same sale, it would be extremely interesting to know who assembled such a fine group of drawings at such an early date, but as yet no further details are known.

A painting of London Bridge is mentioned by George Vertue in his notebook in June 1749 (see p. 19). That may well be the view of it by Canaletto sold by Griffier Fagel at auction (Coxe, Burrell and Co.) in London on 22 May 1801 (lot 8) for twenty guineas (see Finberg 1921, p. 59, and Constable under no. 738). Untraced since, it is one of the very few recorded paintings of Canaletto's English years that has not come down to us.

4

Saint Paul's Cathedral

1754
Oil on canvas
20½ × 24¼ in. (52 × 61.6 cm.)

Yale Center for British Art, Paul Mellon Collection

Provenance:

Painted in 1754 for Thomas Hollis (1720–1774), Corscombe, Dorset.

Bequeathed by him, with all of his property, to 'his dear friend and fellow traveller' Thomas Brand (1719–1804), who subsequently took the name Brand-Hollis, The Hyde, near Ingatestone, Essex.

Bequeathed by him, with all of his property, to The Rev. John Disney (1756–1816), The Hyde, near Ingatestone, Essex.

His son, John Disney, barrister-at-law and antiquary (1779–1857), The Hyde, near Ingatestone, Essex.

His son, Edgar Disney (d. 1881), The Hyde, near Ingatestone, Essex.

His widow, Mrs Edgar Disney; sale, Christie's, London, 3 May 1884, lot 132 (66 guineas to Hay).

John Hay, U.S. Secretary of State.

His daughter Mrs James Wadsworth.

Her daughter Evelyn Wadsworth Symington.

With Hirschl and Adler, New York, 1960.

With Agnew's, London.

Paul Mellon, by whom purchased from the above in 1961 and given to the present owner in 1976 (Acc. no. B1976.7.95).

Selected Exhibitions:

London 1987, no. 75.

Turin, Montreal, Washington, and Marseille 1999–2000, no. 625 (exhibited Montreal and Washington only).

Selected Literature:

Finberg 1921, pp. 42, 43 and 63 (as untraced).

Constable I, pp. 96 and 145; II, no. 422.

Puppi 1968, no. 300.

Constable / Links 1976, I, pp. 96 and 145, pl. 207; II, no. 422.

Links 1981, no. 254, illustrated.

Links 1982, p. 173, pl. 170.

Corboz 1985, I, pp. 213–5, fig. 254; II, p. 706, no. P 375, illustrated.

Constable / Links 1989, I, pp. lxxv, 96 and 145, pl. 207; II, no. 422.

Links 1994, p. 191, pl. 169 (colour).

The first cathedral dedicated to Saint Paul on the site was founded in 604. Its subsequent history is one of a succession of fires. Fire destroyed the Saxon cathedral in 1087, delayed completion of its Romanesque successor in 1135, and destroyed the spire in 1561, before the Great Fire of London of 1666 obliterated the greatest cathedral of medieval Britain. Its ruins were demolished to make way for the Baroque masterpiece by Sir Christopher Wren which graces the city to this day. The foundation stone of that was laid on 25 June 1675, the choir was opened on 2 December 1697, and the cathedral was finally declared complete in 1711. While Saint Paul's Cathedral plays an inevitable subsidiary role in many of Canaletto's views of the Thames, it is perhaps surprising that this should be the only painting in which it takes centre stage. It should be remembered, however, that the painter (in striking contrast to Panini) never depicted Saint Peter's in Rome, the building which contemporaries considered Saint Paul's to emulate.

The history of the painting is known with unusual comprehensiveness. An inscription on a label on the reverse was transcribed by Constable in 1960 as follows:

Fatto nel anno 1754 in Londra per la prima | ed ultima volta con ogni maggior attentzione | ad istanza del Sig.n cavaliere Tomaso Hollis | Padrone mio stimatiss.o | Antonio Canal detto Il Canaletto || It was necessary to new line the picture in 1850 | so that the inscription is now hid | John Disney 1850.

Similar inscriptions have been found (in varying states of preservation) on labels on the reverse of four of the other five paintings executed for Thomas Hollis (Fig. 2), three also giving the date 1754 and one 1755, and there is no reason to doubt that they record inscriptions by Canaletto himself. Hollis was described by Horace Walpole as 'a gentleman of ample fortune; an antiquary, collector, of the most virtuous morals, and the most bigoted of all republicans, to a degree of being unable to converse with men of other principles' (see p. 10 and Cat. nos 4, 15, 33, 37 and Figs 10, 28.1). He had befriended Joseph Smith during a visit to Venice on his Grand Tour (he was there 8 December 1750–28 February 1751) and may have met Canaletto at the same time. Hollis is not known to have acquired any other paintings of this kind, and it is not known why he waited until 1754 to commission the set of six views from Canaletto.

A rapid sketch (Fig. 4.1; Constable I, pl. 161; II, no. 849) must surely be preparatory for this painting, although the viewpoint is lower, the portico is shown with only a single order of columns and what seems to be an equestrian monument is shown in place of Francis Bird's statue of Queen Anne in front of the façade. The indications of shadow correspond closely with the painting. It comes from the same sketchbook as those used for the view of *The Old Horse Guards and the Banqueting House, Whitehall, from Saint James's Park*, a painting executed some five years earlier (Figs 16.1, 16.2).

A lost drawing of the façade of the cathedral is recorded in an engraving by Fambrini published in Venice by Giacomo Aliprandi, which is inscribed 'An.t Canaletto Veneziano disegno / in Londra'; although Constable stated that 'no example of the engraving has been found', a unique impression belonging to F.J.B. Watson was recorded by Links and is here reproduced for the first time (Fig. 4.2; Constable II, under nos 422 and 849; Constable / Links 1976, II, no. 743*).

Canaletto was not the only Venetian artist to paint St Paul's Cathedral. A view of it, taken from a slightly different angle, by his near contemporary Jacopo Fabris was sold at Sotheby's, London, 12 June 2003, lot 108.

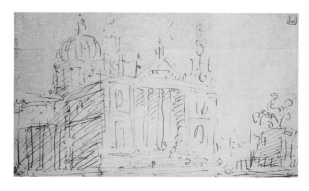

Figure 4.1
A Domed Church, with a Statue, probably St Paul's Cathedral, pen and brown ink, 4¼ × 7½ in. (10.8 × 19.1 cm.). Gallerie dell'Accademia, Venice

Figure 4.2
F. Fambrini, after Canaletto, *The Façade of St Paul's Cathedral,* engraving, unique impression. Whereabouts unknown

5

The City from the Terrace of Somerset House

6

The City of Westminster from the Terrace of Somerset House

5

The City from the Terrace of Somerset House

Engraved 1750
Oil on canvas
15 ¼ × 28 ⅝ in. (38.6 × 72.9 cm.)

Yale Center for British Art, Paul Mellon Collection
Exhibited at Yale only

Provenance:
Thomas West, by 1 August 1750.
(Possibly) Robert Ludgate, 14 Sussex Place, Regent's Park,
    London; sale, Christie's, London, 8 May 1830, lot 49,
    as 'A View of London – Looking towards St. Paul's,
    taken from the Gardens of Old Somerset House'
    (with the pendant: 15 guineas).
Thomas Harcourt Powell, Drinkstone Park, Bury St.
    Edmunds.
His great-nephew T. Harcourt Powell; sale, Christie's,
    London, 26 November 1965, lot 68 (with the pendant:
    28,000 guineas to Agnew's).
Paul Mellon, by whom purchased from Agnew's in
    February 1966 and presented to the present owner in
    December 1976
    (Acc. no. B1976.7.96).

Selected Literature:
Constable II, no. 428(b) and possibly no. 428(d),
    as untraced.
Constable / Links 1976, I, pl. 207; II, no. 428(b) and
    possibly no. 428(d).
Corboz 1985, II, p. 716, no. P 408, illustrated.
Constable / Links 1989, I, p. lxviii, pl. 207; II, no. 428(b)
    and possibly no. 428(d).

Engraved:
Fig. 5.1. By Edward Rooker for Robert Sayer of Fleet Street,
London, with the inscription 'Canaleti Pinx^t. in the
Collection of M^r. Thos West …', published 1 August 1750,
republished 20 August 1751 (Constable I, pl. 182).

6

The City of Westminster from the Terrace of Somerset House

Engraved 1750
Oil on canvas
15 ¼ × 28 ¼ in. (38.7 × 71.8 cm.)

Yale Center for British Art, Paul Mellon Collection
Exhibited at Yale only

Provenance:
As for no. 5 (described in the 1830 sale catalogue as 'View
of the River Thames, from the Terrace of Somerset House
Gardens, looking towards Westminster Bridge'; lot 69 in
the 1965 sale
(Acc. no. B1976.7.97).

Selected Literature:
Constable II, no. 429(a) and possibly no. 429(b),
    as untraced.
Constable / Links 1976, I, pl. 207; II, no. 429(a) and
    possibly no. 429(b).
Links 1981, under no. 229.
Constable / Links 1989, I, p. lxviii (mistakenly referred
    to as no. 429(b) rather than no. 429(a)), pl. 207;
    II, no. 429(a) and possibly no. 429(b).

Engraved:
Fig. 6.1. By Johann Sebastian Müller for Robert Sayer of
Fleet Street, London, with the inscription 'Canaleti Pinx^t.
in the Collection of M^r. Thos West …', published
1 August 1750, republished 20 August 1751 (Constable I,
pl. 182).

The terrace of Somerset House, located on the great bend
in the River Thames almost equidistant from St Paul's
Cathedral and Westminster, afforded fine views of both the
City of London and the City of Westminster. The vantage
point is clearly shown on the left in *The Thames and the City
from Richmond House* at Goodwood (Fig. 25). Canaletto
almost certainly derived the idea of pendant views of the
City and of Westminster from Antonio Joli, who had
executed several paired paintings of these subjects in the
1740s, although his Westminster views are not taken from
the terrace of Somerset House but from a point further
upstream. It is tempting to relate both artists' evident access
to the terrace to the fact that the Venetian envoy is recorded
as having an apartment in Somerset House, at least by 1763.

In *The City from the Terrace of Somerset House* the celebrated skyline of the city is the focal point of the composition
in a manner only rivalled elsewhere in Canaletto's œuvre
by *The Thames and the City on Lord Mayor's Day* (Fig. 6).
Silhouetted against the sky are St Paul's Cathedral and
more than three dozen of Sir Christopher Wren's spires
and towers of churches dating from his reconstruction of
the City after the Great Fire of 1666. Towards the right
the Monument, the wooden tower of Pieter Moritz's
waterworks, Old London Bridge and four spires and towers
are shown from very much the same angle as in Canaletto's
drawing of *Old London Bridge* (Cat. no. 3). In the left foreground are the river stairs of Somerset House, constructed
to the design of Inigo Jones in 1628–31. In *The City of
Westminster from the Terrace of Somerset House* Westminster
Bridge is shown newly completed, with, beyond its right-
hand (West) end, the four towers of the Church of Saint
John the Evangelist, Smith Square, and Westminster
Hall, and further to the right Westminster Abbey and the
Banqueting House, Whitehall (for which see Cat. no. 15).
All those buildings survive today, but further to the right
and partly obscured by trees is the wooden tower of the York
Buildings waterworks (now destroyed; see Cat. no. 13).

When these paintings re-emerged at Christie's, London,
in 1965, Constable (who was 'Fine Art Consultant' to
Christie's at the time) identified them as 'almost certainly'
those from the collection of Thomas West which were
engraved by Rooker and Müller for Robert Sayer (Figs 5.1,
6.1). Although there are variations in the cloud formations,
the correspondence between paintings and engravings
is otherwise so close as to exclude the possibility that the

paintings are other than Thomas West's, given that the prints clearly compress the images into a less horizontal format. In both engravings almost all of the other bank of the Thames is omitted, and in *The City from the Terrace of Somerset House* the stern of the large boat at the lower right, which helps to balance the composition, is accommodated by being moved to the left. Further confusion has resulted from a failure to recognise that, despite being in mid-eighteenth century English carved giltwood frames, both paintings have clearly been slightly reduced in size, the cropping of the lower edge being particularly obtrusive in *The City of Westminster from the Terrace of Somerset House*.

Although it has always been stated that the first edition of Müller's print of *The City of Westminster from the Terrace of Somerset House* is that of 20 August 1751, it was in fact published simultaneously with that of the pendant on 1 August 1750, impressions of that date being in the Royal Collection (Inv. no. 807842) and in the collection of the Yale Center for British Art (Acc. no. B1977.14.18461). In any case, the paintings must date from shortly before Canaletto's temporary return to Venice and must therefore be the first painted versions of these influential compositions. Numerous derivations by other painters are known, mostly taken from the prints. It has even been suggested, by Philip Conisbee, that the composition of Claude-Joseph Vernet's *The Port of Bordeaux from the Château Trompette* of 1759 (Paris, Musée du Louvre) may have been influenced by Rooker's engraving of *The City from the Terrace of Somerset House* (Conisbee 1976, under Cat. no. 36).

Figure 5.1
Edward Rooker, after Canaletto, 'A West View of London with the Bridge taken from Somerset Gardens', engraving. Yale Center for British Art, Paul Mellon Collection

Figure 6.1
Johann Sebastian Müller, after Canaletto, 'A North East View of Westminster with the New Bridge taken from Somerset Garden', engraving. Yale Center for British Art, Paul Mellon Collection

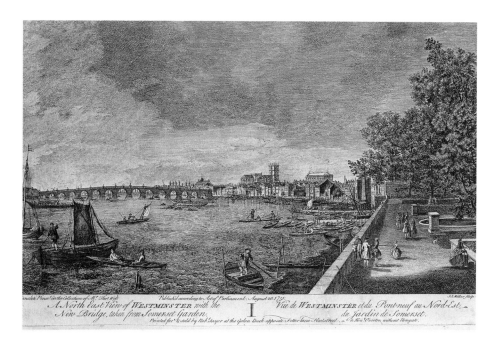

7

The City from the Terrace of Somerset House

Probably 1750
Pen and brown ink with grey wash over pencil,
stylus and extensive pin pointing
7⅞ × 19⅛ in. (20 × 48.5 cm.)

The Royal Collection

Provenance:
Joseph Smith (*c.* 1674–1770), Venice (where he served
   as British Consul 1744–1760).
Sold by him to King George III in 1762 with most, if not
   all, of his collection of work by Canaletto, as well as
   paintings, drawings and prints by other artists, gems,
   cameos, coins, books and manuscripts.

Selected Exhibitions:
London 1980–1, no. 86.
Venice 1982, no. 54.

Selected Literature:
Finberg 1921, pp. 37–8 and 64.
Parker 1948, no. 114, pls 69, 70.
Constable I, p. 143, pl. 138; II, no. 745.
Corboz 1985, I, p. 76, fig. 62 (detail); II, p. 733, no. D 114,
   illustrated.

8

The City of Westminster from the Terrace of Somerset House

Probably 1750
Pen and black ink with grey wash over pencil,
stylus and extensive pin pointing
8¾ × 19⅛ in. (22.3 × 48.6 cm.)

The Royal Collection

Provenance:
As for Cat. no. 7.

Selected Exhibitions:
London 1980–1, no. 87.
Birmingham 1993–4, no. 15.

Selected Literature:
Finberg 1921, pp. 37–8 and 73–4.
Parker 1948, no. 115, pls 71, 72.
Constable I, pp. 95 and 143, pl. 139; II, no. 746.
Corboz 1985, II, p. 755, no. D 153, illustrated.
Constable / Links 1989, I, pp. lxvii–lxviii, 95 and 143,
   pl. 139; II, no. 746.

Figure 7.1
London: The Thames and the City from the Terrace of Somerset House,
not later than 1750, pen and brown ink with grey wash on paper,
9¼ × 28¾ in. (23.5 × 73 cm.). Samuel Courtauld Trust,
Courtauld Institute of Art Gallery

Stefano Orlandi tells us in his *Abecedario*, published in
1753, that on his return to Venice in the latter part of 1750
Canaletto 'brought with him various sketches of views
and of the most notable sites of that large city, which it is
hoped that, at his convenience, he will want to consign to
canvas.' It may be presumed that those included the six
drawings of London which passed from the collection of
Joseph Smith into the British Royal Collection (see also
Cat. nos 26, 29, 30), as it seems less likely that these were
acquired by Smith after 1755. All of them apart from *The
City from the Terrace of Somerset House* feature Westminster
Bridge prominently. In striking contrast with the other
components of Smith's unrivalled collection of Canaletto
drawings now at Windsor Castle, all but one have been
considered somewhat deficient in quality, and other versions
are known of four. They would, however, have served
perfectly well as a 'pattern book' from which Smith could
choose which compositions to commission paintings of.
In the event, these two subjects were to be the only ones
'consigned to canvas' for Smith (see Cat. nos 9–10).

   The City from the Terrace of Somerset House is a replica
of a drawing formerly in the Fauchier-Magnan collection
and in that of Count Antoine Seilern at Princes Gate,
London, which now belongs to the Courtauld Institute of
Art (Fig. 7.1). Although less well preserved than the version
in the Royal Collection, the Courtauld sheet is considerably
larger and is unanimously regarded as being of distinctly
finer quality and displaying a greater sense of distance. The
slight variations between the two indicate that it was already
the basis for the earliest known painted rendition of the
view at Yale (Cat. no. 5) before being used for that in the
Royal Collection (Cat. no. 9). It must also have been used

for a second 'small' version in an English private collection, which has as a pendant a different view of Westminster from much nearer the bridge, a close version of Cat. no. 27 in this exhibition (Constable I, pl. 79; II, no. 428(a); exhibited Birmingham 1993–4, no. 14).

It must be presumed that there was a corresponding drawing, now lost, of the pendant composition of *The City of Westminster from the Terrace of Somerset House.* The surviving version of that, however, differs notably from both the painting at Yale (Cat. no. 6) and that in the Royal Collection (Cat. no. 10), showing the terrace wall at a much less acute angle and omitting most of the tree on the right as well as several of the more prominent boats. It does, however, correspond closely, but for certain additions (two small boats with single male occupants towards the lower left and a prelate conversing with the lady on the terrace) and other minor variations with a second 'small' version of the subject, which has no known pendant (Fig. 7.2). First recorded in the mid-twentieth century in the collection of the Duke of Hamilton and Brandon, it was presented by Paul Mellon to the Yale Center for British Art in 1977 and de-accessioned in 1988, subsequently being sold at Christie's, London, 17 November 1989 (lot 3); it has since been in a London private collection (Constable I, pl. 79; II, no. 430).

Figure 7.2
London: The City of Westminster from the Terrace of Somerset House, c. 1750/1, oil on canvas, 16¼ × 28¼ in. (41.3 × 71.8 cm.).
Private Collection, London

9

The City from the Terrace of Somerset House

1750–51
Oil on canvas
42⅝ × 74¼ in. (108.3 × 188.6 cm.)

The Royal Collection
Exhibited at Dulwich only

Provenance:
As for Cat. no. 7.

Selected Exhibitions:
London 1980–1, no. 38.
London 1987, no. 71

Selected Literature:
Finberg 1921, pp. 37–8 and 64, pl. XXII.
Constable I, pp. 143 and 148, pl. 79; II, no. 428.
Puppi 1968, no. 285 A, illustrated.
Links 1981, no. 228, illustrated.
Links 1982, p. 163, pl. 153 and pl. 155 (colour detail).
Corboz 1985, I, pp. 76, 107, 127 and 294, fig. 112; II, p. 717, no. P 411, illustrated.
Constable / Links 1989, I, pp. lxvii–lxviii, 143 and 148, pl. 79; II, no. 428.
Links 1994, p. 177, pl. 157 (colour).

The City of Westminster from the Terrace of Somerset House

1750–51
Oil on canvas
41¾ × 72¾ in. (106 × 184.8 cm.)

The Royal Collection
Exhibited at Dulwich only

Provenance:
As for Cat. no. 7.

Selected Exhibitions:
London 1980–1, no. 39.
London 1987, no. 72

Selected Literature:
Finberg 1921, pp. 37–8 and 73, pl. XXIII.
Constable I, pp. 143 and 148, pl. 79; II, no. 429.
Puppi 1968, no. 286 A, illustrated.
Links 1981, no. 229, illustrated.
Links 1982, p. 163, pl. 154 and pl. 156 (colour detail).
Corboz 1985, II, p. 717, no. P 412, illustrated.
Constable / Links 1989, I, pp. lxvii–lxviii, 143 and 148,
    pl. 79; II, no. 429.
Links 1994, p. 177, pl. 156 (colour).

Although not as large as the five largest paintings of Canaletto's English years, which measure 46 × 93 in. (see Cat. no 17; Fig. 34.1), these are significantly larger than any other painting executed by the artist in this period. They dwarf the other paintings by Canaletto of these compositions and only here is the full potential of the subjects fully realised. It may not be a coincidence that by far the largest of Antonio Joli's pairs of paintings of these views, which must be of slightly earlier date, is of very similar dimensions (43 × 68 in.; 109 × 173 cm.).

The two paintings were the last by Canaletto – and the only English views – to be acquired by his great patron and agent Joseph Smith for his collection in Venice, where he was in these years serving as British Consul. They are unique among the artist's English views in being on a Venetian type of canvas, coarser than that customarily employed by Canaletto in England, and in the ground being russet as in the painter's work in his native city, rather than light grey as in much of his English production. This strongly suggests that they were among the 'affairs' which Vertue mentions as the reason for the painter making 'a Tour to his own country at Venice' in 1750–1. One may presume that Smith chose these compositions from among the graphic material shown to him by Canaletto on his temporary return from London, which included the six drawings of London views which were to remain in his collection. Nevertheless, neither of the paintings is actually based on either of Smith's drawings (Cat. nos 7–8). For *The City from the Terrace of Somerset House* the artist clearly reverted to the drawing now in the collection of the Courtauld Institute (Fig. 7.1) which he must, characteristically, have carried with him to Italy (and back to London again afterwards). He also, with typical agility, adjusted the composition to better suit the much larger scale of the canvas. The viewpoint is set back along the terrace, which is shown from a slightly different angle, and the pedestal, absent from both drawings but shown in the small Yale version (Cat. no. 5) and in Rooker's engraving of it (Fig. 5.1), is reintroduced at lower left. St Paul's Cathedral, the only area in which *pentimenti* are apparent, is uniquely seen from below rather than as if from more or less equal height as in all the other renditions. The buildings are smaller in relation to the picture surface and the figures smaller and more numerous. The pendant composition of *The City of Westminster from the Terrace of Somerset House* does

not derive from the drawing but from Müller's print (Fig. 6.1), an impression of which was also owned by Smith, who presumably received it from Canaletto at this time. Here again there are augmentations and variations to make the composition more appropriate to the unusual size of the canvas. Directly in front of the transept of Westminster Abbey is shown the tower of St Margaret's Church, curiously omitted from all the other representations of the view. The tower of the York Buildings Waterworks is not obscured by trees as in the small Yale version (Cat. no. 6) and the engraving, but even more prominently free-standing than in the drawing (Cat. no. 8) and the second small version.

As Sir Oliver Millar has noted, 'when the two pictures are placed beside each other they create a long panoramic view of the curve in the river, the equivalent on the Thames of Canaletto's wide-angled views of the Bacino (London 1980–1).' That may well have been a factor in Smith's choice of these compositions, since he was to display them in his palazzo on the Grand Canal among paintings of predominantly Venetian subjects.

The two paintings are in the original Venetian frames of the type particularly associated with Smith's collection, and, unlike those on the other paintings by Canaletto now in the collection of Her Majesty the Queen, were returned to their original form in the late 1970s by the removal of accretions put on during the reign of King George IV.

9

The City from the Terrace of Somerset House

10

The City of Westminster from the Terrace of Somerset House

11

Old Somerset House from the River Thames

Probably before 1750
Oil on chamfered mahogany panel
22½ × 42⅞ in. (57.2 × 109 cm.)

Private Collection, courtesy of Simon C. Dickinson Ltd

Provenance:
(Possibly) Henry Rhodes, by 1834; his sale, Christie's,
    London, 24 March 1846, lot 641, as 'Old Somerset
    House from the Thames, with boats and figures'
    (91 guineas to Goldsmid).
(Possibly) Mrs Russell Gurney; sale, Christie's, London,
    3 March 1883, lot 143, as 'Old Somerset House from the
    river' (155 guineas to Martin Colnaghi).
Probably the painting, said to be from the Ashburnham
    Collection, which was purchased by Agnew's, London,
    from A. J. Sulley & Co., London, in 1907, and sold by
    them back to Sulley in 1909 (see below).
With W. Freeman & Co., London, from whom purchased
    in 1923 for £550 for a Yorkshire private collection, from
    which sold through Simon C. Dickinson Ltd to the
    present owner in April 1998.

Selected Literature:
(Probably) Constable II, no. 423(a) and/or no. 423(c)
    and/or no. 423(d).
Links 1998, p. 39, no. 423*.

Built in 1547–50 for Edward Seymour, Duke of Somerset
and Lord Protector of England, Somerset House was
by far the most important of the large mansions of the pre-
Reformation era which backed onto the Thames. After
Somerset's execution in 1552 it was used occasionally by
Princess, later Queen, Elizabeth, and subsequently became
the residence of a succession of British queens, Anne of
Denmark (1603–19), Henrietta Maria (1625–45 and
1660–5) and Catherine of Braganza (1665–93). It was for
Henrietta Maria that the gallery was added to the river front
in 1662–3, probably by John Webb, possibly to a design
by Inigo Jones, who certainly designed the river stairs of
1628–31 and the Queen's Chapel of 1630–5. Jones had an
apartment in the house and died there in 1652. Between 1693
and 1775 Somerset House was mostly let out as grace and
favour residences, its tenants including foreign ambassadors;
the Venetian envoy was living there by 1763. In 1775 it was
demolished, to be replaced by the present building designed
by Sir William Chambers and begun in 1776, the Strand
block of which housed the Royal Academy of Arts from
1780 until 1836 and now houses the Courtauld Institute
of Art.

This painting, one of the foremost Canaletto redis-
coveries of recent years, has hitherto remained unpublished
apart from a brief mention by J. G. Links, and a probable
listing (or listings) by Constable (see below). Until the
mid-1990s a larger version on canvas was accepted as the
prototype (31⅜ × 46⅜ in., 79.5 × 118 cm.; Constable I,
pl. 77; II, no. 423; Links 1982, p. 171, pl. 166). It was sold
as such at Christie's, New York, 2 June 1988 (lot 97), and
exhibited as such at the Minneapolis Institute of Arts (by
which it was acquired in 1940); at Somerset House itself in
1977, when it was illustrated on the cover of the catalogue of
the exhibition *London and the Thames* (London 1977); at the
Metropolitan Museum of Art, New York (on loan, 1986);
in the Birmingham 1993–4 exhibition (no. 31) and at the
Courtauld Institute Galleries (on loan, 1990 and 1997).
That must now be seen as a copy of the exhibited painting,
albeit of early date and of superior quality to most copies.
While the colouring is identical, it differs from the exhibited
painting in showing more water at the bottom and more sky

at the top, and in a number of minor details. Most telling
among those is its omission of the dog beyond the round
pond, which renders meaningless the gesture of the boy
raising his stick. Another, weaker early derivation, also
corresponding in colour, was sold at Christie's, London,
in 1911 and 1924 as by Canaletto, and is now in the
Philadelphia Museum of Art (Constable 1927, pp. 17–
18, pl. I B; Constable II, no. 423(b)), with a pendant of
Northumberland House also based on a Canaletto composition
(see Cat. no. 14). That would seem to further testify to the
availability of the exhibited painting to contemporary
copyists.

This painting is one of only three known paintings on
panel by Canaletto, the others being views of *The Interior
of Henry VII's Chapel, Westminster Abbey* in the Museum
of London (Fig. 20.1) and of *The New Horse Guards* in a
private collection (Fig. 18.1). It might be surmised that the
artist's use of this support – unusual at this date – may have
been influenced by his lodging with a cabinet maker. The
surfaces of the exhibited painting and that in the Museum
of London both have indentations around the edges,
suggesting that they were framed before the paint was
completely dry.

Although Links states that 'nothing is known of the
origin' of the painting, according to a note in the family
records of the last owner it was purchased in 1923 for
£550 from W. Freeman & Co. of London. That would
seem to make probable its identification as the painting
which was with Agnew's, London, in 1907–9. Constable
records the size as almost identical and states that it
'differs from the Minneapolis picture in details … From
a photograph … certainly by Canaletto'; the only discrepancy is that the support is given as canvas, but in this he
might have been repeating the error he also made over
The Interior of Henry VII's Chapel, Westminster Abbey in the
Museum of London (Fig. 20.1), which he also described
as on canvas. Conversely, Constable II, nos 75 and 157 are
described as on panel, but are in fact on canvas laid down.
The photograph Constable saw should confirm or refute
this, but it is not among his papers. He records that the
painting was 'said to be from the Ashburnham Collection'.

That would be of particular interest, as, if correct, it might establish Sir Humphrey Morice (1723–1785), a director of the Bank of England, as yet another owner of Venetian views by Canaletto who also bought English period paintings from the artist. His pair of views on copper of the Venetian waterfront (Constable II, nos 89 and 117) was bought with the rest of his collection by the 2nd Earl of Ashburnham in 1786, remaining in the family until their sale at Sotheby's, London, in 1953. This painting is not, however, recorded in the Ashburnham sales at Christie's, London, in 1850 or 1860. If the Ashburnham provenance is incorrect, this painting could easily be that owned by Henry Rhodes between 1834 and 1846 and/or that owned by Mrs Russell Gurney in 1883 (Constable II, nos 423(c) and (d)).

12

Old Somerset House from the River Thames

Probably before 1750
Pen and brown ink with grey wash
16⅜ × 28⅝ in. (41.6 × 72.7 cm.)

Yale Center for British Art, Paul Mellon Collection

Provenance:
Christopher Head (d. 1911).
Lady Du Cane, London, by 1921.
By inheritance to a London private collector.
With Colnaghi, London, from March 1966.
Paul Mellon, by whom purchased from the above in
    December 1966 and presented to the present owner
    in December 1977
    (Acc. no. B1977.14.6111).

Selected Literature:
Finberg 1921, p. 63, pl. XXXIV.
Constable I, pl. 138; II, no. 743.
Corboz 1985, II, p. 763, no. D 202, illustrated.

This impressive finished drawing was probably intended either to provide a patron with a fairly accurate impression of what a painting of the view might look like, or for sale as an independent work of art (or both). In any case it must have been produced before the painting (Cat. no. 11) and used in its execution. For, while it corresponds closely in composition and in the boats, and while most of the figures in the drawing are transferred to the painting, there are differences in the painting which must be interpreted as refinements. There is less sky and the tree on the left is reduced, while the trees on the right are more individuated and have a more varied profile. The sail on the boat at lower right is omitted and the rowing boat to the right of centre carries a second seated man. Most significantly, the unkempt foliage along the river wall around the pond – which gives the drawing a rustic atmosphere probably more in keeping with the building's dilapidated state – is abandoned in the painting and replaced by additional figures of perambulating townsfolk, giving it a smarter air.

Christopher Head also owned two other drawings by Canaletto probably of the English period, both *capricci* and for both of which similarly no earlier provenance is known: *A Renaissance Pavilion flanked by two ruined classical Arches over a Waterway by the Venetian Lagoon* (Links 1998, p. 53, no. 825*, pl. 240) and *The Interior of a round Church* (Links 1998, p. 53, no. 828**, pl. 240).

13

The City of Westminster from near the York Water Gate

c. 1746/47
Pen and brown ink with grey wash
15¼ × 28¼ in. (38.7 × 71.8 cm.)

Yale Center for British Art, Paul Mellon Collection

Provenance:
(Possibly) Sale, 1766 (sold for £2 10s).
Robert Prioleau Roupell; sale, Christie's, London,
    12 July 1887, lot 734 (£96 to Thibaudeau, presumably
    for J.P. Heseltine).
John Postle Heseltine (1843–1929), by 1888; his
    (posthumous) Sotheby's, London, 28 May 1935, lot 136
    (£390 to Ellis & Smith).
With Montagu Bernard, London.
With Colnaghi, London.
Paul Mellon, by whom purchased from the above on
    10 August 1961 and presented to the present owner in 1976
    (Acc. no. B1977.14.4630).

Selected Exhibitions:
New York 1989–90, no. 111.
Birmingham 1993–4, no. 18.

Selected Literature:
Finberg 1921, pp. 43, 69 and 75, pl. XXXIII.
Finberg 1922, p. 77, no. 4.
Constable I, pp. 94 and 141, note 1, pl. 139; II, nos 747
    and 749(c).
Walker 1979, p. 240, pl. 23.
Kingzett 1982, p. 54.
Links 1982, p. 147.
Corboz 1985, II, p. 733, no. D 115, illustrated.
Constable / Links 1989, I, pp. lx, 94 and 141, note 1,
    pl. 139; II, nos 747 and 749(c).
Links 1994, p. 165, pl. 138 (colour).

The composition shown in this exceptional sheet is effectively a variant of that showing Westminster from the rather more distant terrace of Somerset House (Cat. nos 6, 8 and 10). York Water Gate, seen on the right, was built in 1626 by Nicholas Stone, possibly to the design of Inigo Jones, for George Villiers, Duke of Buckingham. Originally at the bottom of the garden of Buckingham's home, York House, which was demolished in the 1670s, the Water Gate now stands incongruously inland in Embankment Gardens, the only surviving relic of the great mansions between the River Thames and the Strand. Shown on the extreme right is part of the house of Sir Philip Botiler, with, next to it, no. 14 Buckingham Street, where Samuel Pepys had lived between 1688 and 1701 and which in Canaletto's day housed the Office of the Commissioners of the Salt Tax. In front of that is the York Buildings Waterworks, established in 1675 following the demolition of York House, with its seventy foot high wooden tower, erected in 1691–2, dominating the foreground. The waterworks, which survived until 1829, pumped water as far as the Marylebone Reservoir. In 1712 they became the first to use steam power with 'a machine for raising water by fire', the Newcomen engine whose twin chimneys are seen to the right of the tower, but in 1731 this was abandoned and replaced by horses. Beyond the trees in the garden of Northumberland House are the Queen's Treasury and the long low building of the Small Beer Buttery, then partly residential and partly occupied by the Office of the Board of Green Cloth. The row of houses beyond, among the most fashionable in London at the time, included the residences of Mrs Dunch, Sir Thomas Robinson, Lady Townshend, the Earl of Pembroke, the Countess of Portland, the Duke of Montagu and the Duke of Richmond.

The drawing is highly finished, suggesting that it was intended to be sold as a work of art in its own right. Two related paintings by Canaletto are, however, known. One corresponds with only minor variations and is of only slightly larger dimensions (19 × 32 in.; 48 × 81 cm.; Constable I, pl. 78; II, no. 427); first recorded in the collection of the Duke of Grafton in 1921, this subsequently belonged to Lord Lyle and to Mrs Charles Wood before being sold at Christie's, London, 21 November 1975 (lot 44), and is last recorded with Colnaghi (New York 1983, no. 7). A rather larger version showing Westminster Bridge complete and with more differences in the boats was recently acquired by the National Trust from the Douglas-Pennant family to remain *in situ* at Penrhyn Castle (Fig. 13.1; Constable II, no. 427(a)); that alone shows

part of the Banqueting House, Whitehall, behind the Queen's Treasury.

Two topographical anomalies in the drawing remain unexplained. While Links was wrong to emphasize the inaccuracy of the depiction, in this and in the ex-Grafton painting, of Westminster Bridge with five arches completed towards the Westminster bank (Links 1982 and 1994), he correctly observed, following Walker and Kingzett, that the state of the bridge is that of several years before Canaletto's arrival in England (in Constable / Links 1989, p. lx). As Kingzett points out, a date between June 1742 and May 1743 is implied (compare the diagrams in Walker 1979, p. 282). Furthermore, in the drawing the tower of St Margaret's Church, Westminster is omitted but for its flagpole, apparently having been blended with the North transept of the abbey in a misunderstanding by Canaletto of his own sketches. Perhaps even more curiously, the tower is clearly shown in the ex-Grafton painting but again omitted (including its flagpole) from the Penrhyn version, although it is, of course, absent from all versions of *The City of Westminster from the Terrace of Somerset House* except for the large painting in the Royal Collection (Cat. no. 10).

These details are significant in the analysis of the relationship between Canaletto's versions and three paintings of the composition by his English contemporary Samuel Scott. Richard Kingzett designated Scott's three versions A, B and C; in all three the tower of St Margaret's is omitted but the Banqueting House is included. In Version B the composition is cropped on the left and Westminster Abbey is depicted with a spire over the crossing, projected by Sir Christopher Wren but never built, while in Version C (sold at Sotheby's, London, 9 November 1994, lot 80, and Sotheby's, New York, 24 January 2002, lot 39), the bridge is shown complete. Version A (Fig. 13.2; sold at Christie's, London, 21 November 1975, lot 42, and with Simon C. Dickinson Ltd in 2000), however, corresponds closely with Canaletto's drawing in all topographical respects (except for Scott's inclusion of the Banqueting House) as well as in some of the boats, and Kingzett has suggested that Canaletto was following Scott. Although this hypothesis would conveniently explain how Canaletto was aware of the state of Westminster Bridge in 1742–3, the residual presence in the exhibited drawing of the flagpole of St Margaret's and the fact that both paintings show Hawksmoor's West towers of the Abbey as completed in 1745 would seem to argue against it.

A version of this drawing executed predominantly in grey wash is in the British Museum (Acc. no. 1862.5.24.20); Constable was inclined to accept this as Canaletto's work (Constable II, under no. 747), but it must be a copy.

For the possible identification of the exhibited drawing as that sold at auction in 1766 see under Cat. no. 3.

Figure 13.1
London: The City of Westminster from near the York Water Gate, probably late 1740s, oil on canvas, 29¾ × 42 in. (75.5 × 106.5 cm.). Penrhyn Castle (The National Trust)

Figure 13.2
Samuel Scott, *London: The City of Westminster from near the York Water Gate*, probably late 1740s, oil on canvas, 21½ × 44 in. (54.5 × 111.8 cm.). Private Collection, courtesy of Simon C. Dickinson Ltd

13

The City of Westminster from near the York Water Gate

14

Northumberland House

c. 1752
Pen and brown ink with grey wash
11⅜ × 18¾ in. (28.9 × 47.6 cm.)

The Minneapolis Institute of Arts, John DeLaittre
Memorial Collection, Gift of funds from Mrs Horace Ropes

Exhibited at Yale only

Provenance:
(Possibly) George Reveley (1699–1766).
His son Henry Reveley (1737–1798), Bryn-y-Gwyn,
    Dolgelley, Merionethshire, North Wales, and by
    inheritance there until 1923 through:
His son Hugh Reveley, Ll.B. of Christ Church, Oxford
    (1772–after 1851?).
His grandson Hugh John Reveley (1812–1889), by 1876.
His daughter Fanny Jane Jelf-Reveley (d. 1942).
With Robert Langton Douglas, London, from whom
    purchased in 1923
    (Acc. no. 23.50.54).

Selected Exhibitions:
Canada 1964–5, no. 114.
New York 1989–90, no. 114.

Selected Literature:
Reveley 1820, p. 249.
Finberg 1921, p. 60 (as untraced).
Constable I, p. 96, pl. 137; II, no. 740.
Corboz 1985, II, p. 763, no. D 197, illustrated.

Northumberland House stood where the west end of the
Strand met the south end of St Martin's Lane, on a site
between the corner of the present Trafalgar Square, formed
in the 1820s, and Charing Cross Station, built in 1863.
Built for Henry Howard, 1st Earl of Northampton in
1605–9, it was, in the words of Sir Nikolaus Pevsner
'the grandest Jacobean house in London' and 'the proud
possessor of one of those fantastic frontispieces of superimposed orders which one knows from Oxford Colleges
and the Old Bodleian ... decorated in the craziest taste with

termini pilasters, and much intricate strapwork' (Pevsner and Cherry 1973, pp. 54, 372). After Northampton's death in 1614, 'eaten up by debts incurred in building his new house', it passed to his great-nephew Theophilus Howard, Earl of Suffolk, and thence in 1642 to his son-in-law Algernon Percy, 10th Earl of Northumberland. After nearly a century of neglect the house was inherited in 1748 by Algernon Seymour, 7th Duke of Somerset, who immediately employed Daniel Garrett to carry out extensive works. In April 1749 the Duchess wrote 'We have a vast old house in London not only to furnish from top to bottom but to lay new Floors put up new Ceilings, Chimney-pieces, Sashes and Doors, for everything is gone into ruin'. Somerset, who had in 1749 been created Earl of Northumberland of the fifth creation, died in February 1750 and was succeeded by his daughter Elizabeth and her husband, the former Sir Hugh Smithson, later to be 1st Duke of Northumberland and one of the greatest of Canaletto's patrons during his English years. They continued to employ Garrett to conduct renovations in the years 1750–3, including the remodelling of the Strand façade with sash windows and – the new Countess being the Percy heiress in her own right – with a crowning ornament for the portico in the form of a Percy lion cast in lead, six feet high and eleven and a half feet long. A magnificent picture gallery was completed by James Paine, the grand opening taking place in May 1757, presumably with Smithson's six Canaletto views of England on display (Cat. nos 24, 25, 35, 41; Figs 12, 14.1). Further modifications to the interior were carried out for him by Robert Adam in 1770–5. The house survived, with its Strand façade unchanged since Canaletto's depictions of it, well into the age of photography, being demolished only in 1874 to make way for Northumberland Avenue, all that was preserved being the lead lion which was moved to the East front of Syon House, now the principal Northumberland residence in the south (for which see Cat. no. 35).

Canaletto's superb painting of the Strand front (Fig. 14.1; Constable I, pl. 76; II, no. 419; exhibited New York 1989–90, no. 70) was executed for Smithson presumably immediately after its completion, since in 1753 an engraving of it by Thomas Bowles was published by Robert Sayer. That helped to make it the most imitated of all Canaletto's English views (for one early derivation by an English hand, now in the Philadelphia Museum of Art, see under Cat. no. 11). In the right foreground Hubert Le Sueur's bronze

equestrian statue of King Charles I of 1633 is shown where it was re-erected in 1675 on approximately the site it occupies today in Trafalgar Square, rather than in an imaginary setting in Whitehall as in Cat. no. 15. The painting also provides, in the words of J. G. Links 'one of those street scenes of Georgian London which one wishes he had painted more often' (Links 1982, p. 171, and 1994, p. 188).

While most of Canaletto's 'finished' drawings which connect with paintings do so in a fairly straightforward manner, this drawing has a more subtle relationship with the painting, to the point that it has been stated that it 'is not a preparatory study for the Duke of Northumberland's picture … but is instead an independent, finished drawing' (New York 1989–90). It certainly does not have the character of a study, but it is hardly independent. Indeed the mother and child in the lower right corner and the bench and baskets beside them correspond fairly closely, as do the planks of wood lying in front of the statue and the cartwheel to their left. The cart near the centre and all but the most distant coach in the painting are similarly positioned, and the arrangement of the figure groups is similar, though not the figures themselves. The bollards in the foreground and in front of Northumberland House and the nearest of the four obelisks supporting lamps in the painting are omitted in the drawing, and the row of stalls behind the statue in the drawing is omitted in the painting. However, the main difference is in the shifting of the viewpoint, which for the drawing is distinctly further to the right, so that four bays

of an additional building are included on the far right and the angle of every receding line is subtly altered. All these differences point to the drawing being executed before the painting in order to be presented to Smithson for approval, and that he requested that more emphasis be given to Northumberland House to make the painting less of a London street scene and more a view of his newly acquired London home.

Whether or not the drawing was presented to Smithson, it certainly belonged to his first cousin. It is first recorded in the book on drawings prepared by Henry Reveley (1737–1798) and published posthumously by his son Hugh in 1820. In this, Henry Reveley, a notable collector of drawings and prints, identifies himself as its owner, along with another drawing by Canaletto of the Piazza San Marco (Constable II, under no. 525). His grandson Hugh John Reveley (1812–1889), who is known to have inherited most of his grandfather's collection (Lugt 1921, p. 242), also owned Canaletto's painting of *The Bacino di San Marco, Venice, on Ascension Day* (Thyssen-Bornemisza Collection, Monasterio de Pedralbes, Barcelona; Constable / Links 1976, II, no. 340(aa)). The original owner of all of these may well have been Henry Reveley's father George (1699–1766), whose older sister Philadelphia had married Langdale Smithson of Stanwick and was the mother of none other than Sir Hugh Smithson, as Baetjer and Links have pointed out (New York 1989–90).

Figure 14.1
London: Northumberland House, c. 1752, oil on canvas, 33 × 54 in. (84 × 137 cm.). Collection of the Duke of Northumberland

The Banqueting House and the Holbein Gate, Whitehall, with the Equestrian Statue of King Charles I

1754/5
Oil on canvas
20½ × 24 in. (52 × 61 cm.)

Private Collection
Not exhibited

Provenance:
Painted for Thomas Hollis, presumably in 1754/5, and as for Cat. no. 4 until 1884; 1884 sale, lot 131 (90 guineas to Martin Colnaghi).
With Agnew's, London.
J. Pierpont Morgan, by whom acquired from Agnew's in *c.* 1912.
With Knoedler, New York, 1944.
Mrs B. Rionda Braga, Alpine, New Jersey, by 1962; her [anonymous] sale, Christie's, New York, 18 January 1984, lot 168 (purchased by the present owner).

Selected Exhibitions:
Canada 1964–5, no. 107(b) (exhibited in Montreal only).

Selected Literature:
Finberg 1921, pp. 43–4 and 76, pl. XXXII.
Constable I, p. 145, pl. 87; II, no. 472.
Links 1981, no. 256.
Links 1982, pp. 173 and 185–6, pl. 183.
Corboz 1985, I, p. 283, II, p. 706, no. P 376, illustrated.
Constable / Links 1989, I, pp. lxxvi and 145, pl. 87; II, no. 472.
Links 1994, pp. 191 and 208, pl. 184.

The Banqueting House is the only surviving part of Whitehall Palace, which was otherwise almost entirely destroyed by fire in 1698. Designed by Inigo Jones, the Banqueting House was begun in 1619, three years after his Queen's House at Greenwich (for which see Cat. no. 1), but finished much sooner, in 1622, thus becoming the first completed Renaissance building in England. Its much more prominent location made its impact even greater, and this can be assessed by a comparison with the façade of the neighbouring Northumberland House finished only about a decade before (see Cat. no. 14). Always admired, the Banqueting House was considered by Horace Walpole 'so complete in itself that it stands as the model of the most pure and beautiful taste'. The interior, an exact double cube, retains its ceiling of nine canvases by Rubens on the theme of *The Apotheosis of James I*, installed in 1635. It was from one of the upper windows that Charles I stepped out onto the scaffold to be beheaded on 30 January 1649. On the left in this painting is seen the weather vane added by James II to warn him of a 'Protestant wind' which might carry his son-in-law, the future William III, over the sea from Holland. Through the eighteenth century the Banqueting House was the Chapel Royal and it remained in use as a chapel until 1890. The adjacent Holbein Gate, built about 1532, was also a survivor of the 1698 fire, although it was to be demolished soon after this depiction of it, in 1759, in order to facilitate the passage of traffic to and from Westminster Bridge.

The imaginary aspects of this painting are exaggerated by Finberg, Constable and Links, the only fantasy element being the transposition of Hubert Le Sueur's bronze equestrian statue of King Charles I of 1633 from the other end of Whitehall, where it is shown in Canaletto's views of Northumberland House (see Cat. no. 14). It had been re-erected close to its present site in Trafalgar Square in 1675. In other respects the view merely reverses that shown in the distance in the Bowhill and Goodwood views of Whitehall (Figs 8 and 25), with Richmond House shown in the background, the same buildings being shown, from slightly different viewpoints, in a painting of only a few years earlier by Antonio Joli (Fig. 15.1), and in the background of a caricature published on 5 March 1752 (London 2003, no. 4.17). The only major difference, the inclusion of the statue of King Charles I adjacent to the place of his execution is a conceit which must have held a strong appeal for Canaletto's

patron, the staunchly republican Thomas Hollis.

Of the six paintings executed for Hollis, this is the only one which does not have a label on the reverse with an inscription transcribing that on the back of the canvas covered by relining in 1850 (see Cat. nos 4, 33, 37; and Figs 10, 28.1). Those found on the other five paintings of the set date four of them to 1754 and one to 1755, and it may safely be presumed that this painting also dates from 1754/5. Constable was critical of the quality of the five Hollis paintings known to him, and particularly scathing about this one, of which he even states that 'the authenticity … has been doubted'. In his low opinion of the group he was followed by Links, who went as far as to propose that 'There is … a suggestion of old stock about Hollis's purchase, refurbished with labels to please the buyer' (Constable / Links 1989 I, p. lxxvi). On the contrary, the six paintings display a stylistic homogeneity characteristic of Canaletto's sets of paintings at all moments in his career, and are of particular interest in the ways in which they, uniquely among his English output, anticipate the stylistic traits of his late period, after his return to Venice in 1755. When sold in 1984, this painting set a new auction record for a work by the artist.

Figure 15.1
Antonio Joli, *London: The Banqueting House and the Holbein Gate, Whitehall*, late 1740s, oil on canvas, 16½ × 28 in. (42 × 71 cm.). Offered at Sotheby's, London, 25 November 2004, lot 11

16

*The Old Horse Guards and the Banqueting House,
Whitehall, from Saint James's Park*

Probably 1749
Oil on canvas
18⅝ × 30¼ in. (47.3 × 76.8 cm.)

Private Collection
Exhibited at Dulwich only

Provenance:
Dr Edward Wilmot (1693–1786), created a baronet in
    1759, and by descent through Sir Henry Sacheverel
    Wilmot, 4th Bt. (1801–1872), by 1857, to Sir Robert
    Wilmot, 8th Bt. (1939–1974); sale, Christie's, London,
    27 June 1975, lot 31.
With Roy Miles, London, 1975.
Paul Mellon, by whom purchased from the above; his
    sale, Christie's, London, 17 November 1989, lot 4.
A UK pension fund, by whom purchased at the above sale
    and sold, Christie's, London, 4 July 1997, lot 121
    (purchased by the present owner).

Selected Literature:
Watson 1949, p. 20, fig. 25.
Watson 1950, p. 316, fig. 12.
Constable I, pp. 37, 94 and 142, pl. 76; II, no. 416 and
    under nos 735–6.
Puppi 1968, no. 280, illustrated.
Links 1981, no. 222, illustrated.
Links 1982, pp. 161–2, pl. 151 (colour).
Corboz 1985, II, p. 716, no. P 405, illustrated.
Constable / Links 1989, I, pp. lxvii, 37, 94 and 142,
    pl. 76; II, no. 416.
Links 1994, pp. 172–3, pl. 154 (colour).

The ninety acre St James's Park, the oldest of London's
royal parks, had three avenues, lined with three hundred
and fifty limes planted by Queen Anne's gardener to shade
the walks. Since the reign of King Charles II it had been
open to all and was the most fashionable place for the *beau
monde* to take the air in the afternoon, to gossip, to pick up
'ladies of the town' or to watch members of the royal family
escorted by Yeomen of the Guard. Riding in chairs, on
horseback or in carriages was severely restricted, royal
permission to use coaches only being granted to the Duke
of Portland, the two Principal Secretaries of State and
the First Lord of the Treasury, who needed access to
neighbouring Downing Street.

Horse Guards Parade on the east side of the park,
shown here, was then as now used for military parades.
The red brick building is the Horse Guards, built in
1663–5, which was the headquarters of the General Staff
of the army and housed the horse guards and some of the
foot guards. By 1745 it was in such a dilapidated state that
the colonels of the Horse Guards complained to the
Secretary at War that it was 'in very rotten and decayed
condition … having been supported many years by
props … is now become so dangerous that it is not safe for
the Coaches of his Majesty and the Royal Family to pass
under the Gateway, and the Men and Horses doing duty
there, are in perpetual danger of loosing their lives by the
falling down of the Buildings' (quoted by Einberg 1992).
Its demolition was begun in the latter part of 1749. It was
replaced by the present building, designed by William Kent
shortly before his death in 1748 and executed by John Vardy
(the architect of nearby Spencer House) and William
Robinson between 1750 and 1759, the exterior being
finished by November 1753. Behind the Horse Guards is
seen the Banqueting House, Whitehall, and part of the
Holbein Gate (for which see Cat. no. 15). In the left
foreground is a Knight Companion of the Order of the
Bath, the Order whose number Canaletto was to paint
in procession from Westminster Abbey sometime after
26 June 1749 (see Cat. no. 19), and whose chapel in
Westminster Abbey he was to paint twice (see Cat. no. 20).

It is generally presumed that this painting dates from
1749 when the old Horse Guards was already condemned,
and thus, like the larger view of the same subject (Cat. no.
17), it was presumably painted around May or June of that
year, since the trees are similarly in full leaf. Of particular

interest is the almost unique survival of two rough sketches evidently used in the execution of the painting.

These are on pages from a sketchbook formerly in the collection of Dr Alfredo Viggiano, Venice, and since 1968 in the Venetian Accademia, which also includes a sketch which seems to represent St Paul's Cathedral (see Fig. 4.1); they show the Old Horse Guards and Little Walsingham House, largely obscured by trees on the left of the composition (Figs 16.1, 16.2; Constable I, pl. 136; II, nos 735–6, where it is incorrectly stated that the Holbein Gate is not shown in the painting, and that the second drawing relates to 'the right-hand part of the distant buildings' rather than the left foreground; see also Venice 1982, nos 43–4, and, for the first drawing, Links 1982, pl. 150, and Links 1994, pl. 153). The two drawings were first published by Watson, who pointed out that both are

> *of an unusually summary character, and so bespattered with notes on colours and architectural characteristics as to suggest at first sight that they are sketches made on the spot, perhaps in a notebook held in the artist's hand … The painting agrees closely with the drawings, and follows the notes as to colour, treatment of architecture and material, with great care. The proportions of the Horse Guards building have been modified to accord with the direction* piu largo *and the plastered walls of Little Walsingham House follow the indication* sporco. *Dirty they may well have been, for the house had already been described as 'little, old and ruinous' as early as 1658, although it was not demolished until 1786* (Watson 1950).

The 1975 sale catalogue records that the painting was 'traditionally thought to have been in the collection of Dr Meade'. Richard Mead was the leading physician of his day, numbering among his patients King George I, King George II, Alexander Pope, Sir Robert Walpole, Bishop Burnet and the French painter Jean-Antoine Watteau, who came to England specially to consult him about his consumption. A very distinguished man of letters, Mead formed a large collection of paintings, books, manuscripts, coins and antiquities. In the words of the author of his entry in the Dictionary of National Biography 'Of the many men who have grown rich in professions, few have expended their riches during their lives so generously and wisely as Mead', and Professor Francis Haskell described him as 'the most stimulating art collector of early eighteenth-century England' (Haskell 1980, p. 301). His collection, most of

which was dispersed in a series of sales at Langford's, London, 20–22 March 1754 (paintings), 13–28 January, 11–19 February and 11–15 March 1755, included Holbein's portrait of Erasmus and Massys' portrait of Aegidius, both now in an English private collection, and some of the finest paintings from the collection of Cardinal Massimi (Haskell 1980, p. 118).

Mead was a friend of Joseph Smith and certainly owned a pair of Venetian views by Canaletto, showing 'St Mark's Place at Venice, in the Carnival Time' and 'A view up the Grand Canal'. Sold at Langford's on 21 March 1754, lots 30 and 31, these were subsequently in the collections of Charles Jennens and the Earls Howe before passing into that of Conte Borletti, Milan (Constable no. 35, but with the provenance of 35(c), and 248). A label found on the stretcher of the exhibited painting at the time of the 1989 sale establishes that it was already by 1857 (when it was lent for exhibition) in the collection of a forebear of the 1975 vendor, Sir Robert Wilmot, 8th Bt. The first baronet, Edward Wilmot (1693–1786) was not only a colleague of Mead but also, as the husband of his daughter Sarah, his heir, Mead's only son having died without issue. Edward Wilmot is known to have inherited other paintings from his father-in-law which were not in his posthumous sale, Michael Dahl's portrait of Mead and Jacopo Amigoni's portrait of Queen Caroline commissioned by him (Kerslake 1977, I, p. 185). Thus the family tradition that the painting came from Mead's collection is quite possibly correct. On the other hand, Canaletto's view of *The Interior of Henry VII's Chapel in Westminster Abbey* in the Museum of London (See Fig. 20.1) also has a Wilmot provenance and presumably entered the family collection at the same time as *The Old Horse Guards*. Probably of very similar date and sharing a relevance to a patron interested in the Order of the Bath and the military, the two paintings would seem to have had more relevance to Edward Wilmot himself, since he was Physician-General to the Army from 1740, and could have been stimulated to an interest in Canaletto's work not only by his father-in-law but also by his friend George Garnier, Apothecary-General to the Army (for whom see pp. 12–14 and Cat. no. 54) and his patient the Duke of Richmond (see pp. 38–41 and 45; Figs 25, 26).

A large version, corresponding closely but with loftier trees, was formerly in the collection of the Lords Hesketh at Easton Neston, and subsequently of Major the Hon.

Figure 16.1
London: The Old Horse Guards and the Banqueting House, Whitehall, from St James's Park, not later than 1749, pen and brown ink over pencil, 4½ × 8½ in. (11.4 × 21.7 cm.). Gallerie dell'Accademia, Venice

Figure 16.2
London: Little Walsingham House, not later than 1749, pen and brown ink, 5¼ × 7⅜ in. (13.4 × 18.9 cm.). Gallerie dell'Accademia, Venice

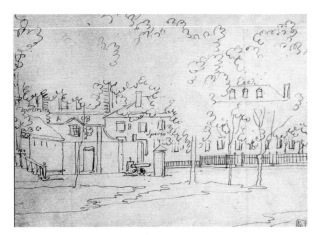

J.B. Fermor-Hesketh. Constable called it a 'school version', noting its 'scratchy handling', and that verdict was shared by the art market when it was offered unsuccessfully as the work of Canaletto at Christie's, London, 8 July 1988, lot 130. Despite having an eighteenth-century French provenance, it is presumably the work of an English hand and its authorship should be further investigated. Constable also refers to paintings of both this view and the New Horse Guards by Samuel Scott, but none are included by Kingzett in his catalogue of Scott's work (Kingzett 1982).

17

The Old Horse Guards from Saint James's Park

1749
Oil on canvas
46 × 93 in. (117 × 236 cm.)

The Sir Andrew Lloyd Webber Art Foundation

Provenance:
Exhibited by the artist for sale at his studio July–August 1749.
John Robartes, 4th and last Earl of Radnor of the 1679 creation (*c.* 1686–1757), Radnor House, Cross Deep, Twickenham, Middlesex, by June 1756.
Bequeathed by him on his death without issue to James Harris, M.P., of the Close of Sarum, Salisbury and the Manor House, Great Durnford, Wiltshire.
His son James Harris, created Baron Malmesbury of Malmesbury in 1788, and in 1800 Earl of Malmesbury and Viscount Fitzharris of Heron Court, Christchurch, Hampshire, and by descent until sold, Christie's, London, 15 April 1992, lot 59 (purchased by the present owner).

Selected Exhibitions:
Canada 1964–5, no. 104.
Birmingham 1993–4, no. 19.

Selected Literature:
Finberg 1921, p. 35 (as untraced).
Constable 1927, pp. 17 and 18, pl. II A.
Constable I, pp. 37, 95 and 142, pl. 76; II, no. 415.
Puppi 1968, no. 281, illustrated, and colour pl. LXII (detail).
Links 1981, no. 219, illustrated, and with a colour detail on p. 85.
Links 1982, pp. 161–2, pl. 149 (colour).
Corboz 1985, II, p. 706, no. P 372, illustrated.
Constable / Links 1989, I, pp. lxvii, lxxiii, 37, 95 and 142, pl. 76; II, no. 415.
Einberg 1992.
Links 1994, pp. 172–3, pl. 152 (colour).

The change in viewpoint from that adopted for the smaller painting of the same subject (Cat. no. 16) has resulted in a shift of focus from the park to the buildings, and indeed allowed a panoramic view of those bordering St James's Park on its East side, although the Banqueting House and the Holbein Gate are not visible from this angle. Behind the trees to the left of the Horse Guards are the Office of the Paymaster General, built in 1732–3, and Admiralty House, the residence of the First Lord of the Admiralty. The large block adjoining that to the left is the Admiralty, built in 1722–6, behind which is the spire of the church of St Martin-in-the-Fields by James Gibbs, also of 1722–6. Above the roofs to the right of the Horse Guards is seen the tower of the York Buildings Waterworks (for which see Cat. no. 13). In the right foreground are the Portland stone Treasury, by William Kent, built in 1733–6, and the brick nos 2 and 1 Downing Street. Of the buildings on the park, the Admiralty, the Office of the Paymaster General and the Treasury all survive. At lower left is the tip of the straight strip of water known as the Canal, created by King Charles II in 1660–2, which stretched six hundred yards to a point in front of Buckingham House (on the site of Buckingham Palace); the main feature of the park, it was replaced by the present serpentine pond in 1828.

On 25 July 1749 Canaletto placed an announcement in the *Daily Advertiser*, stating that

Cat. no. 17

Signor Canaleto hereby invites any Gentleman that will be pleased to come to his House, to see a Picture done by him, being A View of St James's Park, *which he hopes may in some Measure deserve their Approbation. The said View may be seen from Nine in the Morning till Three in the Afternoon, and from Four till Seven in the Evening, for the Space of fifteen Days from the Publication of this Advertizement. He lodges at M*ʳ. *Richard Wiggan's, Cabinet-Maker, in Silver-Street, Golden Square.*

This was duly recorded by George Vertue (*Note Books*, III, p. 151). There can be no reasonable doubt that this is the painting referred to, not least because of its size. Although that was slightly exaggerated by Constable (a mistake which was not rectified in later editions of his catalogue), at 46 × 93 in., it is still as large as any of Canaletto's English views. Of the four other paintings of almost exactly the same measurements, the *Chelsea College and Ranelagh* (for which see Fig. 34.1) was certainly also executed as a speculative venture, and the *Whitehall and the Privy Garden looking North* now at Bowhill (Fig. 8) presumably so. The other two paintings of these dimensions are those acquired by Prince Lobkowicz at least one of which may also have been painted as a speculation (Figs 5, 6).

Since the trees in this painting are shown in full leaf it may be supposed that the paint was barely dry when it was exhibited to the public in July 1749. Although the small painting of the same subject is presumed to be close to this in date, the two differ dramatically in character as well as scale. This, as Constable stated (1927) 'combines breadth

of design and atmospheric quality with delicate and vivacious detail, in a way rivalled only by the *Whitehall* in the collection of the Duke of Buccleuch, and the *Whitehall* and the *Thames from Richmond House* [at Goodwood]', and in it, as Sheila O'Connell has pointed out, 'Canaletto has created a grandeur and spaciousness that had not previously been associated with London views' (London 2003, p. 187).

Elizabeth Einberg has suggested that the artist may have hoped that the painting would catch the eye of Sir Watkin Williams Wynn (1692–1749), Member of Parliament for Denbighshire and one of the richest Tory landowners in the country, whose London house, No. 1 Downing Street in the right foreground, is shown being prepared for occupation for the London season; if so, nothing had happened by 26 September when Sir Watkin died unexpectedly as the result of a fall from his horse while out hunting. It may also be noted that the Duke of Bolton, who lived at No. 2 Downing Street, already owned a set of four Venetian views by Canaletto (Links 1998, nos 85**, 133*, 233(bb) and 240*). It must, however, be observed that if Canaletto did paint his large 'speculations' with particular clients in mind, the strategy found remarkably little success. In the event, this painting did find a less obvious taker at some point between 1749 and 1756 in the 4th Earl of Radnor, who paid 80 guineas for it. In a letter of June 1746 to James Harris, M.P., father of the 1st Earl of Malmesbury, he expressed his admiration for his purchase: 'The Canaletti, the subject being that part of St James's Park towards the Horse Guards, is, I think, the most capital picture I ever saw of that master'. He also expressed his intention of bequeathing it to Harris, along with a fine painting by Meindert Hobbema and possibly another by Ruysdael. When he died the following year he left his house and most of his collection of paintings to his steward Frederick Atherton Hindley, but his intention towards his friend Harris was fulfilled, only the Ruysdael being omitted in favour of a view of *The Tower of London from the Pool of London*, the largest version of a popular composition by Samuel Scott. At 45 × 98 in., this is of similar size to the Canaletto and possibly, in Kingzett's opinion, of similar date; thus the Earl of Radnor may have intended them to hang as a pair, although it remains impossible to establish which he purchased first.

The price paid for this painting in 1992 remained the record for a work by the artist at auction until July 2005.

18

The Old Horse Guards from Saint James's Park

1749
Pen and brown ink and grey wash over black chalk
13 ⅜ × 27 ⅛ in. (34.6 × 68.8 cm.)

Lent by the Trustees of the British Museum
Exhibited at Dulwich only

Provenance:
(Probably) Sale, 1766 (sold for £4).
George Hibbert, by 1809; sale, Christie's, London,
   12 June 1833 [=3rd day], lot 159 (6½ guineas to Tiffin).
With Colnaghi, London, from whom purchased in 1868
   (Acc. no. 1868-3-28-305).

Selected Exhibitions:
Birmingham 1993–4, no. 20.
London 2003, no. 4.2.

Selected Literature:
Finberg 1921, pp. 35 and 57, pl. XIXb.
Finberg 1922, p. 77, no. 1.
Constable 1927, p. 18.
Constable I, pp. 94 and 142, pl. 136; II, no. 734.
Links 1982, p. 161.
Corboz 1985, II, p. 732, no. D 106, illustrated.
Constable / Links 1989, I, pp. lxxiii, 94 and 142, pl. 136;
   II, no. 734.
Links 1994, p. 173.

This drawing corresponds closely with the larger of Canaletto's two paintings of *The Old Horse Guards* (Cat. no. 17), although it omits the guards at drill on the Parade, while including a gentleman with a raised cane in the centre foreground, two other figures accompanying the youth seated on the grass towards the right, and a gentleman directly behind those, immediately to the left of the steps to Downing Street. As Finberg and Constable point out, it must have been retained by Canaletto for some years after its execution, being used for a painting of *The New Horse Guards from St James's Park* which was probably painted between November 1752 and November 1753, as the scaffolding for putting the clock in place is still on the turret and the south wing has not yet been built (Fig. 18.1; Constable I, pl. 76; II, no. 417; sold after being offered at Christie's, London, 6 July 1984, lot 87, it is now in an European private collection). That painting also corresponds closely, including some of the figures not present in the large version of 1749, although, apart from the New Horse Guards having replaced the Old Horse Guards, the trees in the Treasury garden have grown, and there are some additional figures towards the right. It is one of the three known paintings for which Canaletto used a panel as the

support, and, at 23 × 43¼ in. (58.5 × 110 cm.), is of almost identical size to the *Old Somerset House* (Cat. no. 11). Its provenance is regrettably unknown before the mid-twentieth century, when it was owned by Mrs Robin Buxton of Itchen Abbas, Hampshire.

Another painting of *The New Horse Guards*, showing them complete, was also accepted as Canaletto's work by Finberg (1921, p. 58) and Constable (Constable / Links 1976 and 1989, I, pl. 207). Apart from the updating of the buildings, however, and the absence of the scaffolding from the turret, the painting corresponds surprisingly closely with the ex-Buxton version on panel, even in size, and its authenticity was doubted when it was last exhibited in public in 1968 (as 'Circle of Canaletto', although the attribution has never been questioned in any of the literature on the artist). The painting was in the Drury-Lowe Collection at Locko Park, Derbyshire, by 1901 and until at least 1973, but recent attempts to trace it have not borne fruit.

For the probable identification of this drawing with that sold at auction in 1766, see under Cat. no. 3.

Figure 18.1
London: the New Horse Guards from St James's Park,
probably between Nov. 1752 and Nov. 1753,
oil on panel, 23 × 43¼ in. (58.5 × 111 cm.). Private Collection

19

Westminster Abbey with the Knights Companion of the Order of the Bath in Procession, 26 June 1749

1749
Oil on canvas
39⅜ × 39⅜ in. (100 × 100 cm.)

Lent by the Dean and Chapter of Westminster Abbey

Provenance:
Joseph Wilcocks (1673–1756), Dean of Westminster and Bishop of Rochester, by whom presumably commissioned.
Bequeathed by his son to the abbey and hung at the Westminster Deanery ever since.

Selected Exhibitions:
Venice 1982, no. 103.
London 1987, no. 73.
New York 1989–90, no. 67.
Birmingham 1993–4, no. 27.

Selected Literature:
Finberg 1921, pp. 35 and 68–9, pl. XX.
Constable I, pp. 37, 95 and 142, pl. 80; II, no. 432.
Puppi 1968, no. 283, illustrated, and colour pl. LIX.
Links 1981, no. 221, illustrated, and with a colour detail on p. 87.
Links 1982, p. 162, pl. 152.
Corboz 1985, II, p. 716, no. P 407, illustrated.
Constable / Links 1989, I, p. lxvi, 37, 95 and 142, pl. 80; II, no. 432.
Links 1994, pp. 173 and 177, pl. 155 (colour).

The coronation and burial church of English monarchs, Westminster Abbey, alone of all the great English abbeys, survived the Reformation due to its unique connection with the crown and state. Of the first church on the site nothing is recorded, but King Edward the Confessor is known to have begun to rebuild it and the monastic buildings in the mid-11th century. The great abbey church which replaced it and which survives today was begun on 6 July 1245 and was ready to receive the remains of Saint Edward the Confessor on 13 October 1269. The nave was completed after 1375, in the style of the previous century, but the church was only finished, with the erection of the West towers, very shortly before Canaletto's arrival in London. Sir Christopher Wren had recommended in 1713 that they be built 'in the Gothick Form' because 'to deviate from the old Form, would be to run into a Disagreeable Mixture, which no Person of good Taste could relish' (quoted by Pevsner and Cherry 1973, p. 400). The work was eventually begun to the design of Nicholas Hawksmoor, Wren's successor as Surveyor to the Fabric, in 1734 and was continued after Hawksmoor's death in 1736 by John James until the completion of the towers in c. 1745 (the inscription above the West window misleadingly gives the date 1735).

The Order of the Bath had been revived by King George I on 18 May 1725 and was at the time limited to the sovereign, the Great Master and thirty-six Knights Companion, almost all of whom were invested on 27 May and installed on 17 June of that year. The installation ceremony was subsequently held every four years, that on 26 June 1749 including the Knights Companion who had been invested on 2 May. This painting shows the knights leaving their chapel in the abbey (for which see Cat. no. 20) after the ceremony and proceeding back to the Princes' Chamber of the House of Lords.

Canaletto was presumably requested to use a square canvas, an awkward shape which he otherwise avoided. The visual interest of the painting is redeemed by the moving of the façade of the abbey church over to the right, and by using the V-shaped line of crimson-cloaked knights to help balance the composition. This also made it possible to accommodate all of the procession while emphasizing its tail end. The last person was usually the Great Master but on this occasion John Montagu, 2nd Duke of Montagu, who had been Great Master since 1725, was prevented by illness from attending (he died ten days later on 5 July 1749),

and his place was taken by John West, 7th Baron De La Warr. The penultimate component was the Dean of the Order, an office always held by the Dean of Westminster, on this occasion Joseph Wilcocks (1673–1756), who was concurrently Dean of Westminster and Bishop of Rochester from 1731 until the time of his death. Wilcocks is presumed to have commissioned the painting, doubtless with the intention of commemorating, as much as anything, the completion of the towers, in which he took a particular interest – although Canaletto's inclusion of the procession in this manner also allowed particular prominence to be given to his stately figure.

The painting is generally presumed to have been executed not long after the event. Jane Farrington states that 'it cannot be assumed that Canaletto witnessed the event and he may have relied on visual and written accounts' (Birmingham 1993–4). There is no reason to believe, however, that he did not, and particular attention is given to the diverse attitudes of the onlookers and to details such as the time on the abbey clock (shortly after midday) and the houses of King Street in the left background, up which the procession passed before turning into New Palace Yard.

20

The Interior of Henry VII's Chapel in Westminster Abbey

Probably early 1750s
Oil on canvas
30½ × 26¼ in. (77.5 × 67 cm.)

Private Collection
Exhibited at Dulwich only

Provenance:
(Possibly) Lord W, in the Samuel Dickenson sale,
    Christie's, London, 12 March 1774, lot 37 (sold with lot
    38, 'The inside of King's College at Cambridge, its
    companion': £6 11s to Captain Thompson).
(Possibly) Martin F. Tupper, 1857.
(Possibly) Anon. sale, Christie's, London, 1858
    (63 guineas to Pearce).
With Arthur Tooth & Sons, London.
Ernest Kleinwort, Heaselands, Haywards Heath, Sussex,
    by whom purchased from the above on 24 February 1947.
His widow, Mrs J.N. Kleinwort; her posthumous sale,
    Sotheby's, London, 9 July 1997, lot 69 (purchased by the
    present owner).

Selected Literature:
Finberg 1921, p. 69 (as untraced).
Constable I, pl. 80; II, no. 433.
Puppi 1968, no. 276 A, illustrated.
Links 1981, no. 225, illustrated.
Corboz 1985, II, p. 714, no. P 400, illustrated.

The chapel, one of the masterpieces of the Late Perpendicular style, was begun by King Henry VII in 1503 as a new Lady Chapel for Westminster Abbey, as a chantry chapel for himself, and with a view to being a shrine to Henry VI. It was completed by Henry VIII in c. 1512. Built of Huddleston stone, it is remarkable above all for its spectacular vault, a technically ingenious groin ornamented to resemble a fan-vault, and for the richness of the sculptural decoration of the interior, consisting originally of 107 figures of which 95 remain, their almost complete survival unparalleled in any English church. The focal point of the interior is the tomb of Henry VII and Elizabeth of York, a screen of c. 1507–9 surrounding a tomb chest with the celebrated gilt bronze recumbent effigies by the Florentine Pietro Torregiano of 1512–18. When King George III revived the Order of the Bath on 18 May 1725, the building was designated its chapel, and the heraldic banners of living knights were hung over their stalls.

Another depiction by Canaletto of the subject is in the Museum of London (Fig. 20.1; Constable II, no. 433(a), incorrectly described as on canvas and as 'improbably by Canaletto'; Links 1998, p. 40, no. 433*, pl. 274). That is slightly smaller, on panel and in less satisfactory condition. It is less ambitious in composition in showing the view along the central axis of the chapel, while including more figures and banners over the stalls. The stylistic differences between Canaletto's two depictions of the chapel suggest that they are of different dates. If that in the Museum of London may be of approximately the same time as the view of the other end of the Abbey (Cat. no. 19), as Finberg suggested (1921, p. 35), the exhibited painting should date from several years later. Links, who in 1981 had dated it within 1746–50, later revised this opinion to the early 1750s (private communication, 1995).

Paintings of interiors are rare in Canaletto's work, the only examples in his Italian *oeuvre* being three different views of *The Interior of the Basilica of San Marco*, dating from widely varying moments in the artist's career (Constable I, pl. 25; II, nos 77–9). While in England, however, he also painted two different views of *The Interior of the Rotunda at Ranelagh* (see Cat. no. 33) and presumably a representation of *The Interior of King's College Chapel, Cambridge*, of which at least two paintings given to Canaletto are recorded, one in an auction as early as 1774 (see under Provenance above) and another in the collection of Horace Walpole. Constable

accepted one as Canaletto's work (Constable I, pl. 74; II, no. 411, as 'Attributed to Canaletto'; exhibited Canada 1964–5, no. 105, as by Canaletto) and it was recently bequeathed to the Virginia Museum of Fine Arts, Richmond, Virginia. However, in the opinion of the present writer, it should be regarded as reflecting a lost original (despite the difficulties involved in assessing the quality of a painting in such unsatisfactory condition).

Given the designation of Henry VII's Chapel as that of the Order of the Bath, Canaletto may have hoped that one of his two paintings would attract the interest of one of the illustrious Knights Companion who he had depicted in procession on 26 June 1749 (see Cat. no. 19). In the event, the Museum of London painting was acquired by the same patron as the smaller of his two depictions of *The Old Horse Guards*, probably of approximately similar date (Cat. no. 16), in which one of the Knights Companion is shown in the foreground. It should come as no surprise that a view of the Old Horse Guards, headquarters of the army's general staff, should be purchased by the same client as a view of the chapel of the then purely military Order of the Bath, nor that the client should be the Physician-General to the Army, Dr (later Sir) Edward Wilmot (for whom see under Cat. no. 16).

In both Canaletto's views of *The Interior of Henry VII's Chapel* particular prominence is given by the lighting to the tomb (on the left) of John Sheffield, 1st Duke of Buckingham and Normanby (1648–1721), designed by P.D. Plumière and executed by Peter Scheemakers and Laurent Delvaux. The duke was the builder in 1702–5 of Buckingham House, the precursor of Buckingham Palace, which was owned from 1721 until its sale to King George III in 1762 by his illegitimate son Sir Charles Sheffield. Whether Canaletto was trying to catch the eye of this particular patron we will never know, and the early history of this painting remains to be established.

Figure 20.1
London: The Interior of Henry VII's Chapel, Westminster Abbey, 1749?, oil on panel, 27½ × 23⅛ in. (70 × 58.7 cm.). Museum of London

21

The Thames and the City from Richmond House

Probably 1746
Pen and brown ink with grey wash
13¼ × 21¼ in. (33.7 × 54 cm.)

Birmingham Museums and Art Gallery
Gift MGC/V&A Purchase Grant Fund
Exhibited at Dulwich only

Provenance:
Michael William Coplestone Dillon Onslow, 7th Earl of
     Onslow; sale, Sotheby's, London, 2 July 1984, lot 124.
Acquired by the present owner in 1994
     (Acc. no. 1994 P28).

Selected Exhibitions:
Venice 1982, no. 52.
Birmingham 1993–4, no. 11.
Rome 2005, no. 68.

Selected Literature:
Constable I, p. 140, pl. 138; II, no. 744.
Links 1982, p. 154, pl. 141.
Corboz 1985, I, p. 85, fig. 78; II, p. 733, no. D 113,
     illustrated.
Links 1994, p. 168, pl. 143.
Links 1998, p. 53.
Baetjer 2002, p. 215, fig. 3.

Inscription:
On the reverse: 'Vista del Tamigi / dal Duca de Richmond,
a Londra', considered probably autograph by Jane
Farrington (Birmingham 1993–4) and possibly autograph
by Links (1998).

When Canaletto came to England in May 1746 he brought with him a letter from Joseph Smith to Owen MacSwinny asking him to arrange an introduction for the painter to the 2nd Duke of Richmond. It was MacSwinny who had been responsible for the Duke's purchase in the 1720s of two Venetian views on copper by Canaletto and one if not both of the *Allegorical Tombs* painted in large part by the artist (Constable II, nos 232, 235 and 516–7). MacSwinny heeded this request, which was transmitted to the Duke by his former tutor Tom Hill in a letter of 20 May 1746, in which he says 'I told him the best service I thought you could do him w^d be to let him draw a view of the river from y^r dining-room which would give him as much reputation as any of his Venetian prospects' (quoted by Constable I, p. 33). Although nothing is known of the early provenance of this drawing, there is no reason whatsoever to doubt that it was executed as a direct result of Hill's letter. With its flotillas of boats, nowhere else does Canaletto succeed to such a degree in giving the Thames the character of the Bacino di San Marco, the terrace in the foreground even resembling the Piazzetta which is similarly flanked by buildings. This would support a dating in the latter part of 1746, soon after his arrival in London, given his previous almost total inexperience of environments other than that of Venice.

Its high degree of finish suggests that it was executed for presentation to the Duke, and one may presume that the differences between it and the resultant painting now at Goodwood (Fig. 25), generally considered to have been executed in the summer of 1747, reflect, at least to some degree, his response to it. Most of these derive from the change in format, the painting having to be almost square in order to function effectively above one of the two chimneypieces in the Great Hall at Goodwood. Thus, while the depiction of the left part of the skyline, with St Paul's Cathedral and the spires of St Mary-le-Strand, St Clement Danes and St Brides, corresponds closely, the composition is curtailed in the painting immediately to the right of the Monument, the right-hand part of the drawing, amounting to more than a third of the composition, being omitted. The part of Richmond House Terrace which projects into the river is, however, included in order to balance the composition by being moved to the left to appear in the bottom right corner of the painting.

Aesthetically far more significant is the change in Canaletto's treatment of the foreground, which in the painting is seen not straight on but at an angle, giving the composition far greater visual interest. There the eye is led in not by the projecting wing of Richmond House, omitted on the right, but by part of Montagu House introduced on the left. The number of craft on the river is also drastically reduced.

The drawing has always been highly regarded despite the discoloration of the fugitive ink which has changed the tonal values. A drawing in a horizontal format corresponding in a similarly approximate manner with the pendant Goodwood painting of *Whitehall and the Privy Garden from Richmond House* (Fig. 26) also survives (Fig. 9; Constable I, pl. 142; II, no. 754). It was, however, to be carried through eventually to a painting, although with a significant shift in viewpoint, the canvas now in the collection of the Duke of Buccleuch (Fig. 8).

22

Richmond House Terrace and the West End of Westminster Bridge

Probably 1747
Pen and brown ink over black chalk
7⅞ × 12¾ in. (20 × 32.4 cm.)

Private Collection

Provenance:
Baron Karl Eduard von Liphart, Florence; his posthumous
sale, Leipzig, 26ff. April 1898, lot 186.
A.W.M. Mensing; his posthumous sale, Amsterdam,
26 October 1937, lot 38.
Anon. sale [Ir. A.B. Reintjes and others], Frederik Muller,
Amsterdam, 25 July 1940, lot 407 (bought by P. de Boer).
The P. and N. de Boer Foundation, Amsterdam; sale,
Christie's, London, 4 July 1995, lot 70.
With Trinity Fine Art, London, 1998, from whom
purchased by the present owner.

Selected Literature:
Watson 1950, pp. 316 and 319, fig. 13.
Constable I, p. 149, pl. 142; II, no. 753.
Corboz 1985, I, p. 350, fig. 425; II, p. 732, no. D 109,
illustrated.
Baetjer 2002, pp. 215–20, figs 4–5.

Inscription:
Extensively annotated in the artist's hand: *pon. novo | Londra*
[new bridge, London]; on the western abutment of
Westminster Bridge, *copi* or just *c* [tiles], *pion.º* [for *piombo*,
lead], *tole* [boards or weather-boarding], *cener.ᵉ* [ash-
coloured], *tole cen.ᵉ* [ash-coloured weather-boarding],
cot.º or *co.º* [terracotta]; on the central chimney, *coto uech.º*
[old brick], *zaleto* [yellow], *B. za.º* or *B.z.º* [whitish yellow],
pie.ᵃ ui.ᵃ [old stone], *oc.ᵃ* or *o.ᵃ* [ochre].

Similar annotations to those on this drawing are found on the two sketches of the *The Old Horse Guards and the Banqueting House, Whitehall,* and the *Old Horse Guards and Little Walsingham House* in the Accademia, Venice (Figs 16.1, 16.2). Although these help to give all three sheets the appearance of sketches made on the spot, this was contested by Sir Francis Watson when he published them for the first time in 1950. Canaletto's use of the two other sketches for the smaller of his two paintings of *The Old Horse Guards* has already been discussed (see Cat. no. 16). Publishing this drawing as a *Veduta ideata based on the Riverside Terrace of Old Montagu House,* Watson describes it as 'a travesty of reality', and suggests that it 'was in all probability made after the artist's return to Italy'. Although Constable catalogued the drawing under 'English views' rather than '*capricci*', neither he nor Links ever questioned Watson's assertions. It was left to Katharine Baetjer to point out that the terrace is not that of Old Montagu House but that of Richmond House, and that Canaletto has not departed nearly as far from the facts as was imagined (Baetjer 2002, pp. 217–18). Indeed the only element which is certainly imaginary is the statue on the end of the bridge, although a degree of artistic license over the water level may well have been necessary in order to bring into view the boat at lower left.

On the right are the two projecting wings of Richmond House, also shown in simplified form on the far right of Cat. no. 30. The chimney of the nearer of the two wings, which could not be accommodated in the upper right corner, is sketched against the wall below. The viewpoint is thus towards the right end of the other part of the terrace shown in Cat. no. 21, in which the flowerpots around the corner of the building are also depicted. Unlike Cat. no. 21, the sheet would appear to be from a sketchbook, and there are scattered sketches, including a sailing skiff with two figures, on the *verso* (see Baetjer 2002, Fig. 5).

Although the detailed colour notes suggest that Canaletto intended to produce a painting of the subject, none is currently known, although Constable mentions one 'said to be in a Norfolk private collection' which he was unable to trace. The drawing was certainly used as the basis for a series of three drawings in which the element of fantasy is increasingly evident (see Cat. no. 65 and Fig. 65.1).

The drawing presumably dates from around the same time as Canaletto's other drawing and two paintings taken from Richmond House for the 2nd Duke of Richmond (Cat. no. 21; Figs 25, 26), since no contact between artist and patron is recorded after 1747 and the duke died in 1750. Canaletto may understandably have been hopeful of a further commission for a painting which would combine Richmond House and Westminster Bridge, of which the duke was one of the Commissioners.

Cotº
uech.º

Cepi

B. Rª

B. ¿.º

Pion.º

ꝃole. uº

C

pon. nouo
fondra

Pion.

C.ti

Coi

tole.

cº

B.

Ceneꝟ.º

ꝃole cenª

piè uiᵉ

zaleto

23

Westminster Bridge from the North with the Lord Mayor's Procession, 29 October 1746

1746–47
Oil on canvas
37¾ × 50¼ in. (95.9 × 127.6 cm.)

Yale Center for British Art, Paul Mellon Collection

Provenance:
Presumably commissioned by George Garnier (1703–63),
    and by inheritance at Rookesbury Park, Wickham,
    Fareham, Hampshire, to John Carpenter Garnier
    (1839–1926); sale, Christie's, London, 13 July 1895,
    lot 26 (280 guineas to P. & D. Colnaghi).
William Henry Montagu-Douglas-Scott, 6th Duke of
    Buccleuch and 8th Duke of Queensberry (1831–1914).
His grandson, Walter John Montagu-Douglas-Scott,
    8th Duke of Buccleuch and 10th Duke of Queensberry
    (1894–1973).
With Edward Speelman, London, by whom acquired from
    the above in 1962.
Paul Mellon, by whom purchased from the above in
    April 1962 and presented to the present owner in 1976
    (Acc. no. B1976.7.94).

Selected Exhibitions:
New York 1989–90, no. 63.

Selected Literature:
Finberg 1921, p. 72, pl. XV.
Constable 1923, p. 283.
Constable I, pp. 34, 94 and 141, note 1, pl. 80; II, no. 435
    and under nos 425 and 749(b).
Puppi 1968, no. 267, illustrated.
Walker 1979, pp. 167 and 238–9, pls 31–2.
Links 1981, no. 213, illustrated.
Links 1982, pp. 148–9, pl. 135 (colour).
Corboz 1985, II, p. 711, no. P 390, illustrated.
Constable / Links 1989, I, pp. lxi–lxii, 34, 94 and 141,
    note 1, pl. 80; II, no. 435 and under nos 425 and 749(b).
Links 1994, pp. 165–6, pl. 139 (colour).
Redford 1996, p. 78, pl. 23 (colour).
Eglin 1999, p. 110, fig. 22.
Eglin 2001, pp. 131–2.

Engraved:
R[ichard] Parr, after a drawing by Samuel Wale, published
by John Brindley, New Bond Street, London, March 1747.

During the first half of the eighteenth century, the need
became acute for a bridge to help relieve the burden on the
narrow and increasingly congested Old London Bridge
(see Cat. no. 3). London was not only the economic, social,
intellectual and cultural centre of the country, the seat of
government and law, but also by far the largest city in the
world, and its expansion had greatly increased the need to
facilitate the passage of food and other goods to and from
other parts of the country. While the road system had greatly
improved, even after the construction of the wooden bridge
at Fulham in 1729, that and Old London Bridge remained
the only bridges across the Thames below Kingston. For
decades discussion of a new bridge had been met with
virulent opposition from parties who perceived a threat
to their interests, notably short-sighted bodies in the City,
residents of Southwark and the notoriously offensive
Thames watermen, who operated ferry and taxi services
across the river at numerous 'stairs'. Finally, however, on
20 May 1736 a parliamentary bill received the royal assent
and became law as 'An Act for Building a Bridge across the
River Thames, from the New Palace Yard in the City of
Westminster to the opposite shore in the County of Surrey'.
Powers sufficient to carry the project through to a successful
conclusion were accorded to a body of about 175 commissioners, who included several past and future patrons of
Canaletto, notably Sir Hugh Smithson, the Duke of
Richmond, the Duke of Bedford and Sir Robert Walpole.
The importance given to the enterprise was such that it was
decreed that anyone hindering construction or endangering
users of the bridge would suffer death 'without benefit
of clergy'.

The construction of the bridge was one of the great
engineering feats of the eighteenth century. Most of the credit
for it must go to Charles Labelye, an engineer of Swiss
origin who, after showing to the commissioners the caisson,
a machine for laying the foundations of the piers which he
seems to have invented, was appointed on 10 May 1738
engineer in charge of the foundations. Although it had been
assumed for some time that only a stone bridge would be
appropriate, it was only confirmed in February 1740 that the

upper part of the bridge as well as the piers would be of
stone rather than wood. In April of that year Labelye's
design for this was approved, and he was confirmed as the
engineer for the whole undertaking.

The bridge was to consist of thirteen semi-circular
arches, twelve piers and two abutments, the middle arch to
be 76 feet wide and the remainder decreasing by four feet
each. The design was altered in 1744 to include a small arch
in each of the abutments, so that the bridge finally consisted
of fifteen arches and fourteen piers. When it was completed
in 1750 it was calculated to have cost no less than £218,800,
some of which came from state lotteries but most from
parliamentary grants. The first stone was laid by the Earl
of Pembroke on 29 January 1739 and, despite attempts at
sabotage, the first pier, built of regular courses of Portland
stone, was complete by 23 April. That was one of the
middle piers, the second of which was completed in
August. The last pier was completed on 21 February 1744,
Labelye proudly pointing out that 'The building of both
Abutments and all the Piers of this Bridge were happily
compleated in Five Years & twenty-three Days from the
laying of the first Stone …' (Labelye 1751). Only a month
after that the four arches nearest the Westminster side were
complete but for their cornice and balustrade, progress
having been more rapid there than on the Surrey side.

Canaletto's views of Westminster Bridge outnumber
by far those of any other English subject. Although they
show the bridge in a wide variety of states, it should not be
assumed that the sequence represents the order of execution.
Indeed, this painting, which appears to show the bridge
complete, may well be the artist's earliest depiction of it,
since an engraving after it was published in March 1747.
Lord Mayor's Day, when the new Lord Mayor of London
processed by river from the City to Westminster to be
sworn in office before the Barons of the Exchequer and
subsequently presented to the king, took place annually
on 29 October (until 1752, when the date was changed to
9 November), and the one represented must thus be that of
1746. The barge carrying the new Lord Mayor, William
Benn of the Fletchers' Company, shown broadside in
the foreground, was accompanied by other colourfully
decorated barges either owned or hired by all the City livery
companies. The indistinctness of the standards prevents
their precise identification in the painting, but they are
named in the glossary on Parr's print: from left to right,

the Skinners', the Goldsmiths' and the Fishmongers'; navigating under the arches of the bridge the Clothworkers', the Vintners' and the Merchant Taylors'; behind the Lord Mayor's the Mercers' and on the far right the Drapers'. The last stone of the bridge had been laid only four days earlier by the Earl of Pembroke, who had 'laid the first stone but seven years, eight months and twenty-seven days before'. The balustrade was not to be finished for another year, however, and the last four centres, of arches on the Surrey side, were not struck until September, November and December 1746, and April 1747. Canaletto has also anticipated incorrectly the form which the bridge was to take above pavement level. A semi-octagonal, half-domed, Portland stone shelter for pedestrians is shown over every pier, whereas in fact only twelve of these were provided, four over the corners of the central arch and of the last arch at each end. Furthermore, the statues of Thames and Isis shown over the central arch, although projected at one time, were never installed. Any celebration of the imminent completion of the bridge proved to be premature, as in the months following May 1747 it became increasingly clear that the fifth pier from the Westminster abutment was settling and the opening of the bridge was consequently delayed until November 1750 (see Cat. no. 26).

Lord Mayor's Day and other river processions (see Cat. nos 27 and 30) provided perfect excuses for Canaletto to enliven the foreground of views of the Thames with festive river craft, the City end of the same pageant being shown in one of the two paintings acquired by Prince Lobkowicz (Fig. 6). Cat. no. 23 has often been chosen to demonstrate how Canaletto was unable to differentiate the individual characteristics of the unfamiliar northern subject and ended up making it look like Venice, complete with an inappropriate number of boats and Mediterranean sunshine. The 'decorative' quality of the painting (in a pejorative sense) is enhanced by the bridge being almost exactly parallel with the picture plane. This is not the case in any other depiction of the subject, and the contrast in mood with the Lobkowicz *Westminster from Lambeth* (Fig. 5) is striking. It seems probable, however, that these aspects of the painting which have been seen as weaknesses were entirely intentional, for there is every reason to believe that it was intended to hang *en suite* with three earlier Venetian views, two real and one ideal, with which it is first recorded

in the 1895 sale. While *The Molo from the Bacino di San Marco on Ascension Day, with the Bucintoro* (Cat. no. 54) is slightly larger, the patron must have requested that this painting follow the same unusual dimensions as the two Grand Canal views, *The Rialto Bridge from the South* (Fig. 54.2) and the *Capriccio of the Grand Canal with Palladio's Design for the Rialto Bridge, the Basilica Palladiana and the Palazzo Chiericati* (Fig. 54.3). In all three of those paintings the whole of the foreground is filled with water punctuated by numerous boats, while in *The Molo from the Bacino di San Marco on Ascension Day, with the Bucintoro* (Cat. no. 54), remarkably similar to this in colouration, the buildings are similarly parallel with the picture plane, forming a horizontal band between water and sky.

It has been suggested that Canaletto's Whig patrons' display of his views of Venice was intended in part to express their admiration for the political structure of the Venetian Republic, and that for the same reason the artist deliberately made London resemble Venice, and, for instance, the Thames at Walton resemble the Brenta Canal (in which respect it may be noted that his view of *Old Walton Bridge*, Cat. no. 37, and that of *Dolo on the Brenta*, Fig. 11, are not only of identical date but strikingly similar in mood). In the words of Professor Bruce Redford 'Canaletto manipulates topography, perspective, composition, and allusive detail so as to bring Venice and London into mysterious relation' (Redford 1996, p. 76). Redford uses this painting to demonstrate this argument, pointing out that 'only the Lord Mayor's barge … is positioned horizontally to the picture plane, thereby achieving maximum visual kinship with the Bucintoro. Indeed every important aspect of the picture – the banded composition, the massing of the boats, the studied legibility of the splendid central barge – defines the event as a northern analogue to the Sposalizio [the ceremony of the Marriage with the Sea on Ascension Day]' (Redford 1996, p. 78). Although the example he uses for comparison is *The Molo from the Bacino di San Marco on Ascension Day, with the Bucintoro* in the Royal Collection (Fig. 54.1), how much more supportive of his theory is the fact that Cat. no. 23 was designed to hang in the same room as the present picture, so that the parallel between the Lord Mayor's barge and the Bucintoro, both towards the right side and facing left, could hardly have been more direct.

Although Links speculated that the painting may have been commissioned by John Brindley, publisher of the engraving after it, it seems highly likely that the group of paintings sold from Rookesbury Park by John Carpenter Garnier (1839–1926) in 1895 had been commissioned by his forebear George Garnier (1703–63), and had passed quietly by inheritance at Rookesbury for 150 years until their dispersal (see pp. 12–14 and Cat. no. 54). It has already been suggested that the imminent completion of Westminster Bridge may have been one of the factors which drew Canaletto to England. The proximity to each other in date of the last two components of the group, one, *The Molo from the Bacino di San Marco on Ascension Day, with the Bucintoro* (Cat. no. 54) probably painted shortly before Canaletto's departure for London, the other almost immediately after his arrival there, suggests that Garnier's patronage may even have been one of the reasons for the artist undertaking the journey to England.

24

The City seen through an Arch
of Westminster Bridge

1747
Oil on canvas
23½ × 38⅜ in. (59.7 × 97.5 cm.)

Collection of the Duke of Northumberland

Provenance:
Commissioned by Sir Hugh Smithson (1714–86), 4th Bt.,
who succeeded to the Earldom of Northumberland in
1750 and was created 1st Duke of Northumberland of
the third creation in 1766, and by inheritance to the
present owner.

Selected Exhibitions:
London 1977, no. 10.
Birmingham 1993–4, no. 6.

Selected Literature:
Finberg 1921, pp. 28–9 and 70–1, pl. XIIb.
Constable I, pp. 34, 94, 141, note 1, and 143, note 3,
    pl. 74; II, no. 412.
Puppi 1968, no. 265, illustrated.
Walker 1979, pp. 158, 171 and 239.
Links 1981, no. 209, illustrated.
Links 1982, pp. 151–2, pl. 138.
Corboz 1985, I, p. 76, fig. 63 (detail); II, p. 711, no. P 388,
    illustrated.
Constable / Links 1989, I, pp. lxiii, 34, 94, 141, note 1,
    and 143, note 3, pl. 74; II, no. 412.
Links 1994, pp. 166–7, pl. 140 (colour).

Engraved:
R[ichard] Parr after a drawing by Samuel Wale, published
by John Brindley 3 June 1747.

25

Westminster Bridge under Construction,
from the South-East Abutment

1747
Oil on canvas
23⅜ × 38¼ in. (59.3 × 97.3 cm.)

Collection of the Duke of Northumberland

Provenance:
As for Cat. no. 24.

Selected Exhibitions:
London 1977, no. 11, illustrated.

Selected Literature:
Finberg 1921, pp. 28, 29 and 70, pl. XIIIb.
Constable I, pp. 34, 94 and 141, note 1, pl. 80; II, no. 434.
Puppi 1968, no. 266, illustrated.
Walker 1979, pp. 171 and 240, pl. 35.
Links 1981, no. 208, illustrated.
Corboz 1985, II, p. 711, no. P 389, illustrated.
Constable / Links 1989, I, pp. lxi, lxiii, 34, 94 and 141,
    note 1, pl. 80; II, no. 434.

24

The City seen through an Arch of Westminster Bridge

25

Westminster Bridge under Construction, from the South-East Abutment

Cat. no. 24 is one of the most striking of all Canaletto's English compositions, and it was disseminated almost immediately after its completion by an engraving published on 3 June 1747 (although there the strength of the design is slightly diluted by the addition of a boat in the stretch of open water in the centre). The print was distributed as a pendant to that of Cat. no. 23, which had been published three months earlier. The painting shows one of the timber centres constructed initially by James King, and from 1743 by his foreman William Etheridge, who a few years later was to design and build Old Walton Bridge (see Cat. nos 37–9). That for the middle arch was completed by 11 June 1741 and the arch turned by 3 February 1742, although the centre was not in fact removed until December 1744. The first of the centres to be struck had, however, left the west 68-foot arch standing free on 14 December 1743. From February 1744 a new design of centre invented by Charles Labelye and using straight rather than circular wedges was employed, and it is that which is shown here. This must be the last centre to be struck, the completion of which Labelye reported on 7 April 1747, although it seems that the timbers may have remained for some months, since he recorded in 1751 that 'on 25th July 1747 the last Center was taken down and all the fifteen Arches of this Bridge were left entirely free and open' (Labelye 1751). Cat. no. 25 similarly shows work on the bridge nearing completion, before the subsidence of the fifth pier from the Westminster abutment necessitated repair and delayed its opening for three years (see Cat. no. 26). It represents the bridge as it appeared in April–May 1747, and unlike Cat. no. 23, which is of only slightly earlier date, shows even the half-domed recesses correctly. Although Constable suggests that the painting may have been made at a later date on the basis of a drawing, there is no reason to believe that it is not contemporary with its pendant, which must have been finished some time before 3 June 1747.

Despite Constable's introduction of an element of doubt, there can be no question that both paintings were commissioned by Sir Hugh Smithson, Bt., to whom the engraving is dedicated and from whom the paintings have passed by inheritance to the present owner. They are thus the only paintings of the bridge executed by Canaletto for one of the commissioners, and indeed one who had regularly attended meetings, particularly in the period 1743–5, although he was also one of the few present at the important meeting of 10 January 1749 when Labelye's proposals for rebuilding the sunk pier were approved.

Smithson was the son of Langdale Smithson, whose grandfather had made a fortune from haberdashery. In 1729 he succeeded his grandfather Sir Hugh Smithson of Stanwick, Yorkshire, as the 4th baronet, and he rebuilt Stanwick Park to his own designs in c. 1739–40. On 16 July 1740 he married Lady Elizabeth Seymour (1716–76), daughter of Algernon, 7th Duke of Somerset, and through her he enjoyed an unexpected and meteoric rise to eminence through a succession of deaths between 1744 and 1750. The death of George Seymour, Viscount Beauchamp, the only son of Smithson's father-in-law, at Bologna on 11 September 1744, on his nineteenth birthday, was followed on 2 December 1748 by that of Charles Seymour, 6th Duke of Somerset at the age of 86. On 7 February 1750 Smithson's father-in-law, who in the previous year had been created 1st Earl of Northumberland of the fifth creation with remainder in favour of Smithson, died at the age of sixty-five. Smithson then assumed the name and arms of Percy, becoming 2nd Earl of Northumberland and inheriting the vast Percy estates, including Northumberland House, Syon House, Alnwick Castle and Warkworth Castle. Apart from managing those with considerable success, he was returned as Member of Parliament for Middlesex in November 1747, and was appointed a trustee of the British Museum in 1753; in 1754 Thomas Chippendale dedicated his *Gentleman and Cabinet-Maker's Director* to him. He was made a Knight of the Order of the Garter in 1757, the 1st Duke of Northumberland of the third creation in 1766, and Master of the Horse in 1778. His illegitimate son James Smithson (1765–1829) was the founder of the Smithsonian Institution Washington, D.C.

Smithson's first commission to Canaletto, dating from around the time of his marriage, was for two magnificent and large canvases of Venetian views, *The Piazza San Marco looking West from the North End of the Piazzetta* and *The Courtyard of the Doge's Palace with the Giants' Staircase* (Constable II, nos 36 and 80; exhibited Rome 2005, nos 56–7). These were evidently delivered by 31 June 1741, when one was mentioned in a letter by Frances, Countess of Hertford, and were painted for Stanwick Park, where they remained until their removal to Alnwick shortly before the demolition of Stanwick in 1923. It is possible that Smithson knew of Canaletto from his great patron of the early–mid 1730s, the Duke of Bedford; on the establishment of the Society for the Encouragement of Learning, in May 1736, the duke was president and Smithson one of two vice-presidents. After commissioning these two paintings from Canaletto in 1747, Smithson was presumably influential in his father-in-law's commission of the views of Windsor Castle, completed on 11 June of the same year (Cat. no. 41), and Syon House of 1749 (Cat. no. 35) which Smithson inherited in 1750. The group was to be completed in the early 1750s by the views of Northumberland House (Fig. 14.1) and Alnwick Castle (Fig. 12).

These paintings, and the others belonging to the Duke of Northumberland (Cat. nos 35, 41) have been cleaned specially for this exhibtion, and are reproduced after cleaning.

26

Westminster Bridge under Repair, from the Westminster South Causeway

1749
Pen and brown ink with grey wash over pencil and extensive pin-pointing
11½ × 19 in. (29.3 × 48.4 cm.)

The Royal Collection

Provenance:
As for Cat. no. 7.

Selected Exhibitions:
London 1980–1, no. 89.

Selected Literature:
Finberg 1921, p. 73.
Parker 1948, no. 118, pl. 76.
Constable I, pp. 95 and 143, pl. 141; II, no. 751.
Walker 1979, pp. 177, 196, 199 and 240, pl. 36.
Links 1982, p. 154, pl. 142.
Constable / Links 1989, I, pp. lxvii–lxviii, 95 and 143,
    pl. 141; II, no. 751.
Links 1994, p. 168, pl. 145 (colour).

The composition of this drawing is similar, although in reverse and taken from the opposite bank, to that of the painting executed for Sir Hugh Smithson in 1747 (Cat. no. 25). Here, however, the bridge is shown with the two arches supported by the fifth pier from the Westminster abutment being dismantled in April–May 1749. In the months following May 1747 it had become increasingly evident that this pier was settling and the Works Committee decided in a meeting on 8 September that, although the subsidence seemed to have slowed, the balustrade, plinth, cornice and pavement over the two arches should be removed as a precaution, and that the gravel between the spandrels should be extracted so that the Purbeck stone counter-arch could be inspected. Charles Labelye and William Etheridge were to discuss what sort of centres would be appropriate, if it was to transpire that they were needed to save the arches. A week later a large block of stone from the fifth arch fell into the river, and construction of the centres was authorized at the end of October. Those, designed by Labelye and built by Etheridge, and clearly shown in this drawing, were not in place until June 1748. The pier was then loaded with a weight greater than it was intended to bear, with the result that by 21 June it had sunk to a mean level 2 ft 11 in. below that of its neighbours, that disparity also being carefully recorded here. The commissioners of the bridge decided in July that the two Purbeck arches should be dismantled and the pier taken down to water level, and the upper, Purbeck arches were removed in October. In December Labelye submitted a proposal to strengthen the sunk pier with piles and then rebuild it in line with the others. The old centres were then to be reused and the arches reconstructed in a manner which put less weight on the unreliable pier. That was approved by the commissioners on 10 January 1749 and Labelye was instructed on 14 March to begin demolition, but action was evidently slow. A report of late May by Labelye stating that the masons 'had taken down all Portland Stone of the damaged Arches since [ie. by] 20th May' provides a *terminus ante quem* for the scene depicted in this drawing, which thus must date from April or early May.

No other version of the drawing is known, and it is of distinctly higher quality than the other English drawings by Canaletto owned by Consul Smith (see Cat. nos 7–8 and 29–30).

27

Westminster Bridge from the North with the Lord Mayor's Procession, 25 May 1750

1750
Oil on canvas
18⅜ × 30¼ in. (46.7 × 76.7 cm.)

Private Collection, courtesy of Simon C. Dickinson Ltd

Provenance:
Painted for William Barnard, Bishop of Derry (d. 1767),
    the King's House, Chapelizod, near Dublin, and
    subsequently Ranelagh, County Dublin.
Peter Purcell, County Kildare.
His grandson Colonel McDonnell.
On the Dublin art market.
Thomas Bodkin, Dublin, by 1926.
Donald Howard, 3rd Baron Strathcona and Mount Royal
    (1891–1959), Colonsay House, Isle of Colonsay, Argyll,
    by 1956.
His son, Donald Howard, 4th Baron Strathcona and
    Mount Royal.
With David Carritt Ltd., London, 1986.
Private Collection, Washington, D.C.
Anon. sale, Ader Tajan, Paris, 29 March 1994, lot 63.
Acquired by the present owner through Simon C.
    Dickinson Ltd in March 1997.

Selected Exhibitions:
London 1977, no. 13.

Selected Literature:
Constable 1927, p. 23.
Constable I, pp. 95 and 143; II, no. 436 (incorrectly
    described as pl. 80).
Puppi 1968, no. 284 A (incorrectly illustrated).
Walker 1979, p. 241.
Links 1981, no. 227 (incorrectly illustrated).
Constable / Links 1989, I, pp. lxi–lxii, lxiii and lxvii,
    95 and 143, pl. 236; II, no. 436 and p. 738.
Links 1998, pp. 40–1, pls 236 and 231 (the inscription
    on the reverse).

Walker identifies the subject as the state procession of John Blachford of the Company of Goldsmiths to Westminster to be sworn in as Lord Mayor on 25 May 1750. That was much smaller than the usual October pageant, and Blachford 'went in the City Barge, attended only by the Goldsmiths' Barge' (*The Gentleman's Magazine*, 20, 1750, p. 254). Although this identification is accepted by Links, it assumes that the presence of two additional barges is due to artistic licence (Constable / Links 1989, I, pp. lxi–lxii). Although the bridge was by then almost finished, Canaletto has, as in Cat. no. 23, erroneously shown shelters for pedestrians over all the piers, rather than just those in the centre and at both ends, as well as the statues of Thames and Isis which were never installed.

During relining in 1986 the canvas was found to be signed and inscribed on the reverse: 'Antonio Canaleto fecit, con Ogni Stima, e Rispeto / All'Eccellentissi[mo] Sig:[r] Gulielmo Vescovo / di Deri' (Fig. 27.1). As Links points out, this must refer to William Barnard, who became Bishop of Derry on 3 March 1747 (Constable / Links 1989, I, p. lxii). Although he was born in London and spent his last years there, around the time that the painting was executed Barnard was living at the King's House in Chapelizod, near Dublin, which was secured for him by his brother-in-law Archbishop Stone, the primate. Barnard's collection of pictures was much admired by Mrs Delany, who often dined with him in 1750 (Delany 1861–2).

Figure 27.1
Inscription on the reverse of Cat. no. 27

28

Westminster Bridge from the North

Probably 1750
Pen and brown ink with grey wash over black chalk
and pin-pointing
13½ × 29 in. (34.5 × 73.8 cm.)

Lent by the Trustees of The British Museum
Exhibited at Yale only

Provenance:
With Colnaghi, London, from whom purchased in 1868
    (Acc. no. 1868-3-28-305).

Selected Exhibitions:
London 2003, no. 4.25.

Selected Literature:
Finberg 1921, pp. 37 and 73, pl. XVI.
Constable II, no. 749(a).
Corboz 1985, II, p. 733, no. D 112, illustrated.

A refinement of that of Cat. no. 23, with the viewpoint moved to the Surrey bank of the Thames, this is one of the most important of all Canaletto's English compositions, known in three drawn and three painted versions. The prime drawing must be the one first recorded in the collection of Sir Richard Colt Hoare, 2nd Bt (1758–1838), and still at Stourhead, Wiltshire (since 1946 the property of the National Trust; Constable II, no. 749(b)). It differs from the others in showing the bridge rising more steeply toward the centre, and from Cat. no. 28 in including four barges identifying the subject as Lord Mayor's Day; Sir Richard Colt Hoare's grandfather Sir Richard Hoare (1709–54) had been Lord Mayor in 1745 (as had his great-great-grandfather Sir Richard Hoare (1648–1718) in 1712). The third version in the Royal Collection – smaller than the other two and the least delicate in handling, omitting, for instance, the pennant on St Margaret's, Westminster – is the only one which shows the correct arrangement of pedestrian shelters (although still showing incorrectly the statues of Thames and Isis never installed over the central arch); it must be the latest in date, made expressly for Joseph Smith (Constable I, pl. 140; II, no. 749).

The three paintings of the composition all measure approximately 18 × 30 in. The earliest is probably Cat. no. 27, which has been identified as depicting the Lord Mayor's Procession on 25 May 1750. A variant in an English private collection (with a pendant which is a variant of Cat. nos 5 and 9), seems to show the same event, although the barges are differently positioned and more prominent (Constable II, no. 436(a)). Canaletto returned to the composition for what must be his last view of Westminster Bridge, painted in 1754 for Thomas Hollis (Fig. 28.1; Constable II, no. 437(b), as untraced; Links 1998, p. 41, pl. 236; exhibited Venice 1982, no. 107, and London 1987, no. 74). In that work the barges are omitted and the composition is – surprisingly – adapted to show the appearance of the bridge in June–July 1750, with the two arches being rebuilt; Canaletto may well have felt that this variation justified his statement in a 'certificate' on the reverse, similar to those on four of the five other paintings for Hollis (Cat. nos 4, 33 and 37, and Fig. 10, but not Cat. no. 15), he writes that the subject was done for him 'for the first and last time'. All Canaletto's depictions of the composition show imaginary hills in the background on both sides.

Figure 28.1
London: Westminster Bridge under Repair, from the North, 1754,
oil on canvas, 19¼ × 30 in. (49 × 76.2 cm.). Private Collection

29

The City seen through an Arch of Westminster Bridge

Probably 1750
Pen and brown ink with grey wash over pencil and
extensive pin-pointing
11¾ × 19 in. (29.8 × 48.4 cm.)

The Royal Collection

Provenance:
As for Cat. no. 7.

Selected Exhibitions:
London 1980–1, no. 88.
Venice 1982, no. 55.
Birmingham 1993–4, no. 7.

Selected Literature:
Finberg 1921, pp. 29, 37 and 71, pl. XIIa.
Parker 1948, no. 119, pl. 77.
Constable I, pp. 93, 141, note 1, and 143, note 3, pl. 135;
    II, no. 732.
Walker 1979, p. 240, pl. 34.
Corboz 1985, II, p. 731, no. D 105, illustrated.
Constable / Links 1989, I, pp. lxvii–lxviii, 93, 141,
    note 1, and 143, note 3, pl. 135; II, no. 732.

30

Westminster Bridge from the North-East, with a Procession of Civic Barges

Probably 1750
Pen and brown ink with grey wash over pencil and
extensive pin-pointing
10¾ × 19⅛ in. (27.1 × 48.6 cm.)

The Royal Collection

Provenance:
As for Cat. no. 7.

Selected Exhibitions:
Canada 1964–5, no. 111.
London 1980–1, no. 90.
Birmingham 1993–4, no. 17.

Selected Literature:
Finberg 1921, pp. 37 and 71–2.
Parker 1948, no. 117, pl. 75.
Constable I, pp. 94 and 141, note 1, pl. 141; II, no. 750.
Walker 1979, pl. 43.
Corboz 1985, II, p. 737, no. D 131, illustrated.
Constable / Links 1989, I, pp. lxvii–lxviii, 94 and
    141, note 1, pl. 141; II, no. 750.

Of the six drawings by Canaletto of English subjects
owned by Joseph Smith and now in the Royal Collection,
(see also Cat. nos 7, 8 and 26), no fewer than five show
Westminster Bridge. There is every reason to believe that
all of these drawings, with the exception of *Westminster
Bridge under Repair, from the Westminster South Causeway*
(Cat. no. 26), are replicas of earlier compositions, made
especially to be presented to Smith on the artist's return to
Venice in the latter part of 1750, when Smith commissioned
painted versions of two of them (see Cat. nos 7–10). That
supposition is supported by the existence of demonstrably
earlier versions of both of these drawings. A version of
Cat. no. 29 in the Albright-Knox Art Gallery, Buffalo,
corresponds closely in size and in all but very minor details,
but is distinctly more refined in execution, with more use
of the pen (Constable II, under no. 732; exhibited Canada

1964–5, no. 112, illustrated). That is itself based on the
painting executed in 1747 for Sir Hugh Smithson (Cat.
no. 24) but without the centring removed by the end
of July of that year (or the hanging bucket), and with
different boats and figures. The painting does not show
the spire of the church of St Mary le Strand, an omission
thought significant enough that it is corrected in Parr's print;
the spire is shown in both drawings of the composition,
which would seem to confirm that they are of later date.
The drawing at Buffalo may be that of 'London from the
Centre Arch of Westminster Bridge' which was among
the four drawings by Canaletto in an anonymous sale in
1766 (see under Cat. no. 3).

Cat. no. 30 is closely based on a slightly larger drawing
in the British Museum, which is in less satisfactory condition
(Constable II, under no. 750; exhibited London 2003,
no. 2.38, illustrated in colour). Here the execution is more
perfunctory and the detail simplified, a wall and trees have
been introduced to close the composition on the left, and the
pennant on St Margaret's, Westminster, is blowing the other
way to avoid confusion. Constable considered the British
Museum drawing to be later in date since 'the bridge is
complete with all its turrets', but the arrangement of the
shelters for pedestrians is, in fact, shown correctly here, and
is wrongly anticipated in the British Museum version.
Constable also questions the identification of the subject as
Lord Mayor's Day, but an inscription in Canaletto's hand
on the reverse of the British Museum drawing, which reads
'Foncion de Lord Mayor of London', should dispel any
doubt on this issue (London 2003, p. 129).

31

The Grand Walk of the New Spring Garden, Vauxhall, with the
Orchestra Pavilion, the Organ House and the Turkish Dining Tent

32

The Interior of the Rotunda at Ranelagh

31

*The Grand Walk of the New Spring Garden,
Vauxhall, with the Orchestra Pavilion,
the Organ House and the Turkish Dining Tent*

c. 1751
Oil on canvas
20 × 30¼ in. (50.8 × 76.8 cm.)

Compton Verney, Warwickshire, England

Provenance:
Possibly acquired by Arthur Hill (before 1699–1771),
    who took the name Hill-Trevor in 1763 and became in
    1765 the 1st Viscount Dungannon of the second creation,
    and by descent at Brynkinalt, Denbighshire, to his great-
    grandson Arthur Hill-Trevor, 3rd Viscount Dungannon
    (1798–1862).
By inheritance at Brynkinalt on his death without issue to
    his kinsman Lord Arthur Edwin Hill (1819–1894),
    created Baron Trevor in 1890, and by descent at
    Brynkinalt until sold at Christie's, London, 9 July 1999,
    lot 84.
Acquired at the sale by a private collector, from whom
    purchased in June 2006.

Selected Exhibitions:
Canada, 1964–5, no. 107.
New York 1989–90, no. 71.
Birmingham 1993–4, no. 28.

Selected Literature:
Constable 1927, pp. 18 and 23, pl. II B.
Constable I, pp. 42, 95, and 144, note 3, pl. 80; II, no. 431.
Puppi 1968, no. 287, illustrated.
Links 1981, no. 231, illustrated.
Corboz 1985, II, p. 718, no. P 414, illustrated.
Links 1994, p. 186, pl. 164 (colour).

32

The Interior of the Rotunda at Ranelagh

c. 1751
Oil on canvas
20⅜ × 30⅜ in. (51.7 × 77 cm.)

Compton Verney, Warwickshire, England

Provenance:
As for Cat. no. 31.

Selected Exhibitions:
Canada, 1964–5, no. 106.
New York 1989–90, no. 72.
Birmingham 1993–4, no. 29.

Selected Literature:
Sewter 1949, p. 85, fig. 27.
Constable I, p. 146, pl. 77; II, no. 421.
Puppi 1968, no. 303B.
Links 1981, under no. 253.
Corboz 1985, II, p. 723, no. P 430, illustrated.

These two paintings, clearly intended as pendants, depict the two principal fashionable pleasure grounds in eighteenth-century London. The New Spring Garden was opened to the public by 1661, initially benefiting from the change in official attitudes to places of public entertainment which took place after the Restoration of King Charles II the year before. It was, however, inconveniently located on the Surrey side of the Thames, near the East end of the modern Vauxhall Bridge, visitors being dependent for access on the notoriously bad mannered watermen, and the Garden had closed by the time the resourceful entrepreneur Jonathan Tyers (1702–67) secured a thirty-year lease in 1728. He re-launched it in 1732, with an admission price of only a shilling, and under his management the Garden, with the enthusiastic support of the ground landlord Frederick, Prince of Wales, enjoyed a period of sustained prosperity. Twelve thousand people attended the rehearsal of Handel's *Music for the Royal Fireworks* there on 21 April 1749, London Bridge remaining impassable for three hours as a result. Tyers's enterprise gained a significant boost from the opening of Westminster Bridge in 1750, and he was able to buy the freehold of the land in 1758. In the following year Robert Adam was hoping for a commission for a 'Temple of Venus'. The Garden remained in the possession of Tyers's descendants until 1821, becoming officially known as Vauxhall Gardens in 1785 and finally going out of business in 1859.

Canaletto shows the view seen on entering the Garden, looking East up the Grand Walk to the distant statue of Aurora. While this was already established as one of the most satisfactory views of the subject, Canaletto has depicted the warm sunlight as coming from the North, in order to highlight the Garden's central buildings, shown on the right: the octagonal Orchestra Pavilion opened on 2 June 1735, the Organ House of 1737 and the Turkish Dining Tent erected shortly before 1744, the first and last of these possibly designed by William Kent. On the left are some of the supper boxes. Those were decorated with at least fifty-three canvases by Francis Hayman, Peter Monamy and others, most, if not all, executed between 1739 and 1743. An even more significant product of Tyers's patronage of contemporary artists is Louis-François Roubiliac's cele-brated marble statue of Handel of 1738 (London, Victoria and Albert Museum), which originally stood in the South Walk just off to the right of the view in the painting.

Ranelagh, which had a shorter life, occupied the former garden of Ranelagh House, which had been built in about 1690 for Lord Ranelagh, Paymaster General to the Forces, and stood to the east of Chelsea College. The site was purchased by James Lacy in 1740 and developed by him with Sir Thomas Robinson. It catered to a more discerning audience than the New Spring Garden, admission being set at two shillings and sixpence, which included tea or coffee and bread and butter, or five shillings on fireworks nights. Its dominant attraction was the Rotunda, which was built in 1741 to the designs of William Jones and opened in 1742. Constructed entirely of wood, it had an internal diameter of 150 feet and two tiers of fifty-two boxes. Fashionable society could gather in the vast space regardless of weather, to attend balls and masquerades or listen to music, which always played an important part in the entertainment provided in the Rotunda. It boasted a substantial organ, a band and a choir. The central octagon was originally the bandstand, but by Canaletto's day that had been transferred to the side in front of the organ and replaced by a fireplace. The young Mozart performed on the organ on 29 June 1764.

Ranelagh initially enjoyed considerable popularity, Horace Walpole writing in a letter in 1744

Every night constantly I go to Ranelagh, which has totally beat Vauxhall. Nobody goes anywhere else; everybody goes there. My Lord Chesterfield is so fond of it, that he says he has ordered all his letters to be directed thither … You can't set your foot without treading on a Prince, or Duke of Cumberland. (Walpole, *Correspondence*, vol. 37, p. 164)

Changes of fashion led to the falling off of patronage as the century progressed, the Rotunda being closed in 1803 and demolished in 1805. Canaletto's decision to paint the sombre interior of the Rotunda in contrast with the *plein air* gaiety of the New Spring Garden suggests that he was aware of a general perception that Ranelagh was a more serious and restrained establishment than Vauxhall.

The New Spring Garden is the only painting of the subject by a significant artist, and *Ranelagh*, and its variant (Cat. no. 33) are similarly the definitive records of the appearance of the building. However, the rivalry between the two establishments rules out as prospective clients for this pair of views both Tyers – despite his patronage of the visual arts – and those involved with Ranelagh, and it must be presumed that they were executed as a speculation. There is no record

of either of the paintings before the 1920s, nor is there any evidence that they have ever been sold on the open market. It seems highly probable, therefore, that they were acquired from the artist by a forebear of the first recorded owners, the Barons Trevor, most probably Arthur Hill (before 1699–1771), later Hill-Trevor and, from 1765, 1st Viscount Dungannon of the second creation. In 1737 he had married an heiress, Anne Stafford (d. 1799), and in 1751 had inherited Brynkinalt, the house where the paintings are first recorded, and other Trevor property from his father's bachelor half-brother Marcus Hill, who had died in that year.

The date of *c.* 1751 proposed for both paintings by Jane Farrington (Birmingham 1993–4) seems probable on stylistic grounds and gains considerable support from Canaletto's extensive involvement with both subjects in that year. For not only did he include the Rotunda in the panoramic view of *Chelsea College and Ranelagh* which

he exhibited in July 1751 (see Cat. no. 34 and Fig. 34.1), but he also provided Robert Sayer with four drawings of the New Spring Garden and three of Ranelagh, which were among those of London views, all now lost, of which engravings (in reverse) were published on 2 December 1751.

Despite variations of detail, and indeed inaccuracies, both paintings are clearly based on the drawings also used for Edward Rooker's print of '*A View of the Grand Walk &c in Vauxhall Gardens*' (Fig. 31.1) and Nathaniel Parr's print of '*An Inside View of the Rotundo in Ranelagh Gardens*' (Fig. 33.1).

Figure 31.1
Edward Rooker, after Canaletto, '*A View of the Grand Walk &c in Vauxhall Gardens*', published 2 December 1751, engraving

33

The Interior of the Rotunda at Ranelagh

1754
Oil on canvas
18½ × 29¾ in. (47 × 75.6 cm.)

The National Gallery, London

Provenance:
As for Cat. no. 4 until 1884; 1884 sale, lot 129
(90 guineas to Reynolds).
F.D. Reynolds, Dublin; his (posthumous) sale, Christie's,
London, 15 July 1893, lot 62 (46 guineas to Buttery).
With A.H. Buttery, from whom purchased in 1894
(Acc. no. 1429).

Selected Exhibitions:
Venice 1982, no. 109.

Selected Literature:
Finberg 1921, pp. 41–2, 43 and 60–1, pl. XXX.
Constable I, pp. 36, 40, 96, 145–6 and 166, pl. 77;
II, no. 420.
Puppi 1968, no. 303A, illustrated, and colour pls
LX–LXI.
Levey 1971, pp. 29–31, no. 1429.
Links 1981, no. 253, illustrated, and illustrated in colour
on pp. 92–3.
Links 1982, p. 173, pl. 169.
Corboz 1985, I, p. 37; II, p. 707, no. P 378, illustrated.
Constable / Links 1989, I, pp. lxxv, lxxvi, 36, 40, 96,
145–6 and 166, pl. 77; II, no. 420.
Links 1994, p. 186, pl. 168 (colour).

As in the case of four of the other five paintings commissioned by Thomas Hollis (see Cat. nos 4, 33, 37, and Figs 10, 28.1, but not 15), John Disney transcribed the inscription that had been visible on the back of the canvas until relining in 1850 onto a label on the reverse: 'Fatto nel anno 1754 in Londra per la prima ed ultima volta con ogni maggior attentzione ad istanza del signor Cavaliere Hollis padrone mio stimatiss⁰ – Antonio del Canal detto il Canaletto'. This is one of the rare instances of Canaletto spelling his name in the same way that we do. Given the obvious relationship of the composition with the earlier version (Cat. no. 32), the assurance extracted by Hollis from the artist that he was painting the subject (or rather the composition?) 'for the first and last time' has provoked a certain amount of comment, Sewter even accusing him of 'mendacity' (Sewter 1949, p. 85). Other versions are also known of Hollis's *Westminster Bridge*, *The Campidoglio and the Cordonata, Rome*, and *Old Walton Bridge*, the only one certainly of later date (see Cat. no. 38). In all these cases, however, Canaletto has gone to some lengths to differentiate the versions. For this painting he reverted to Parr's engraving of 1751 (Fig. 33.1), thus reversing the composition, as well as providing a largely new cast of figures and varying the positions of the chandeliers (all the versions omit some of these in order to avoid crowding the composition with them). Evidently the painter felt that such changes justified the wording of the 'certificates' written on the reverses.

Figure 33.1
Nathaniel Parr, after Canaletto, *'An Inside View of the Rotundo in Ranelagh Gardens'*, published 2 December 1751, engraving

34

Chelsea from Battersea Reach

1751
Oil on canvas
34 × 42 in. (86.5 × 106.5 cm.) (approximate measurements, as the bottom edge is irregularly cut)

Blickling Hall, Norfolk, England. The Lothian Collection (The National Trust)

Provenance:
Philip Henry Kerr, 11th Marquess of Lothian (1882–1940), Newbattle Abbey, Midlothian, by 1931, and subsequently Blickling Hall, Norfolk; bequeathed with Blickling to the National Trust in 1940.

Selected Literature:
Vertue 1934, p. 158.
Constable I, pp. 37–8, 95 and 143–4, pl. 75; II, no. 413(b).
Puppi 1968, no. 289, illustrated.
Links 1981, no. 233, illustrated.
Links 1982, pp. 167–8, pl. 160.
Corboz 1985, II, p. 706, no. P 373, illustrated.
Constable / Links 1989, I, pp. lxvi, lxxi–lxxii, 37–8, 95 and 143–4, pl. 75; II, no. 413(b).
Links 1994, p. 184, pl. 158.

In July 1751, presumably encouraged by the success of advertising *The Old Horse Guards from Saint James's Park* (Cat. no. 17) almost exactly two years earlier, Canaletto posted a second announcement in the *Daily Advertiser*:

Signior Canaletto | Gives notice that he has painted the Representation of Chelsea College, Ranelagh House, and the River Thames, which if any Gentleman and others are pleas'd to favour him with seeing the same, he will attend at his Lodgings, at Mr. Viggan's, in Silver-Street, Golden Square, for fifteen Days from this Day, the 31st of July, from Eight o'Clock in the Morning to One in the Afternoon, and from Three in the Afternoon to Six at Night, each Day.

This event was duly recorded by Vertue:

Lately … Canaletti. painter has painting [sic] a large picture a View on the River Thames. of Chelsea College. Ranelagh gardens & c. an[d] parts adjacent. with barges & boats figures – this he exposd to publick View at his Lodgings – being a work lately done to shew his skill – this valud at 60. or 70 pounds. haveing made a Tour to his own Country at Venice for some affairs there – in 8 months going and comeing. it is tho[t] that this View is not so well as some works of Canaletti formerly brought into England. nor does it appear to be better than some painters in England can do. (Vertue, *Note Books*, III, p. 158)

Vertue's unenthusiastic response would seem to have been shared by Canaletto's clientele, as the painting remained unsold and was subsequently cut in two, presumably in the view that the parts would be easier to sell than the whole. That had taken place by 1802, when the slightly wider and taller, right-hand part was sold at auction in London on its own. It re-emerged at an auction in 1921 and was subsequently published and connected with the advertisement by Finberg (Finberg 1921, pp. 36, note 1, and 56; Finberg 1922, pp. 76–7, no. 3, pl. XCIV). Later becoming the property of the great Cuban collector Oscar B. Cintas (1887–1957), it passed to the Museo Nacional de Bellas Artes, Havana (Fig. 34.1; Constable I, pl. 75; II, no. 413(a)).

Vertue's disparaging comments about the painting being no better than the work of some of Canaletto's English contemporaries are particularly pertinent in the case of the exhibited, left-hand section. This bears a nineteenth century inscription on the stretcher identifying it as the work of Samuel Scott, to whom it remained attributed until its inclusion in an exhibition of Scott's work in London in 1955 (described as a 'Scene on the Thames at Twickenham'), when its true authorship was recognised by Francis Watson. Nothing is known of the painting's history before it was recorded (as the work of Scott) in 1931 in the

Figure 34.1
Left section: Cat. no. 34;
right section:
Chelsea College and Ranelagh, 1751,
oil on canvas, 37½ × 53½ in. (95.5 × 127 cm.).
Museo Nacional de Bellas Artes, Havana

Outer Hall of Newbattle Abbey, the seat of the Kerr family since the sixteenth century (Robert Wenley has kindly confirmed this). It was retained by the 11th Marquess of Lothian when he donated Newbattle to the nation in 1937, being transferred to Blickling Hall with which it passed to the National Trust on his death in 1940. The attribution to Scott in no way does justice to its quality of execution and majesty of conception, and it is to be regretted both that the painting was mutilated and that the Cuban government has repeatedly declined to lend their part for exhibition abroad. While the Blickling part has suffered more than most of Canaletto's English paintings, its appearance has been improved by recent cleaning. Together the two sections make up the whole width of the painting, and show it to have been of almost identical width to the four largest of Canaletto's English views, *The Old Horse Guards from Saint James's Park* (Cat. no. 17), the two Thames views acquired by Prince Lobkowicz (Figs 5, 6) and the Duke of Buccleuch's *Whitehall* (Fig. 8). Although Links states (1982 and 1994) that 'the painting was more than two metres wide and only a metre high', there is no reason to doubt that its height was originally also similar, between 46 and 46¾ in. Those proportions would seem to be confirmed by an unpublished copy of the whole painting in the Ancaster Collection at Grimsthorpe Castle (28 × 49½ in.; no. 272, as Canaletto; Courtauld Photographic Survey neg. no. B80/973).

The right-hand part of the composition is dominated by the readily recognisable Chelsea College, later the Royal Hospital, designed by Sir Christopher Wren, completed in 1692, and still occupied today by the veteran soldiers known as 'Chelsea Pensioners'. To the right is the Ranelagh Rotunda (for which see Cat. nos 32–3). The exhibited section shows, from right to left: the Infirmary Ward of Chelsea College; the Greenhouse, Art Gallery and octagonal Summerhouse of Walpole House, Sir Robert Walpole's residence; Gough House; Turret House; part of Paradise Row and the Greenhouse of the Chelsea Physick Garden. Canaletto's composition effectively combined those of two engravings by I. Vivarez after J. Maurer, published in 1744 (Phillips 1951, figs 171 and 178), into an ambitious panorama well beyond the powers of imitation of his English competitors. Finberg suggested that a special function seems be in progress, possibly a royal visit to the College, since the Cuban section includes a barge flying

the Union flag being saluted by a hoy flying the flag of the Trinity House. The treatment of the gnarled tree and foliage at the lower left in this part suggests an awareness of seventeenth-century Dutch landscape painters such as Jan Wynants, whose work was also receiving the admiration of the young Thomas Gainsborough at precisely this time. Unlike the other large paintings which Canaletto appears to have executed as speculations, it is far from clear whose patronage he might have been hoping to attract with this particular view.

35

Syon House

1749
Oil on canvas
33⅝ × 54½ in. (85.3 × 138.5 cm.)

Collection of the Duke of Northumberland

Provenance:
Painted in 1749 for Algernon Seymour, 7th Duke of
    Somerset and 1st Earl of Northumberland (1684–1750).
His son-in-law Sir Hugh Smithson (1714–86), 2nd Earl of
    Northumberland, created 1st Duke of Northumberland
    of the third creation in 1766, and by inheritance to the
    present owner.

Selected Literature:
Finberg 1921, p. 63, pl. XXVI(a).
Constable I, pp. 37, 95 and 142, pl. 83; II, no. 440.
Puppi 1968, no. 282, illustrated.
Links 1981, no. 220, illustrated.
Corboz 1985, II, p. 716, no. P 406, illustrated.
Constable / Links 1989, I, pp. lxvi–lxvii, lxxii, 37, 95
    and 142, pl. 83; II, no. 440.
Links 1998, p. 41.

Syon House, at Isleworth in Middlesex, lies on the north
side of the River Thames to the West of London. The site
was originally occupied by a Bridgettine convent which
was moved there in 1431, its cloister clearly influencing the
form of the house begun after 1546 by Edward Seymour,
Duke of Somerset and Lord Protector of England, who
also built Old Somerset House (see Cat. no. 11). After his
execution in 1552, Syon passed to John Dudley, Duke of
Northumberland, and it was there that his daughter-in-law
Lady Jane Grey began her nine days' reign. Reverting to
the crown after Dudley's execution, it was granted in 1594
to Henry Percy, 9th Earl of Northumberland, in whose
family it has remained ever since. When Sir Hugh
Smithson, later to be created 1st Duke of Northumberland
of the third creation, inherited Syon with the Earldom
of Northumberland from his father-in-law in 1750, he
described it as 'ruinous and inconvenient'. In 1761 he

commissioned Robert Adam to transform the interior with
the magnificent suite of reception rooms which are one of
the architect's crowning achievements, while the grounds
were landscaped by Lancelot 'Capability' Brown (see also
Cat. no. 44).

Canaletto's view is taken from the Surrey bank of the
Thames, looking north-west, the viewpoint being by the
road running between Kew Gardens and the river (for a
print of 1750 showing this, see Phillips 1951, Fig. 212). It
shows the south and east façades, the latter with the arcade
traditionally associated with the repairs and improvements
made by Inigo Jones sometime after 1632, which remains
one of the few post-sixteenth century changes to the
castellated exterior.

As Constable already pointed out, the date of the
painting is established by its mention in a letter at Syon
House from Smithson to his mother-in-law the Duchess of
Somerset, written from Syon on 2 July 1749: 'Mr Canaletti
has begun the picture of Syon and by the Outlines upon the
Canvass I think it will have a noble effect and he seems
himself to be much pleas'd with the subject, which I think
will suit his manner of painting perfectly well …'. This
documents the painting as the earliest of Canaletto's three
'portraits' of Northumberland seats, executed some seven
months before Smithson inherited the house. Despite this, it
was always presumed, in the light of his previous patronage
of Canaletto, that it was Smithson who commissioned it,

an issue in no way elucidated by the letter. The question
was, however, resolved by two documents first published
by Links (1998). The record in the account book of the
7th Duke of Somerset in the archives of Hoare's Bank,
of a payment on 21 July 1749 'To Ant. Canal £33.12.'
is corroborated by a receipt in Canaletto's hand found at
Alnwick Castle which reads: 'A di 19 Lug[l]io 1749
Londra / Ricevo dal Mil[ord] Duk de Sormeset trentadue
Ginee e queste per il prezzo di un quadro da Me dipinto
con la vista di Sion afermo io Sotto Scrita di mano propria /
Giò: Antonio Canal' (Fig. 35.1). Thus, although Smithson
must have been instrumental in recommending Canaletto
for the commission, the patron was, in fact, unquestionably
his father-in-law. This should come as no surprise, since the
painting records the appearance of one of the properties
which he had inherited on the death of his father Charles
Seymour, 6th Duke of Somerset, on 2 December 1748.
The documents are also of interest in providing additional
evidence of the prices which the artist's work commanded,
as well as an indication of the length of time required to
produce a painting of this not inconsiderable size.

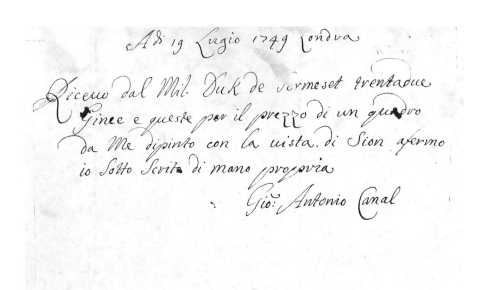

Figure 35.1
Canaletto's receipt for
payment for Cat. no. 35.
(Northumberland Archives,
Alnwick Castle)

36

Hampton Court Bridge

1754
Pen and brown ink with grey wash
9⅛ × 15¼ in. (23.2 × 38.9 cm.)

Lent by the Trustees of The British Museum

Provenance:
Richard Payne Knight (1750–1824), by whom bequeathed
(Acc. no. Pp. 5-146).

Selected Exhibitions:
Birmingham 1993–4, no. 34.

Selected Literature:
Finberg 1921, pp. 41 and 57, pl. XXIX(b).
Constable I, p. 96, pl. 135; II, no. 730.
Constable / Links 1989, I, pp. lxxvi and 96, pl. 135;
II, no. 730.

Engraved:
James Hulett, for Robert Sayer, published 1754.

This seven-arched wooden Chinese bridge stood by Hampton Court Palace, part of which is shown on the left. The first bridge on the site, it was built by Samuel Stevens and Benjamin Ludgator and opened on 13 December 1753. Despite its delicate appearance, it was a road bridge twenty feet wide and the largest Chinoiserie bridge ever constructed. It was rebuilt in 1778, replaced by an iron bridge in 1865 and by the present structure in 1930–3.

The trees in full leaf indicate that this drawing dates from the spring of 1754, since an engraving of it was published by Robert Sayer in that year. As far as we know, Canaletto took no interest in the great Tudor royal palace, with its four splendid ranges by Sir Christopher Wren completed in 1699, but he brought considerable charm to this depiction of the bridge. While Chinoiserie may have held an appeal for him beyond that indicated by the figures in Chinese costume (see, for example, Fig. 17) and boats in several paintings of the period, there is no way of knowing whether the subject was chosen by Canaletto or whether he was responding to a commission from Sayer.

The drawing was bequeathed to the British Museum by the great Regency classical scholar, arbiter of taste and collector Richard Payne Knight, along with the rest of his collection of bronzes, coins, gems, marbles and drawings, which included another drawing by Canaletto, a Venetian *capriccio* (Constable I, pl. 145; II, no. 771).

A weak painting of the composition, slightly extended to the left, was sold at Sotheby's, New York, 22 May 1992, lot 218, as the work of John Paul.

37

Old Walton Bridge

1754
Oil on canvas
19¼ × 30¼ in. (48.8 × 76.7 cm.)

Dulwich Picture Gallery, London
Exhibited at Dulwich only

Provenance:
As for Cat. no. 4 until 1884; 1884 sale, lot 130
  (125 guineas to Denison).
Christopher Beckett Denison, Upper Grosvenor Street,
  London; his (posthumous) sale, Christie's, London,
  13 June 1885, lot 858.
Purchased at the sale for 235 guineas by Henry Yates
  Thompson (Chairman of the Dulwich Picture
  Gallery Committee).
Miss E. Murray Smith, by whom donated in 1917
  (Acc. no. 600).

Selected Exhibitions:
London 1977, no. 15.
Venice 1982, no. 108.
New York 1989–90, no. 73.
Birmingham 1993–4, no. 35.

Selected Literature:
Finberg 1921, pp. 42 and 66, pl. XXXI(a).
Constable I, pp. 40, 96, 145, 146 and 166, pl. 83; II, no. 441.
Puppi 1968, no. 302, illustrated.
Links 1981, no. 255, illustrated.
Links 1982, pp. 173 and 177, pl. 171.
Corboz 1985, I, pp. 34, 37, 74, 268 and 294, fig. 330
  (colour detail); II, p. 705, no. P 371, illustrated.
Constable / Links 1989, I, pp. lxxv–lxxvi, 40, 96, 145,
  146 and 166, pl. 83; II, no. 441.
Links 1994, pp. 191 and 196, pl. 170 (colour).

The bridge, the first on the site, was authorised by an Act of Parliament of 1747 and was opened to the public in August 1750. Crossing the Thames some twenty-five miles upstream from Westminster and greatly facilitating transport across the river in this area, it was designed and built by William Etheridge, who was the master carpenter on London Bridge 1743–9 and was also responsible for the 'geometrical' wooden bridge of Queen's College, Cambridge. But for the four stone piers, it was constructed entirely of latticed timber, by an unusual method known as 'trussing', which permitted any strut to be removed without displacing another. It had a central span of 132 feet with two side spans of 44 feet each. The central arch, which was claimed as 'much the largest Arch in Europe' (*The Daily Advertiser*, 3 March 1747), had a clear height of 26 feet above highest flood level, which made the roadway exceptionally steep and gave the bridge a striking appearance from the sides. The bridge was built at the expense of Samuel Dicker, who was permitted to levy tolls for its use. Dicker was Member of Parliament for Plymouth from 1754 and died in London in 1760; his home at Mount Felix is shown on the raised ground at the left.

Canaletto shows the bridge from what was then the Middlesex bank of the Thames, looking south-west (today both banks are in Surrey). Constable seems to have been alone in regarding this painting as 'mechanical in touch and lacking atmosphere'. It has otherwise long been admired as one of the most charming of Canaletto's English views, as well as the only one in which he attempts to capture unsettled – and thus particularly English – weather conditions. The atmosphere is, in fact, very similar to that of the painter's view of *Dolo on the Brenta* (Fig. 11), which dates from the very same year and is based on one of his own etchings of about 1742. This 'enchanting picture of *Old Walton Bridge*' was particularly esteemed by Links, who saw in it 'the perfect combination of a fairy-tale structure and an artist who responded to it with the sensitivity he had shown in the finest of his etchings' (Links 1982 and 1994).

On the reverse of the original canvas there was an inscription almost identical to those recorded on the back of the *St Paul's Cathedral* (Cat. no. 4) and *Ranelagh* (Cat. no. 33) also painted for Thomas Hollis. There is no basis for Links's remarks that 'there is … a suggestion of old stock about Hollis's purchase, refurbished with labels to please the buyer' (Constable / Links 1989, I, p. lxxvi), nor that 'One cannot help wondering whether the picture may have been painted closer to 1750 … the figures being added later at Hollis's request' (Links 1994, p. 191), nor that 'there is every reason to suppose that more than one of Hollis's pictures had been painted well before the date put on them when he bought them' (New York 1989–90, p. 334).

On the other hand, there is much to be said for Finberg's suggestion that Hollis 'appears to have looked through Canaletto's sketches and drawings, and to have chosen the subjects which pleased his fancy' (Finberg 1921, p. 41). Although no drawings are known nor print sources identified for the *Saint Paul's Cathedral* (Cat. no. 4) or *Whitehall* (Cat. no. 15), the *Westminster Bridge* (Fig. 28.1) is based on an earlier drawing (Cat. no. 28) which had already been used for a painting (Cat. no. 27), *The Interior of the Rotunda at Ranelagh* is certainly based on Parr's engraving of 1751 after a lost Canaletto drawing (Fig. 33.1) and *The Campidoglio and the Cordonata, Rome* (Fig. 10), is based on an engraving by Alessandro Specchi of 1692. As Finberg also pointed out, the painter has shown the bridge in the state in which it appeared in 1750, the stone abutments, absent here, being depicted in the course of construction in an engraving by Luke Sullivan of 1751; this would indeed seem to confirm that it was a drawing dating from when the bridge first opened which pleased Hollis's fancy. There is no known connection between Hollis and the subject. Nor is there, indeed, any particular connection between Hollis and any of the subjects he chose except for the Rome view, which clearly functioned as a souvenir of his Grand Tour; that, however, dates from 1755 and must have been the last to be supplied.

It is hardly surprising that Hollis should have requested to have himself represented among the foreground figures in that, but there is nothing beyond the aesthetic success of the composition to explain the inclusion of the same group in this painting. It is identified in a catalogue of 1809 as showing 'Thomas Hollis, his friend Thomas Brand, his servant Francisco and his dog, Malta'. Brand, later Brand-Hollis, was Hollis's lifelong companion and heir, and 'Francisco' was Francesco Giovannini, a Roman whom Hollis had met in Venice, where he acted as 'a kind of antiquary' to the English traveller and afterwards accompanied him to England. Hollis is presumably the taller of the central pair of gentleman, judging by the description of him left by Giovanni Battista Cipriani: 'Passava sei piedi d'altezza, di figura Erculea, come anco la forza corporale, … largo di petto e di spalle' (see also Fig. 2). In this painting Canaletto has also included an artist, presumably himself, seated on a stool in the centre foreground drawing the scene, as if to indicate his pride in this particular achievement.

38

Old Walton Bridge

1755
Oil on canvas
18⅛ × 48⅛ in. (46 × 122.2 cm.)

Yale Center for British Art, Paul Mellon Collection
Exhibited at Yale only

Provenance:
Painted for Samuel Dicker in 1755.
Mrs Ruth Prideaux, by 1929.
With Spink, London.
Mrs Harris William Skrine, Sintra, Portugal, by 1939;
    sale, Sotheby's, London, 8 December 1971, lot 102.
Purchased at the sale by Paul Mellon, by whom presented
    in 1981
      (Acc. no. B1981.25.86).

Selected Exhibitions:
Canada 1964–5, (Addenda) no. 107(a).

Selected Literature:
Constable 1929, p. 49, pl. B.
Constable I, pp. 40, 42, 97 and 146, pl. 83; II, no. 442.
Puppi 1968, no. 315, illustrated.
Links 1981, no. 257, illustrated.
Links 1982, pp. 177–8, pl. 174.
Corboz 1985, I. pp. 34, 37, 74, 268 and 294, fig. 351;
    II, p. 707, no. P 377, illustrated.
Constable / Links 1989, I, pp. lxxvi, 40, 42, 97 and 146,
    pl. 83; II, no. 442.

This painting, a variant of Cat. no. 37, bears an inscription on the reverse of the lining canvas which must have been copied from that on the back of the original canvas (Fig. 38.1) The wording is very similar to the inscriptions recorded on the back of Cat. no. 37 and four of the other Hollis paintings, but with the 'much esteemed patron' identified this time as 'Signor Cavaliere Dickers' and the date given as 1755. This painting, the drawing after it (Cat. no. 39) and the Hollis view of Rome (Fig. 10) are thus the last evidence of Canaletto's activity in England.

Samuel Dicker, who had paid for the construction of Old Walton Bridge, was a far more obvious client for a painting of the subject than was Hollis. A successful Jamaica merchant with no known connection with Italy, Dicker was, however, acquainted with at least two patrons of Canaletto, the Duke of Bedford and William Beckford (see pp. 23, 45, 46). The presence of this inscription strengthens the supposition that Dicker's commission may have been granted as a result of seeing Hollis's painting of the subject, and that Dicker particularly requested a different composition to be executed for him 'for the first and last time'. He was evidently keen, however, that this include not only his house, again seen on the far left, but also the full extent of the works which he had funded. Those included abutments to facilitate transport across the bridge, and a causeway across the flood plain to link it to Cowey Bridge,

which had been built in 1662 to facilitate access to the ford and ferry used to cross the Thames before 1750. Those features are notably absent from Cat. no. 37. As Dodsley explains (1761), there were 'five other arches of brick work on either side to render ascent and descent more easy, but there is seldom water under any of them, except in great floods and four of them on the Middlesex side are stopped up they being on the high ground above reach of floods'.

An artist and a patron figure are again included in the foreground, but the composition resulting from the need to incorporate all those elements is generally regarded as lacking the magic of Cat. no. 37. The canvas is of much greater width while retaining the same height, giving it unusually narrow proportions, while the position of the bridge almost parallel with the picture plane diminishes the sense of depth. Canaletto has attempted to counter that by including in the foreground to the right of centre a tree not dissimilar to that in a similar position in *Dolo on the Brenta* of 1754 (Fig. 11), but here the result is less successful.

The bridge had already become unsafe by 1780, when Dicker's nephew replaced the three wooden spans with four stone arches and a brick superstructure (painted on two occasions by Turner). In 1864 one of the arches of that gave way and it was replaced by an iron bridge opened in 1853, which still stands although no longer in use by vehicular traffic.

Figure 38.1
Inscription on the lining canvas of Cat. no. 38

39

Old Walton Bridge

1755
Pen and brown ink with grey wash
11⅜ × 26¾ in. (28.9 × 67.9 cm.)

Yale Center for British Art, Paul Mellon Collection

Provenance:
Mrs Heywood Johnstone, Bignor Park, near Pulborough,
    Sussex; her posthumous sale, Christie's, London,
    20 February 1925, lot 21 (to Ellis & Smith).
Adrien Fauchier-Magnan, 135 rue Perronet, Neuilly-sur-
    Seine; sale, Sotheby's, London, 4 December 1935, lot 6
    (£185 to Agnew).
Private collection.
With Agnew's, London, 1959.
Paul Mellon, by whom presented in 1981
    (Acc. no. B1981.25.2409).

Selected Exhibitions:
New York 1989–90, no. 115.

Selected Literature:
Finberg 1921, pp. 42 and 67, pl. XXXI(b).
Constable 1927, p. 23, pl. IA.
Constable I, pp. 40–1, 42, 97, 146, 158–9 and 166, pl. 142;
    II, no. 755.
Links 1982, pp. 177–8.
Corboz 1985, I, p. 74; II, p. 735, no. D 123, illustrated.
Constable / Links 1989, I, pp. lxxvi, 40–1, 42, 97, 146,
    158–9 and 166, pls 142 and 231; II, no. 755.
Links 1994, p. 196, pl. 171 (colour).

Engraved:
Fig. 39.1; Anthony Walker, for the print seller J. Jarvis,
of Bedford Court, Covent Garden.

Inscription:
In Canaletto's hand: 'Disegnato da me Antonio Canal
detto il Canaleto appresso il mio Quadro Dippinto in
Londra 1755 / Per il Signore di^ckers.'

As Canaletto's inscription indicates, this drawing is,
indeed, a faithful copy of Cat. no. 38 and was clearly made
for use by the engraver. Anthony Walker's print follows
it closely except in the centre foreground where a second
cow and three sheep are substituted for two of Canaletto's
beloved dogs (Fig. 39.1). The print is dedicated to Samuel
Dicker and includes a brief key identifying not only
Dicker's house but also that of Miss Eaton beyond and the
Earl of Lincoln's park, seen through the centre arch of
the bridge.

A painting of the subject by Francis Towne, signed and
dated 1785, is in the collection of the Yale Center for British
Art (Acc. no. B1976.7.155); although the central tree is
moved to the right side, the composition is otherwise closely
related to Canaletto's painting and drawing of 1755 and
must have been taken entirely from the print, since the bridge
had been replaced by that date.

Figure 39.1
Anthony Walker, after Canaletto, 'A View of the New Bridge over the Thames
at Walton in Surrey', (Old Walton Bridge), 1750, hand-coloured engraving,
11⅝ × 23¼ in. (29.5 × 60.3 cm.). Yale Center for British Art, Paul Mellon Collection

Disegnato da me Antonio Canal detto il Canaleto appresso il mio Quadro Dippinto in Londra 1755.
Per il Signore Caualiere diKent.

40

Eton College

c. 1754
Oil on canvas
24¼ × 42⅜ in. (61.6 × 107.7 cm.)

The National Gallery, London

Provenance:
Sir John Tobin; sale, Griffiths, Liverpool, 22 March 1860,
   lot 33 (35 guineas).
Wynn Ellis (1790–1875), of Ponsbourne Park, near
   Hatfield, Hertfordshire, Tankerton Castle, Whitstable,
   Kent, and 30 Cadogan Place, London, by whom
   bequeathed in 1876 with 93 other paintings, including
   six by or attributed to Canaletto
   (Acc. no. 942).

Selected Exhibitions:
Birmingham 1993–4, no. 36.

Selected Literature:
Finberg 1921, pp. 29 and 56, pl. XIV(b).
Constable I, pp. 36 and 145, pl. 84; II, no. 450.
Puppi 1968, no. 313, illustrated.
Levey 1971, pp. 27–9, no. 942.
Links 1981, no. 251, illustrated.
Links 1982, p. 192, pl. 187.
Corboz 1985, I, pp. 74–5, 127, 267 and 294, fig. 59 (detail);
   II, p. 725, no. P 435, illustrated.
Constable / Links 1989, I, pp. lxiv, 36 and 145, pl. 84;
   II, no. 450.
Links 1994, p. 211, pl. 187 (colour).

Eton lies across the River Thames from Windsor, to which it is connected by a bridge (seen on the far right in Cat. no. 41). At the other, north end of the High Street, indicated here on the left, is Eton College, the greatest of English private schools, founded by King Henry VI in 1440. The dominant building is the Chapel, finished in 1482, with the brick Cloister Court of 1441–*c.* 1460 shown to its right, with considerable artistic license.

In an article of 1899, H.P. Horne used the rumour recorded by Vertue that the painter working in England was not the 'veritable Cannelletti of Venice' to propose that three paintings attributed to Canaletto were in fact the work of an impostor. Those were this painting, acquired by the National Gallery in 1876, *The Interior of the Rotunda at Ranelagh* purchased by the National Gallery in 1894 (Cat. no. 33) and *Alnwick Castle* (Fig. 12). While that suggestion is clearly without foundation, the execution of *Alnwick Castle* is indeed disappointing compared with that of the other six paintings by Canaletto owned by the Duke of Northumberland and housed in the castle, almost certainly indicating that the artist had no first-hand experience of the subject. Similar weaknesses are even more apparent in this view of Eton College, which takes Canaletto's customary lack of respect for topographical accuracy to unusual extremes. There are numerous inaccuracies in the depiction of the Chapel and College buildings, and the church on the left never existed. The uninspired execution suggests that it too may follow a graphic source by another artist (so far unidentified) or that sketches made by Canaletto on the spot at an earlier date were very summary in nature.

Finberg dates the painting to *c.* 1747, presumably because it nearly shares a viewpoint with Canaletto's *Windsor Castle* of that year (Cat. no. 41); indeed, as Links has pointed out, while sketching Windsor from Mr Crowle's cottage on Romney Island Canaletto 'had only to turn his chair to the right and the view of Eton would confront him' (Links 1994). Such a dating is, however, much too early and that of *c.* 1754 proposed by Levey and Constable is far more satisfactory. The subject would clearly have held an appeal to any of the school's numerous affluent alumni, but there is obviously no way of establishing whether the painting was a commission or a speculation. A copy of it is on the fore-edge of a volume of *The Spectator* for 1846, bound as an Eton leaving present in 1847.

A closely related drawing, but with fewer figures and extended to the right, was first recorded in the collection of Lord Harmsworth at Mereworth Castle; it was offered unsuccessfully at Sotheby's, London, 4 July 1994 (lot 165), Christie's, New York, 30 January 1998 (lot 123) and Christie's, London, 6 July 2004 (lot 69). While it may have been used in the execution of the painting, its style suggests that it is of not dissimilar date.

41

Windsor Castle

1747
Oil on canvas
33 × 54¼ in. (84 × 137.7 cm.)

Collection of the Duke of Northumberland

Provenance:
Painted in 1747, probably for Algernon Seymour,
    Earl of Hertford, later 7th Duke of Somerset and
    1st Earl of Northumberland (1684–1750).
His son-in-law Sir Hugh Smithson (1714–1786),
    2nd Earl of Northumberland, created 1st Duke of
    Northumberland of the third creation in 1766, and by
    inheritance to the present owner.

Selected Exhibitions:
Venice 1982, no. 106.
New York 1989–90, no. 64.

Selected Literature:
Finberg 1921, pp. 29 and 76, pl. XIV(a).
Constable I, pp. 34, 94 and 141, pl. 83; II, no. 449.
Puppi 1968, no. 273, illustrated.
Links 1981, no. 216, illustrated.
Links 1982, p. 152, pl. 139 (colour).
Corboz 1985, I, p. 215; II, p. 713, no. P 396, illustrated.
Constable / Links 1989, I, pp. lxiii–lxiv, 34, 94 and 141,
    pl. 83; II, no. 449.
Links 1994, p. 167, pl. 142 (colour).

Windsor Castle, covering some thirteen acres, is England's largest castle, as well as being one of the principal residences of its monarchs, inhabited continuously for nearly one thousand years. It occupies a commanding position dominating the Thames Valley, easily defensible due to the steepness of the approaches. The first castle on the site, erected by William the Conqueror, was of motte and bailey type. Although of wood, its form is still clearly apparent today, the surviving motte being in the centre of the relatively small middle bailey, there called the Middle Ward, with the bailey to the west called the Lower Ward and that to the east the Upper Ward. The first stone buildings were constructed by

Henry II between 1165 and 1179. The most significant subsequent building programmes were carried out first in the fourteenth century by Edward III, who began the conversion of the building from fortress to home, and based there the Order of the Garter which he founded in 1348, and later, after 1660, by Charles II.

This painting shows the castle before the transformation of its appearance and character during the nineteenth century. In the Lower Ward to the right is seen St George's Chapel, dating from between 1475 and 1511. Dedicated to the patron saint of the Order of the Garter (the most senior and oldest British Order of Chivalry), the chapel is the Order's spiritual home; it is also the burial place of ten English kings. To the left are Henry III's Tower and the Round Tower, Henry II's shell keep of the 1170s, as it appeared before it was heightened by thirty-three feet in the nineteenth century. In front of that is the 'Norman Gate' of 1359, flanked on the left by the north range of the Upper Ward, housing the Royal Library and the State Apartments built by Charles II.

Inserted into the lower edge of the frame of the painting is a label inscribed in an eighteenth-century hand which reads: 'This Picture was painted by Signor Canaletti who took the View from the window of the small Cottage at the end of the Enclosure next Mr Crowle's Garden – & the Figures added by him at Percy Lodge. It was finished June the Eleventh 1747'. Although nothing is known of 'Mr Crowle', the site of his garden can be readily identified. It was on the land now known as Romney Island, which was formed when the wall on the left was demolished in 1794 and a lock-cut was made leading from the Thames to Romney Lock and then back to the river. The railway line to London now runs beyond the lock-cut. Remains of the retaining wall of the channel running across the foreground can apparently still be found.

The date establishes the painting as Canaletto's first view of an English subject outside Greater London, executed a year after his arrival. Links interprets the inscription as meaning that the painting was executed *en plein air* (Venice 1982 and New York 1989–90). Although it seems unlikely that the artist ever worked on finished paintings outside the studio, that testifies to the spontaneity of execution which has made this one of the most admired of all Canaletto's English views. While Links praised the way that it 'conveys the late afternoon light and a sense of the lush landscape',

Constable singled out 'the liveliness [of its] handling, especially in the foreground figures, which rivals that of the two Richmond pictures'.

The painting is first recorded in the collection of Sir Hugh Smithson (1714–86), for whom Canaletto had very recently executed a pair of views of Westminster Bridge (Cat. nos 24–5), and it has been stated repeatedly, by Constable and others, that it was painted for him. The precise circumstances of the commission remain uncertain, however, Links observing that the painting 'may have been painted as a gift to his father-in-law, the Earl of Hertford, or ordered by the earl on Sir Hugh's recommendation. Whatever the case, it belonged to him during his father-in-law's lifetime' (New York 1989–90). There seems to be no basis for this last observation, and all the evidence points to the painting having been commissioned by Algernon Seymour, Earl of Hertford (1684–1750), who was to become 7th Duke of Somerset in 1748 and 1st Earl of Northumberland in 1749. The inscription records that it was completed at Percy Lodge, which was at Iver, Buckinghamshire, only seven miles from Windsor. Originally called Richings Lodge, the house had been purchased by the Earl and Countess of Hertford by 16 July 1740, when their daughter married Smithson there. Both the Earl and Countess died there. Their fondness for the house is demonstrated by their commission in 1749 of a poem about it by Moses Browne, published in 1755. On his mother-in-law's death in 1754 it passed to Smithson, who sold it in 1776, and it was destroyed by fire ten years later. As one of the foremost sights in the area of his new home, Windsor would have held more appeal as a subject to the Earl than to his son-in-law, who had no particular connection with the region. The most conclusive evidence is provided by the recently rediscovered documents establishing that it was the Earl of Hertford rather than Smithson who commissioned the *Syon House* (Cat. no. 35), which is of identical size and still hangs as the pendant to the *Windsor Castle* in the Northumberland Collection.

42

Badminton House from the Park

43

Badminton Park from the House

42

Badminton House from the Park

Probably 1748
Oil on canvas
33⅞ × 48 in. (86 × 122 cm.)

Private Collection
Exhibited at Dulwich only

Provenance:
Painted for Charles Noel Somerset, 4th Duke of Beaufort (1709–1756), and by descent.

Selected Literature:
Finberg 1921, pp. 29, 30 and 55, pl. XVIII(b).
Vertue *Note Books*, III, p. 149.
Constable I, pp. 34, 37, 94 and 141–2, pl. 74; II, no. 409.
Puppi 1968, no. 278, illustrated.
Links 1981, no. 217, illustrated.
Corboz 1985, II, p. 715, no. P 403, illustrated.
Constable / Links 1989, I, pp. lxiv, 34, 37, 94 and
   141–2, pl. 74; II, no. 409.

43

Badminton Park from the House

Probably 1748
Oil on canvas
33⅞ × 48 in. (86 × 122 cm.)

Private Collection
Exhibited at Dulwich only

Provenance:
As for Cat. no. 42.

Selected Exhibitions:
Canada 1964–5, no. 103.

Selected Literature:
Finberg 1921, pp. 29, 30 and 55, pl. XVIII(a).
Vertue *Note Books*, III, p. 149.
Constable I, pp. 34, 37, 94 and 141–2, pl. 74; II, no. 410.
Puppi 1968, no. 279, illustrated.
Links 1981, no. 218, illustrated.
Corboz 1985, I, p. 166, fig. 162; II, p. 715, no. P 404,
   illustrated.
Constable / Links 1989, I, pp. lxiv, 34, 37, 94 and 141–2,
   pl. 74; II, no. 410.

Badminton House was built by Henry Somerset, 3rd Marquess of Worcester (1629–1700), who was created Duke of Beaufort in 1682. The appearance of its north front, depicted by Canaletto, has changed little since its completion in about 1691, what alterations there have been being almost all made in the 1730s and early 1740s for the 3rd Duke. Those include the single-storey wings to east and west remodelled by Francis Smith, ending in pavilions first proposed by James Gibbs and largely executed by William Kent, who was also responsible for the central pediment and the twin cupolas. Kent also designed several buildings in the park, although not all of those shown by Canaletto were in fact constructed. The bridge and Worcester Lodge (directly in line with the north entrance at the end of the 'three-mile ride') certainly were; the latter has been described as 'one of the most spectacular triumphs of the English genius for park buildings' (Verey and Brooks 2000, p. 387).

These paintings were mentioned by Vertue in June 1749 (see p. 19) and thus may well date from the spring or early summer of 1748; the artist may have visited Badminton on his way to or from Warwick, some sixty-five miles away. They were commissioned by Charles Noel Somerset (1709–1756), who had succeeded his brother as 4th Duke of Beaufort on 24 February 1745, and who may possibly have derived an interest in Canaletto's work from his role as one of the commissioners of Westminster Bridge. No doubt they were intended to celebrate both the recent completion of the improvements to the house and the duke's recent inheritance. The view of the north front may be seen as a particularly eloquent essay in the tradition of the English country house portrait, its rigid symmetry being necessary for it to function successfully as a pendant to the view of the park. The striking simplicity of that, with its three zones of brown, green and blue, sets it apart in Canaletto's *oeuvre*; as a painting of a real – rather than imaginary – landscape in which buildings play a role of negligible significance it is unique in the artist's work.

If the supposition that Canaletto never visited Alnwick is correct (see pp. 22, 136), Badminton, 104 miles from London, would seem to be the furthest point from the capital that he ever ventured during his nine years in England.

Warwick Castle: the South Front

1748–9
Oil on canvas
28½ × 47¼ in. (72.4 × 120 cm.)

Yale Center for British Art, Paul Mellon Collection

Provenance:

Commissioned by Francis Greville, 8th Baron Brooke
(1719–73), created Earl Brooke in 1746 and 1st Earl of
Warwick of the fourth creation in 1759, Grosvenor
Square, London.

His son, George Greville, 2nd Earl of Warwick
(1746–1816), London.

Passed by gift or exchange to Sir James Peachey, 4th Bt.
(d. 1808), Lord High Chamberlain to King George III,
created Baron Selsey in 1794 (father-in-law of the above
1771–2), West Dean Park, Sussex.

Frederick Bower (born 1827), by whom purchased (with
other paintings) with West Dean Park in the 1870s, and
removed before 1892 to Broomfield Hall, Sunningdale;
his posthumous sale, Christie's, London, 12 February
1906, lot 50 (240 guineas to Ashworth).

Miss F. Batty.

With Agnew's, London, by whom purchased from the
above in 1929.

With Leggatt, London.

John Jacob Astor (1886–1971), created Baron Astor of
Hever 1956, by whom purchased from the above in 1930.

His son the Hon. Gavin Astor (1918–84), from 1971 2nd
Baron Astor of Hever, by 1968.

Samuel T. Fee, U.S.A., by whom acquired from the above
through Agnew's in 1980; his sale, Christie's, New York,
9 May 1985, lot 18 (unsold).

With Agnew's, London (*Venetian Eighteenth-Century
Painting*, 5 June – 19 July 1985, no. 26).

Paul Mellon, by whom purchased from Agnew's in July
1985 and presented to the present owner in August 1994
(Acc. no. B1994.18.2).

Selected Literature:

Finberg 1921, p. 68.
Constable I, p. 142, note 1, pl. 84; II, nos 444 and 448(b).
Puppi 1968, no. 290 C.
Links 1981, under no. 234.
Links 1982, pp. 156 and 158.
Corboz 1985, II, p. 723, no. P 429, illustrated.
Buttery 1987, pp. 440–2 and 445, figs 18 and 21.
Constable / Links 1989, pp. lxv–lxvi, 142, note 1, pl. 84;
    II, nos 444 and 448(b).
Buttery 1992, pp. 22, 23, 27and 60, pls 13–14 (colour).
Links 1998, p. 42.

Warwick Castle stands on a sandstone cliff above a bend
in the River Avon, the obvious natural defences of the site
resulting in a fortification being constructed there as early
as 1068 by William the Conqueror. As at Windsor, that was
of motte and bailey form, the surviving motte being clearly
visible on the left in this painting. Although the walls would
presumably have been of stone by the end of the twelfth
century, the impressive towers of the east front were built
by Thomas Beauchamp, 11th Earl of Warwick (d. 1369)
and his son Thomas Beauchamp, 12th Earl of Warwick
(c. 1339–1401). The castle had fallen into a ruinous state
by 1604, when it was granted by King James I to Sir Fulke
Greville (1554–1628), who was created Baron Brooke in
1621. He saved it from destruction and by 1634 it could
again be described as 'a fayre and stately castle'. Greville
made the building into a comfortable and sumptuous home,
and he was also responsible for laying out the garden. That
included the path winding up the motte (also seen here),
which was popular with seventeenth-century visitors, one
in 1681 leaving a record of how he

> went up a fine winding walk set with herbs and various trees till
> we came to the top of the mount where grew within a circle of
> laurel a Scottish fir tree … I must confess it was very pleasant
> to behold the curiosities below … the pleasant walks and … the
> site of a goodly vale and hills … all together it is one of the best
> inland prospects our country doth afford. (Quoted by Buttery
> 1992, pp. 18–19)

The state rooms were remodeled for Robert Greville, 4th
Baron Brooke in 1669–78 by Roger and William Hurlbutt,
who introduced sash windows with glazing bars in the
principal new rooms. Little needed to be done to the castle
in the following decades, Daniel Defoe describing it in 1724
as 'old, but several Times repair'd and beautify'd by its
several Owners, and 'tis now a very agreeable place both
within and without' (Defoe 1724–7, II, p. 128).

In 1740 the castle was inherited, on his coming of age,
by Francis Greville, 8th Baron Brooke (1719–73), who was
created Earl Brooke in 1746 and 1st Earl of Warwick of the
fourth creation in 1759. In 1748 he began what was to be a
thirteen year employment of Lancelot 'Capability' Brown
as both architect and landscape gardener. Proud of his property and his improvements to it, Brooke was portrayed with
plans of the castle by both Joshua Reynolds and Thomas
Gainsborough, and he commissioned from Canaletto no

Figure 44.1
Warwick Castle: the South Front, probably 1748,
oil on canvas, 16⅞ × 28¼ in. (42.9 × 71.8 cm.).
Wrightsman Collection, New York

Figure 44.2
Warwick Castle: the South Front, probably 1748,
oil on canvas, 29½ × 47⅜ in. (75 × 120.5 cm.).
Museo Thyssen-Bornemisza, Madrid

fewer than five paintings and three drawings of it. Brooke had made an extended Grand Tour in 1735–40, as a result of which he seems to have acquired at least one notable Venetian view by the artist (see p. 12). He had been orphaned at the age of eight and brought up by his maternal aunt Frances, Countess of Hertford and her husband, Algernon Seymour, Earl of Hertford, alongside their own daughter Lady Elizabeth Seymour (1716–76), who married Sir Hugh Smithson in 1740. Thus if Brooke needed any encouragement to renew his patronage of Canaletto, he would have received it from his uncle and aunt's *Windsor Castle* (Cat. no. 41) and his cousin's pair of Westminster Bridge views (Cat. nos 24–5), all of 1747.

Of Canaletto's five paintings of the castle, three show the south front, the side which looms above the River Avon and includes all the residential accommodation. One of those, in the Wrightsman Collection, New York, is significantly smaller than the other four and is presumed to be the first executed for Brooke (Fig. 44.1; Constable II, no. 443). There, work is already in progress at the foot of the motte to remove the formal gardens created by Sir Fulke Greville in accordance with Capability Brown's plans, but the castle is shown as it appeared before the replacement of the windows of the Cedar Room. A visitor to Warwick in August 1748 noted: '… the state apartments, consisting of 5 well-proportioned lofty rooms, the largest of which is wainscoted with cedar; the windows of it are new, but made in the Gothic style and very pretty'. These new windows are clearly evident, with their brilliant white paint, in the exhibited painting, which otherwise corresponds closely but for different figures and for the castle being shown from a slightly nearer viewpoint and at a slight angle. The main difference is in the size, which is nearly four times that of the first painting. The third view is taken from a position nearer the castle, on the island which divides the River Avon at this point, and thus shows the building at even more of an angle (Fig. 44.2; Constable I, pl. 84; II, no. 445). Of less impressive quality, this omits the castle mill and weir, while fully-grown trees are shown at the foot of the motte and on the adjacent riverbank. The wooden bridge over the Avon, which was to be removed in 1753, and the Scots pine tree crowning the motte are only present as *pentimenti*. The fenestration with sashes and window bars is much more consistent. All these features indicate that the Thyssen painting shows the view as Brooke intended it to appear

after the completion of Brown's improvements.

Although Vertue makes no mention of Canaletto's views of Warwick, three documented payments help to establish the dates of the paintings. The ledger of Lord Brooke's account at Hoare's Bank in London records payments to 'Sigr Canall' of £58 on 19 July 1748, and to 'Sigr G. Antº Canale' of 30 guineas on 3 March 1749, while the estate account ledgers record a payment in 1748 to 'Seignr Canal for his Drawings of Warwick Castle' of 10 guineas. Confusingly, a receipt for this sum in Canaletto's hand, dated 28 July 1748, now in the Greville archive at the Warwick County Record Office, identifies it as not for drawings but for '*un quadreto da me dipinto …*' [a small painting painted by me]. Buttery, who published these documents for the first time, identifies the first payment as for both the first, small painting and for that in Madrid. The 1749 payment would thus be for the exhibited painting, described by Buttery as 'the last and grandest' of the three depictions of the south front; the aptness of the figure of 30 guineas has since been confirmed by the discovery that 32 guineas were paid in the same year for the slightly larger Syon House (Cat. no. 35). This sequence is surely correct, but it does not account for the interim payment of 10 guineas, which is related by Buttery to a drawing of the south front, corresponding with the exhibited painting but for differences in some of the figures, sold by the Earl of Warwick at Sotheby's, London, 2 July 1997, lot 53 (Constable I, pl. 143; II, no. 758). That solution depends on Canaletto having described a drawing as a 'small painting' but, as Links observed, 'no better explanation can be offered'. Buttery further suggests that Canaletto must have visited Warwick twice during the execution of these paintings, but there is no reason to believe that one visit would not have sufficed.

Unlike the other four paintings of the castle, which remained the property of the Earls of Warwick until 1977/8 when the castle itself was sold by the 7th Earl to Madame Tussaud's, this one had left the collection within at most sixty years of its execution, passing to Sir James Peachey, 4th Bt., Lord High Chamberlain to King George III, who was created Baron Selsey in 1794. While the precise circumstances remain unknown, Peachey was briefly the father-in-law of George Greville, 2nd Earl of Warwick, who married his daughter Georgiana in 1771, but she died only a year later.

44

Warwick Castle: the South Front

45

Warwick Castle: the East Front

46

Warwick Castle: the East Front from the Courtyard

45

Warwick Castle: the East Front

1752
Oil on canvas
29½ × 48⅜ in. (75 × 123 cm.)

Birmingham Museum and Art Gallery (Bought together with Cat. no. 46 by public subscription with assistance of special Government grants and contributions from Charitable Trusts, Industry, Commerce, the City of Birmingham, West Midlands County Council, NACF, and Friends of the Museum and Art Gallery)

Provenance:
Commissioned by Francis Greville, 8th Baron Brooke
　(1719–73), created Earl Brooke in 1746 and 1st Earl of
　Warwick of the fourth creation in 1759, 29 Grosvenor
　Square, London.
His son, George Greville, 2nd Earl of Warwick
　(1746–1816), Green Street, London.
His son, Henry Greville, 3rd Earl of Warwick
　(1779–1853), by whom transferred from Carlton
　Gardens, London to Warwick Castle between 1844
　and 1846.
By inheritance there to Charles Greville, 7th Earl of
　Warwick (1911–84).
With Marlborough Fine Art, from whom purchased as
　a pair with Cat. no. 46 in 1978.

Selected Exhibitions:
Venice 1982, no. 105.
Birmingham 1993–4, no. 23.

Selected Literature:
Finberg 1921, pp. 41 and 67.
Constable I, pp. 37 and 142, pl. 84; II, no. 446.
Puppi 1968, no. 291 A, illustrated.
Links 1981, no. 236, illustrated.
Links 1982, pp. 158 and 171, pl. 145 (colour).
Corboz 1985, II, p. 720, no. P 418, illustrated.
Buttery 1987, pp. 444–5, fig. 22.
Constable / Links 1989, I, pp. lxv–lxvi, lxxiii, 37
　and 142, pl. 84; II, no. 446.
Buttery 1992, pp. 22, 40, 42 and 60, pls 17–19 (colour).
Links 1994, pp. 168 and 188, pl. 146 (colour).
Links 1998, p. 42.

46

Warwick Castle: the East Front from the Courtyard

1752
Oil on canvas
29½ × 48⅜ in. (75 × 123 cm.)

Birmingham Museum and Art Gallery (Bought together with Cat. no. 45 by public subscription with assistance of special Government grants and contributions from Charitable Trusts, Industry, Commerce, the City of Birmingham, West Midlands County Council, NACF, and Friends of the Museum and Art Gallery)

Provenance:
As for Cat. no. 45.

Selected Exhibitions:
New York 1989–90, no. 69.
Birmingham 1993–4, no. 24.

Selected Literature:
Finberg 1921, pp. 41 and 67.
Constable I, pp. 37 and 142, pl. 84; II, no. 447.
Puppi 1968, no. 291 B, illustrated.
Links 1981, no. 237, illustrated.
Links 1982, pp. 158 and 171, pl. 146 (colour).
Corboz 1985, II, p. 721, no. P 421, illustrated.
Buttery 1987, pp. 444–5, figs 24 and 26.
Constable / Links 1989, I, pp. lxv–lxvi, lxxiii, 37 and
　142, pl. 84; II, no. 447.
Buttery 1992, pp. 22, 40, 42 and 60, pls 23–4 (colour)
　and frontispiece.
Links 1994, pp. 168 and 188, pl. 147 (colour).
Links 1998, p. 42.

In 1752 Canaletto was recalled to Warwick, resulting in two further payments recorded in the ledger of Lord Brooke's account at Hoare's Bank, to 'Sig.r Canaletti' of 32 guineas on 24 March 1752, and to 'Antonio Canal' of £50 on 18 July 1752. Buttery establishes convincingly that the first payment is for one of these two views of the east front, possibly that of its exterior, while suggesting that the second was for the pendant and for the two related drawings (Cat. nos 47–8). If this is correct it provides further evidence that a drawing by the artist could command as much as 10 guineas (see the preceding entry). The impressive fortifications of the east front were the natural focus for the artist's attention after his definitive record of the south front. Here the Gatehouse and Barbican are flanked by Caesar's Tower, also prominent in the views of the south front, and by the twelve-sided Guy's Tower. The range outside the curtain wall between the Barbican and Caesar's Tower housed the laundry and brewhouse, and the exterior view also shows how closely the town encroached on the castle moat until the grounds were extended to the north towards the end of the eighteenth century. In this painting there is an exceptionally felicitous array of promenading gentlefolk, and Canaletto's fondness for dogs finds unrestrained expression. The view of the interior, offering only a glimpse of the residential block of the castle, is perhaps a less obvious choice as a subject, and in its relationship to the pendant is unparalleled in the painter's work, suggesting that it may have been dictated by the patron. The spire of the church of St Nicholas, also shown in all the views of the south front, is neatly framed by the entrance gateway, while the two young trees in supporting frames on the right must, as Buttery points out, be part of Capability Brown's landscaping of the courtyard. While being consistent in size with the two larger views of the south front, these two paintings are the only ones framed identically.

As Buttery observes, the lighting of both paintings from the left required the view from the courtyard to be painted in afternoon light, while all four of the other paintings show the castle in the light of early morning, and the time shown by the single hand of the clock on the castle gatehouse is accurate in this respect.

47

Warwick Castle: the East Front

1751–2
Pen and brown ink with grey wash
12⅜ × 22⅛ in. (31.6 × 56.2 cm.)

The Metropolitan Museum of Art, Robert Lehman
Collection, 1975 (1975.1.297)
Exhibited at Yale only

Provenance:
Francis Greville, 8th Baron Brooke (1719–73), created
Earl Brooke in 1746 and 1st Earl of Warwick of the
fourth creation in 1759.
His son, George Greville, 2nd Earl of Warwick
(1746–1816).
Paul Sandby, R.A. (1730–1809; his collector's mark),
presumably by gift from the above; his posthumous sale,
Christie's, London, 17 March 1812, lot 91 (with the
pendant: £10 to Colnaghi).
Lady Eva Dugdale (daughter of George Greville, 4th Earl
of Warwick), Royal Lodge, Windsor Great Park; sale,
Sotheby's, London, 18 November 1920, lot 42 (with the
pendant: £92 to F. Sabin).
With Frank T. Sabin, London.
Adrien Fauchier-Magnan, 135 rue Perronet, Neuilly-sur-
Seine; sale, Sotheby's, London, 4 December 1935, lot 4
(£220 to Colnaghi).
Philip Hofer, Cambridge, Mass.
Robert Lehman, by 1950.

Selected Exhibitions:
New York 1989–90, no. 112.
Birmingham 1993–4, no. 25.

Selected Literature:
Finberg 1921, p. 68, pl. XXVII(a).
Constable I, p. 142, pl. 143; II, no. 759.
Corboz 1985, II, p. 734, no. D 120, illustrated.
Buttery 1987, pp. 444–5, fig. 23.
Constable / Links 1989, I, pp. lxvi, lxxiii and 142,
pl. 143; II, no. 759.
Buttery 1992, pp. 22 and 42, pl. 26 (colour).
Links 1998, p. 42.

48

Warwick Castle: the East Front from the Courtyard

1751–2
Pen and brown ink with grey wash over black chalk
12½ × 22⅜ in. (31.8 × 56.8 cm.)

The J. Paul Getty Museum, Los Angeles
Exhibited at Yale only

Provenance:
As for Cat. no. 47 until 1935; 1935 sale, lot 5
(£210 to Tooth).
With Arthur Tooth & Sons, London.
Sir George Leon, Bt., by whom acquired from the above
(by exchange) on 9 June 1937.
With Eugene V. Thaw & Co., New York.
John R. Gaines, Lexington, Kentucky; his sale, Sotheby's,
New York, 17 November 1986, lot 25, when acquired
by the present owner
(Acc. no. 86. GG. 727).

Selected Exhibitions:
New York 1989–90, no. 113.

Selected Literature:
Finberg 1921, p. 68, pl. XXVII(b).
Constable I, p. 142, pl. 143; II, no. 760.
Corboz 1985, II, p. 735, no. D 121, illustrated.
Buttery 1987, pp. 444–5, fig. 25.
Constable / Links 1989, I, pp. lxvi, lxxiii and 142,
pl. 143; II, no. 760.
Buttery 1992, pp. 22 and 42, pl. 29 (colour).
Links 1998, p. 42.

While closely related to the paintings of the same compositions (Cat nos 44–6), these drawings differ from them in minor but significant ways. Both show less of the foreground and this is seen from a less elevated viewpoint. In the drawing of the exterior of the east front there are some variations in the figures, the group of dogs is absent and a flock of birds circles the top of Guy's Tower. In the drawing of the view from the courtyard the lower part of Guy's Tower is obscured by trees, it has a door rather than the lancet at ground level which can still be seen today, and the few figures are entirely different; perhaps most significantly, the spire of the church of St Nicholas (the focal point of the painting) is not seen through the gateway arch, and the clock indicates a time in the morning which conflicts with the light source. These variations, and the fluency of handling, leave no doubt that the drawings precede the paintings. No doubt they were executed to give Brooke a (fairly accurate) idea of what the artist proposed to paint. If Buttery is correct in his suggestion that Brooke's final payment to Canaletto, of £50 on 18 July 1752, was for these drawings as well as for one of the paintings – and no other solution can be offered – Canaletto evidently valued them highly in their own right (at around £10 each); there is also a suggestion that the patron's acquisition of them was something of an afterthought. Highly finished, and clearly intended no less as pendants that the resulting paintings, they have long been among the most admired of Canaletto's drawings of English subjects.

Like the painting of the south front, these drawings left the collection of the Earls of Warwick at an early date, passing into that of Paul Sandby, R.A. (1730–1809). While Sandby is known to have been a friend of Charles Greville, second son of the 1st Earl of Warwick, they are more likely to have been given or exchanged by his elder brother, the 2nd Earl, to whom Sandby dedicated four aquatints of Warwick Castle in 1776. The Castle inventory of 1809 lists twelve drawings by Sandby, and a number of watercolours of the castle are recorded in the painter's posthumous sales.

47

Warwick Castle: the East Front

48

Warwick Castle: the East Front from the Courtyard

49

Warwick: Saint Mary's Church and Church Street

Either 1748/9 or 1751/2
Pen and brown ink with grey wash
14 × 11⅛ in. (35.6 × 28.3 cm.)

Lent by the Trustees of the British Museum

Provenance:
Thomas Toon, from whom purchased in 1900
 (Acc. no. 1900-11-12-1).

Selected Exhibitions:
Birmingham 1993–4, no. 26.

Selected Literature:
Finberg 1921, pp. 41 and 67, pl. XXVIII.
Constable I, pp. 142 and 148, pl. 143; II, no. 757.
Links 1982, p. 158, pl. 148.
Corboz 1985, II, p. 755, no. D 151, illustrated.
Buttery 1992, pp. 42, 48 and 54, pl. 30 (colour).
Links 1994, p. 168, pl. 150.

The drawing is accompanied by a label inscribed in Canaletto's own hand 'Ingresso nella Piazza de Varik'. As Constable pointed out, this is on paper similar to that of the drawing, but with the grain running vertically rather than horizontally; thus if it was originally part of the same sheet, it must have been at the side.

The great fire of Warwick in September 1694 destroyed much of the centre of the town, including the bell tower, nave and rood screen of the collegiate church of St Mary, although the Perpendicular East end, with its superb Beauchamp and Dudley tombs, was spared. The bell tower and nave were rebuilt soon afterwards by the renowned local master builder Francis Smith 'of Warwick' (for whom see also Cat. nos 42, 43) and his brother William, to the designs of Sir William Wilson, which were chosen over those of Sir Christopher Wren. Work was begun in 1698, but settling required the tower to be repositioned in 1700 outside the West wall and it was not completed until 1704. Canaletto has underplayed the height of the tower, which dominates the surrounding area, including the nearby castle, and has taken further liberties with the arches on it, which are in fact all pointed. He has, on the other hand, remained particularly faithful to the appearance of the Court House on the right, designed and built by Francis Smith in 1725–30, showing how much more comfortable he was with classical than with gothic forms; standing on the corner of Church Street and the High Street, this still looks remarkably similar, even down to the rainwater pipe, although there are no finials above the balustrade (see Buttery 1992, pl. 34).

The church is depicted from the opposite direction in an equally finished (but less well preserved) drawing showing it, the castle and the roofs of the town from the gardens of the Priory (Yale Center for British Art; Constable I, pl. 142; II, no. 756). Nothing is known of the provenance of either work before the twentieth century, and it seems improbable that they formed part of the commission from Lord Brooke. As views of a relatively low-key subject – a county town in the Midlands – and of unknown function, they are unique in Canaletto's English *oeuvre*. Perhaps, as Jane Farrington has suggested, he hoped to sell them to an engraver (Birmingham 1993–4), but the overriding impression is one of the artist amusing himself on afternoons off from drawing the castle.

Ingresso nella Piazza di Varik.

50

Rome: The Basilica of Maxentius and the Church of Santa Francesca Romana

c. 1752/4
Oil on canvas
51 × 42⅞ in. (129.5 × 109 cm.)

Private Collection, Milan
Not exhibited

Provenance:
Colonel Frederick Liddell Trotter (1838–1900),
　Dyrham Park, Barnet, Hertfordshire, by 1884.
His son, Major Frederick Liddell Trotter, Mells Park,
　Somerset; sale, Christie's, London, 19 May 1939,
　lot 116 (270 guineas to Leggatt).
Sir George Leon, Bt., Warfield House, Bracknell.
With Arthur Tooth & Sons, London.
Dr Carlo Broglio, Paris, by whom purchased from the
　above in February 1950.
Anna Campanini-Bonomi, later Anna Bolchini Bonomi,
　Milan, by 1953.
Acquired by the present owner in 2002.

Selected Exhibitions:
Venice 1982, no. 99.
Rome 2005, no. 69.

Selected Literature:
Parker 1948, p. 51, under no. 105.
Constable I, pl. 70; II, no. 380.
Puppi 1968, no. 217 A, illustrated.
Links 1981, no. 174, illustrated.
Corboz 1985, I, p. 68; II, pp. 435–6, fig. 490
　(colour detail), and p. 654, no. P 324, illustrated.

Figure 50.1
*Rome: The Basilica of Maxentius and the Church of Santa Francesca
Romana*, 1719/20, pen and brown ink, with grey wash,
6⅛ × 8⅞ in. (15.7 × 22.7 cm.). British Museum

The three barrel-vaulted chambers of the north aisle of the Basilica of Maxentius, also known as the Basilica of Constantine, remain one of the most imposing monuments of ancient Rome to survive in the centre of the city. The basilica was begun by the Emperor Maxentius, possibly after a fire in 307 which severely damaged the nearby Temple of Venus and Rome, and completed after his death at the Battle of the Milvian Bridge in 312, when it was dedicated by the Senate to his victorious rival Constantine. It was thought to be the Temple of Peace through the eighteenth century, when the lower parts of its walls were yet to be unearthed, and it was used as a shelter by shepherds, which may account for the haystack shown by Canaletto in the furthest chamber. Beyond and to the right are the Colosseum and the church of Santa Francesca Romana, with its twelfth century campanile and baroque façade, completed in 1615.

The painting was until recently consistently dated within the period 1742–5, the years following the visit to Rome of Canaletto's nephew Bernardo Bellotto. That had inspired in the older artist a renewed interest in producing paintings and drawings of the city, which he had not seen since 1720 and was never to see again. Canaletto did indeed make a drawing of this composition in the early 1740s (now in the Royal Collection; Constable I, pl. 133; II, no. 714). In a horizontal format, it is based on one of the twenty-two drawings in the British Museum made by the artist in Rome in 1719–20 (Fig. 50.1; Constable I, pl. 131; II, no. 713(226)).

This painting can, however, be dated with confidence on stylistic grounds within the second half of Canaletto's period in London. It is, indeed, the most vibrant of the

views of Rome executed by the painter in England. The figure of the running boy at lower right, which does not feature in the drawings, recurs in a drawing in the Albertina, Vienna (Constable I, pl. 156; II, no. 828) and is not dissimilar, although in reverse, to that in the lower right corner of the painting and drawing of Northumberland House (Cat. no. 14 and Fig. 14.1).

The early history of the painting is yet to be established. Dyrham Park, its first recorded location, was purchased by John Trotter, grandfather of the first recorded owner, in 1798. Although the size is given by Constable and elsewhere as 59 × 43 in. (150 × 109 cm.), the painting was reduced in size by some 8 in. (20.5 cm.) at some point between 1939 and 1950. While it is clearly impossible to be certain that the missing section – which showed only sky and clouds – was original, there is every reason to suspect that it was, cusping being clearly evident on the other three sides. The reduction was no doubt commercially motivated, for in its previous form the canvas was of unusually tall shape, suggesting that it was intended for a specific location and as part of a decorative scheme, a function also indicated by the breadth of execution. The lopsided composition suggests that it must have had a pendant. A possible candidate for that would be the *Capriccio of the Church of San Giorgio Maggiore set on the Grand Canal* in the North Carolina Museum of Art, Raleigh (Constable I, pl. 86; II, no. 463). That may well also be of the English period, as Constable suggests, but it is slightly larger (66 × 45 in., 167.5 × 114.5 cm.) and distant in both execution, which is much harder, and subject matter.

A small version in a horizontal format is in the Galleria Borghese, Rome (Constable II, under no. 380), the figures and foreground rocks in which leave no doubt that it is based on the British Museum drawing. Although the attribution has often been questioned, it is certainly by Canaletto and the stylistic similarities which it and its pendant of the Colosseum (Constable I, pl. 71; II, no. 388) display with the paintings of the Hollis group suggest a date of *c.* 1754/5, towards the end of the English period. Both paintings were acquired in England by the Galleria Borghese in 1908.

51

Rome: The Arch of Constantine from the South, the Colosseum beyond

c. 1752/4
Signed 'Ant.° Canaleto.fe!' (lower left)
Oil on canvas
32¼ × 48 in. (82 × 122 cm.)

The J. Paul Getty Museum, Los Angeles
Exhibited at Yale only

Provenance:
Miss Whatman, Kent, in whose family's collection the
  painting is said to have been since 1820 and in which it
  remained until after 1937.
John C. Quilter, by 1953.
With Gooden & Fox, London, by whom purchased from
  the above on 8 August 1957.
Henry G. Martin, London, by whom purchased from the
  above in 1957; sale, Christie's, London, 27 November
  1970, lot 51.
Purchased at the sale by Agnew's on behalf of the present
  owner (Acc. no. 70.PA.52).

Selected Literature:
Constable I, p. 166, pl. 71; II, no. 383.
Puppi 1968, no. 212, illustrated.
Constable / Links 1976, I, p. 166, pls 71 and 231
  (detail of the signature); II, no. 383.
Links 1981, no. 176, illustrated.
Corboz 1985, I, pp. 68, 69 and 230, figs 288 and 289
  (colour detail); II, p. 653, no. P 320, illustrated.

The Arch of Constantine is the largest classical triumphal arch to survive intact. It was dedicated in 315 and bears inscriptions on both sides recording that it was erected by the Roman people after Constantine's victory over Maxentius at the Battle of the Milvian Bridge, 28 October 312. It is adjacent to the Colosseum, the largest and most important amphitheatre in the Roman Empire, which was begun by Vespasian in about AD 69 and inaugurated by his son Titus in 80. The relationship of the two buildings as shown in this painting is, however, to an extent imaginary, as the Colosseum has been moved to the left so that its flank is picturesquely framed by the central arch. In this it does not, unlike *The Basilica of Maxentius and the Church of Santa Francesca Romana* (Cat. no. 50), follow the corresponding drawing in the British Museum, which is dated 1720 (Constable I, pl. 130; II, no. 713(222)). As Corboz has pointed out, the composition corresponds surprisingly closely, although not in the figures, with an engraving by Goussier in *Recueil de planches sur les sciences, les arts libéraux et les arts méchaniques, avec leur explication*, published in Paris in 1762 (Corboz 1985, I, Fig. 290), which strongly suggests that they share a common source, so far unidentified.

The rare signature on this painting suggests that it was the centrepiece of a decorative scheme (as was Cat. no. 69, also signed), as does its unusually symmetrical composition. Like *The Basilica of Maxentius and the Church of Santa Francesca Romana* (Cat. no. 50) this painting has been consistently dated to the first half of the 1740s, despite its clear stylistic divergence from the dated Roman views of that period. In its grey ground, colouration, with pink tinges in the sky, and contrast in handling between the broad strokes of the foreground and larger figures with the detail of the arch and foliage, the painting is entirely characteristic of Canaletto's work in England in the first years of the 1750s. From its style, scale and subject matter it may well, indeed, have formed part of the same scheme as *The Basilica of Maxentius and the Church of Santa Francesca Romana* (Cat. no. 50).

Miss Whatman, presumably Miss Louisa Whatman, who died in 1950 at the age of 92 at Newnham Court, Weavering, near Maidstone, Kent, was the direct descendant of James Whatman, F.R.S. (1702–59), the founder of the famous firm which made paper at the Turkey Mill near Maidstone. By the time of his death this had become the largest papermill in England, and the business was continued and developed by his son, also James Whatman (1741–98), until he sold it in 1794. James Whatman II acquired Vinters, near Turkey Mill, as the family home in 1783, and the house passed by inheritance to Miss Louisa Whatman through his son James Whatman III and grandson James Whatman IV, who inherited it in 1852 and died in 1887. His widow remained there until 1905, after which it passed to several daughters in succession before becoming the property of Louisa, who chose not to live there. Miss Whatman also inherited an important, large and early Canaletto view of *The Grand Canal, looking East from the Campo di San Vio* (Constable II, no. 186). A third painting by Canaletto, a view of *Sansovino's Loggetta of the Campanile* (Birmingham, Barber Institute of Fine Arts; Constable I, pl. 18; II, no. 39) was purchased by James Whatman IV in or after 1864. He sold it at Christie's, London, 20 February 1882, lot 23. His widow is the first recorded owner of an impressive *Portrait of a young Man* by Jan Lievens recently on the London art market (Richard Green), which she sold at Christie's, London, 16 June 1900, lot 65 (as the work of Rembrandt). At least one painting from Miss Whatman's collection, a *Portrait of a Gentleman* by Adriaen van der Werff, dated 1694, recently on the London art market (London 2005, no. 73) is thought to have passed to her by descent from the first James Whatman.

Rome: The Piazza Navona

53

Rome: The Piazza del Quirinale

52

Rome: The Piazza Navona

c. 1750/1
Oil on canvas
15½ × 27 in. (39.5 × 68.5 cm.)

Tokyo Fuji Art Museum, Japan
Exhibited at Yale only

Provenance:
(Presumably) Richard Neave (1731–1814), created a
    baronet in 1795, of 6 Albemarle Street, London, and
    Dagnam Park, Havering, Essex.
His grandson, Sir Arundell Neave (d. 1877), by 1864,
    and by descent at Dagnam Park; Lysdulas, Isle of
    Anglesey; Artramont, County Wexford, and elsewhere
    to Sir Arundell Neave, by whom sold in 1988
    (catalogued for sale at Sotheby's, London, 7 December
    1988, lot 143, but sold before the sale to Edward Speelman
    and Harari & Johns).

Selected Literature:
Constable I, p. 136, note 3, pl. 73; II, no. 401.
Puppi 1968, no. 215, illustrated.
Links 1981, no. 267, illustrated.
Corboz 1985, I, p. 234, fig. 298; II, p. 654, no. P 323,
    illustrated.

53

Rome: The Piazza del Quirinale

c. 1750/1
Oil on canvas
15½ × 27 in. (39.5 × 68.5 cm.)

Tokyo Fuji Art Museum, Japan
Exhibited at Yale only

Provenance:
As for Cat. no. 52.

Selected Literature:
Constable I, p. 136, note 3, pl. 72; II, no. 394.
Puppi 1968, no. 214, illustrated.
Links 1981, no. 266, illustrated.
Corboz 1985, I, p. 234, fig. 296; II, p. 654, no. P 322,
    illustrated.

The two piazze, both of which owe their principal features to late sixteenth- and seventeenth-century popes, remain among the foremost attractions of Rome. In the Piazza Navona, the enlargement of the Palazzo Pamphili, the rebuilding of the church of Sant'Agnese, and Bernini's Four Rivers Fountain were all instigated by Giovanni Battista Pamphili during his pontificate as Innocent X (1644–55). Piazza del Quirinale is dominated by the west wing of the Palazzo del Quirinale commissioned from Domenico Fontana by Sixtus V in 1587 and continued by his successors, the Benediction Loggia over the main entrance being commissioned by Urban VIII from Bernini in 1638. It was also Sixtus V for whom the ancient Roman statues of Castor and Pollux with their steeds, known as the 'horse-tamers' and traditionally attributed to Phidias and Praxiteles, were set up in 1588 by Fontana, who also designed the adjacent fountain. The statues were later moved to their present positions by Pius VI, in order to accommodate the obelisk brought from the Mausoleum of Augustus which now stands between them.

Although both paintings are dated by Puppi (tentatively) and Corboz to the first half of the 1740s, and by Links to 1754–60, their handling and colouration indicate a date in the English period shortly before or after the artist's temporary return to Venice in 1750/1. Since neither subject is represented among Canaletto's Roman drawings, which concentrate on the remains of the ancient city, he was inevitably obliged to turn to the work of another artist as the source of both compositions. As Corboz has pointed out, both derive from engravings by Gomar Wouters issued by Domenico de Rossi in 1692, which are of very similar size to the paintings (45.5 × 70.3 cm.; Corboz 1985, I, p. 234, figs 297 and 299). The *Piazza Navona* follows its prototype surprisingly closely, even in the positions of the carriages and many of the figures. In the *Piazza del Quirinale*, on the other hand, Canaletto has replaced the festivity of Wouters's print with a relatively tranquil scene. Here he has also raised significantly the viewpoint, so that the wing of the palazzo on the Via del Quirinale recedes at a less acute angle, and a view over the rooftops of the city is seen above the building on the left, as well as the top of the Column of Marcus Aurelius and the distant dome of St Peter's.

These are two of the ten paintings by Canaletto which remained together in the possession of the Neave family until the late nineteenth century (the majority until the late twentieth century), which also include a pair of Venetian views similarly datable to Canaletto's English period: *The Churches of the Redentore and San Giacomo* and *The Prisons* (Figs 57.1, 57.2; Constable II, nos 84 and 318), a Venetian *capriccio* probably painted in England, *Capriccio of the Scuola di San Marco from the Loggia of the Palazzo Grifalconi-Loredan* (Fig. 3; Constable II, no. 467), a view of Rome painted late in the English period or shortly after the artist's return to Venice, *The Piazza del Campidoglio and the Cordonata* (Constable II, no. 397, a large version of that painted for Hollis in 1755), and two pairs of Venetian views certainly painted in Italy after 1755 (Constable II, nos 71 and 176; 46 and 74). These form a coherent group, the two unpaired paintings – the *capriccio* and the large Roman view – being of the same size as each other. It must be presumed that the collection was assembled at the time, and thus probably by Richard Neave (for whom see p. 11), although he is not known to have visited Italy and thus nothing is known of the reasons for the choice of these particular subjects.

54

Venice: The Molo from the Bacino di San Marco on Ascension Day, with the Bucintoro

1745/6
Oil on canvas
45¼ × 64 in. (114.9 × 162.6 cm.)

The Philadelphia Museum of Art,
The William L. Elkins Collection, 1924
Exhibited at Yale only

Provenance:
As for Cat. no. 23 until 1895; 1895 sale, lot 25
   (270 guineas to P. & D. Colnaghi).
William L. Elkins (1832–1903), Elstowe, Montgomery
   County, Pennsylvania, by whom bequeathed to the
   City of Philadelphia with life retention by his family
   (Acc. no. E1924·3·48).

Selected Exhibitions:
Canada 1964–5, no. 76.

Selected Literature:
Constable II, no. 344.
Puppi 1968, no. 249, illustrated.
Constable / Links 1976, I, pl. 204; II, no. 344.
Links 1981, no. 205, illustrated.
Corboz 1985, II, p. 661, no. P 353, illustrated.
(all of the above with incorrect height measurement).

Ascension Day, which falls on the Thursday forty days after Easter Sunday, was the most spectacular of Venetian festivals (Fig. 54.1). It was on that day in the year 1000 that Doge Pietro Orseolo had set out from Venice to subjugate the pirates of the Dalmatian coast; after the successful conclusion of the campaign it was decreed that every year on Ascension Day the doge would sail past the Lido into the open sea for a service of supplication and thanksgiving. According to Venetian tradition, Pope Alexander III, during his visit to Venice in 1177, gave Doge Sebastiano Ziani a ring to cast into the waves, transforming the ceremony into the symbolic 'marriage with the Adriatic' which it was to remain until the fall of the Republic in 1797.

The large state vessel called the Bucintoro was used exclusively on this occasion, being transferred from the Arsenal about eight days before. There were several successive models – the one always depicted by Canaletto being that built in the late 1720s to the designs of the architect Stefano Conti, which was to remain in use for all subsequent ceremonies. With the doge's flag at the mast, the doge, his entourage and the Signoria on the upper deck and the oarsmen on the lower deck, its form could be seen as symbolic of the structure of the Venetian State.

This painting shows the doge, his retinue and the Signoria approaching the Bucintoro after processing through the Piazzetta, where booths and stalls have been erected as a market, as was customary. It must therefore represent the morning of Ascension Day, although the scene is lit from the left, the west, an example of the sort of inconsistencies which one often finds in Canaletto's work. He has, however, shown with some care the damage inflicted on the Campanile by lightning on St George's Day, 23 April 1745, the date provided by his inscription on a drawing of it under repair now at Windsor (Constable I, pl. 100; II, no. 552). That was probably brought by Canaletto to England, as it was used for a variant now in the British Museum (Constable I, pl. 100; II, no. 553), and for a painting (Constable / Links I, pl. 189; II, no. 67*), both of which there is reason to believe were executed in London. Here, however, repairs have not yet been begun, and Constable is probably correct in identifying the event depicted as Ascension Day in May 1745, soon

Figure 54.1
Venice: The Bacino di San Marco on Ascension Day, c. 1733–4,
oil on canvas, 30¼ × 49⅜ in. (76.8 × 125.4 cm.).
The Royal Collection

after the damage was incurred. Constable may well also be justified in suggesting that the painting was probably executed before Canaletto's departure for England in May 1746, but it could also date from shortly afterwards, and the probable provenance is of no help in this respect.

Constable did not give this painting the consideration which it deserves. He initially even doubted its authenticity, cataloguing it in 1962 as 'Studio of Canaletto', but he subsequently requested its loan for the Canadian touring exhibition of 1964–5, in the catalogue of which he recorded that 'he is now inclined to accept it as by Canaletto himself'. At the same time he corrected the error over the dimensions of the painting which had led him to question unnecessarily its identification as that in the Carpenter Garnier sale in 1895, but at no point did he – or indeed any subsequent writers on Canaletto – investigate the possible origins of the important group of six paintings by the artist dispersed on that occasion. Those, all identifiable with certainty or with an adequate degree of probability, form such a tightly knit group, all painted between about 1740 and 1747, that it seems inconceivable that they could have been assembled at a later date. There seems no reason whatsoever to doubt that their first owner was George Garnier (1703–63), a forebear of the 1895 vendor, who lived at Rookesbury, the house from

which the paintings were sold. Garnier seems to have been highly cultivated as well as more than adequately affluent, having been granted in 1735 the highly profitable sinecure of Apothecary-General to the Army and having married an heiress in 1736 (see p. 12). Furthermore, we know that he spent time in Venice in the first half of the 1740s, and the paintings included four datable to the first years of that decade, in two pairs. A large view of 'The Rialto' was paired with a 'Composition of Architecture with gondolas and figures', including, according to an annotation in ink in the auctioneers' copy of the catalogue 'Palladio's proposed Theatre'. Judging from their unusual dimensions (38 × 50 in.), the first of these must be *The Rialto Bridge from the South* first recorded in the Hanson Collection in the early twentieth century and now in an American private collection (Fig. 54.2; Links 1998, pp. 23–4, no. 228*, pl. 235). Its pendant is likely to be the *Capriccio of the Grand Canal with Palladio's Design for the Rialto Bridge, the Basilica Palladiana and the Palazzo Chiericati*, the version of which of the appropriate size is first recorded in a New York sale in 1908 (said to have been previously in an English collection) and last recorded in a Bergamo private collection in 1973 (Fig. 54.3; Constable II, no. 458(b); exhibited Bergamo 1969, colour pl. XVIII; and Vicenza 1973, no. 7, as from a

Bergamo private collection). These were accompanied by a much smaller pair of Venetian views, *The Interior of the Basilica of San Marco* (Montreal, Musée des Beaux-Arts; Constable I, pl. 25; II, no. 79; exhibited Rome 2005, no. 66) and *The Courtyard of the Doge's Palace with the Giants' Staircase* (Private collection; Constable I, pl. 26; II, no. 81; exhibited Rome 2005, no. 65). The exhibited painting was both the largest and the latest of the five Venetian paintings presumably acquired by Garnier, but it was not the last painting to join the group. That was the patron's most spectacular purchase from Canaletto, *Westminster Bridge from the North on Lord Mayor's Day, 29 October 1746* (Cat. no. 23).

Figure 54.2
Venice: The Rialto Bridge from the South, c. 1740, oil on canvas, 39 × 51 in. (99 × 129.7 cm.). Private Collection, USA

Figure 54.3
Capriccio of the Grand Canal with Palladio's Design for the Rialto Bridge, the Basilica Palladiana and the Palazzo Chiericati, c. 1740, oil on canvas, 38½ × 51⅛ in. (98 × 130 cm.). Private Collection, Bergamo (?)

54

Venice: The Molo from the Bacino di San Marco on Ascension Day, with the Bucintoro

55

Venice: The Bacino di San Marco and the Dogana from the Piazzetta

Installed 1750
Oil on canvas
51¾ × 64¼ in. (131.4 × 163.2 cm.)

The National Gallery of Victoria, Melbourne,
Thomas Felton Bequest 1986
Exhibited at Yale only

Provenance:
Painted for William Holbech (*c.* 1699–1771) for the
saloon (now the dining room) at Farnborough Hall,
Warwickshire, and by inheritance there to Ronald
Herbert Acland Holbech (1887–1956), by whom
sold in 1929, along with the other paintings by Canaletto
and Panini in the house, to the Savile Gallery, London.
With the Savile Gallery, London, 1930.
With Arthur Tooth & Sons, London, 1944.
With Agnew's, London (and Eugene V. Thaw, New
York), 1976–85, when acquired by the present owner
(Acc. no. E1-1986).

Selected Exhibitions:
Venice 1982, no. 92.

Selected Literature:
Constable I, pp. 147–8, pl. 31; II, no. 128.
Puppi 1968, no. 152 A, illustrated.
Links 1981, under no. 168.
Corboz 1985, I, p. 31, figs 7 (detail) and 8 (colour detail);
II, p. 640, no. P 268, illustrated.

Figure. 55.1
*Venice: Entrance to the Grand Canal, looking East, with the Church of
Santa Maria della Salute*, installed 1750, oil on canvas, 52 × 65 in.
(132 × 165 cm.). Private Collection, USA

This painting originally formed part of a set of four
Venetian views of similar size which decorated the saloon
at Farnborough Hall, along with *The Northeast Corner
of the Piazza San Marco* (Ottawa, National Gallery of
Canada; Constable II, no. 45; I, pl. 188, in the 1976 and
1989 editions), *The Libreria Marciana and the Base of the
Campanile from the North End of the Piazzetta* (Augsburg,
Städtische Kunstsammlungen; Constable I, pl. 18; II,
no. 38), and *The Entrance to the Grand Canal, looking East,
with the Church of Santa Maria della Salute* (Fig. 55.1; Private
Collection, U.S.A.; Constable I, pl. 38; II, no. 173).
These were all set in stucco frames which were finished by
14 November 1750 (by the York plasterer William Perritt,
who had worked in 1741–2 at the Rotunda at Ranelagh,
see p. 12 and Cat. nos 32–3). No further documentation
survives to help date the paintings, and there is no possible
link with the date of the Grand Tour made by the patron
William Holbech between 1732/3 and 1734, on 30 April
of which year he is recorded in Venice. *The Libreria and the
Base of the Campanile from the North End of the Piazzetta* omits
Antonio Gai's bronze gates of the Loggetta, which were
set up in 1742, and a likely dating on stylistic grounds for
both the views of the Piazza San Marco is at the beginning
of the 1740s.

There has been much discussion of a Holbech family
tradition, reported by Constable, that two of the Canaletto
paintings were bought in Italy, and two painted in England.
While Puppi dates all four paintings to 1735–7, and Corboz
places them all together within the bracket 1731–46,

Constable was happy to regard them as two pairs of different
dates (Constable I, pp. 147–8; II, under no. 38). In this he
was initially followed by Links (in Constable / Links 1976,
II, under no. 38), who subsequently became sceptical that
this work – a composition of which no other painting
or drawing is known – could have been made far from the
subject matter (Venice 1982, p. 64). By 1989 he seems to
have satisfied himself that this painting and *The Entrance to
the Grand Canal, looking East, with the Church of Santa Maria
della Salute* (Fig. 55.1) do indeed date from Canaletto's
English years, pointing out that they are on fine weave
canvases quite distinct from the coarse-weave Venetian
canvases of the two Piazza views (New York 1989–90,
p. 203). The stylistic differences between the two pairs of
paintings are pronounced and there is little reason to doubt
the veracity of the family tradition that the later pair was
executed in England, almost certainly in 1749–50 shortly
before their installation in Perritt's frames. It should be noted
that there was an even longer caesura between Holbech's
first acquisition of a painting by Panini, *The Interior of the
Pantheon* (Private Collection, New York State), which is
dated 1734, and his commission of the remaining three, one
of which, *The Interior of Saint Peter's* (Detroit Institute of
Arts), is dated 1750.

What 'little reason' there is for questioning an English
period dating for this painting is inadvertently provided by
Corboz (p. 31), who points out that the central standing
man in profile in a yellow and blue hat is also shown in a
drawing which has generally been presumed to be also the
work of Canaletto (Constable / Links 1976, I, pl. 222; II,
no. 840*****). That drawing, last recorded with Colnaghi
in 2001, is, however, considered by the present writer to
be the work of Bellotto (see Beddington 2004, p. 670).
A first-hand knowledge by Bellotto of this painting would
provide an absolute *terminus ante quem* of 1746, but it must
be presumed that either Canaletto retained a copy of his
nephew's drawing or that both derive from a common
source.

When the four paintings by Canaletto were sold from
Farnborough in 1929, they and three of the four Roman
views by Panini were replaced in Perritt's stucco frames by
copies made by an Indian painter called Mohammed Ayoub
which can still be seen in the house.

56

Venice: The Church of San Giorgio Maggiore

57

Venice: The Church of the Redentore

56

Venice: The Church of San Giorgio Maggiore

Probably late 1740s
Oil on canvas
18⅝ × 30½ in. (47.3 × 77.5 cm.)

Private Collection, UK

Provenance:
Said to have been acquired in London in 1850 or 1852
  from an agent acting on behalf of the duc d'Aumale
  (who lived in London and sold a number of paintings,
  including Italian views, at Christie's on 10 January 1857),
  and by descent until sold at Christie's, London,
  10 December 1993, lot 65.
With Richard Green, London.
Private Collection, England, from which sold at Christie's,
  New York, 27 January 2000, lot 89 (purchased by the
  present owner).

Selected Literature:
Links 1998, p. 30, no. 301**, pl. 268.

57

Venice: The Church of the Redentore

Probably late 1740s
Oil on canvas
18⅝ × 30½ in. (47.4 × 77.3 cm.)

Private Collection, UK,
courtesy of Simon C. Dickinson Ltd

Provenance:
Presumably as for Cat. no. 57 until the mid(?) twentieth
  century.
Anon. Sale, Christie's, London, 13 December 1996,
  lot 81.
With Simon C. Dickinson Ltd, from whom purchased
  by the present owner in October 1997.

Selected Literature:
Links 1998, p. 32, no. 318***, pl. 269.

The churches of San Giorgio Maggiore and the Redentore are among the greatest masterpieces of the hugely influential architect Andrea Palladio (1508–80). Palladio did not receive his first ecclesiastical commission until he was in his fifties, when most of his villas in the Veneto and Vicentine palaces were well behind him. While no secular building was ever constructed to his design in Venice, the majority of his monastic and church projects did come to fruition in the city where his *I quattro libri dell'architettura* was published in 1570 and where he settled in 1570/1. Of those, by far the most significant are these two churches wholly designed by the architect and prominently placed on waterfront sites facing the Molo. The foundation stone of the church of the Benedictine monastery of San Giorgio Maggiore on the Island of San Giorgio Maggiore was laid in March 1566 and the building was virtually complete by 1576, although the façade was not erected (apparently in fairly strict adherence to the architect's model) until 1607–11.

The Redentore, on the Giudecca facing the Giudecca Canal, was commissioned by the Venetian Senate in fulfilment of a vow taken before the deliverance of the city from the devastating plague of 1575–7, in which thirty percent of the population perished. Raised on a podium, the church was to be the culminating site of an annual procession led by the Doge and the Senate every third Sunday in July, for which a causeway of boats was assembled across the canal. Its foundation stone was laid in 1577 and it was completed within fifteen years. While the interiors of both churches reveal the influence of Roman baths, not only in the use of thermal windows but also in the sequence of spaces from the nave to the tribune and the monks' choir, each with a single dome over the crossing, the façades of brilliant white Istrian stone, onto which are superimposed elements of classical porticoes, were unprecedented in Venice in their combination of Counter-Reformation simplicity and classical grandeur, made all the more striking by their waterside settings on and near the Bacino di San Marco.

Figure 56.1
Venice: The Church of San Giorgio Maggiore; probably late 1740s, oil on canvas, 18¾ × 31 in. (47.5 × 79 cm.). Present whereabouts unknown

There can be no doubt that these two paintings were conceived as a pair, although they have never before been publicly exhibited as such. Both were unknown before their re-emergence in London auctions in the 1990s, three years apart but from related Swedish sources. Both had survived in unusually pristine condition and neither canvas had been lined. Other pairings of these subjects are known, of which the earliest is the pair acquired by the Manchester City Art Gallery in 1984 (Links 1998, pp. 30 and 32, nos 301* and 318**, pls 235–6). Also of the 1730s is the version of the Redentore composition which forms part of the large set at Woburn Abbey (Constable I, pl. 59; II, no. 316). The exhibited paintings are intimately related to two other pairs, all of similar size to the Woburn canvases. A version of the *San Giorgio Maggiore* with slight variations in the lighting and differences in the boats and figures is the only component of the group not to have been on the market in recent years and its present whereabouts are unknown (Fig. 56.1; Constable I, pl. 57; II, no. 301). It also had a pendant of the Redentore, although seen from the right rather than the left of the church's central axis and lit from the left rather than the right (Christie's, New York, 27 January 2000, lot 88; Constable I, pl. 59; II, no. 317; Links 1998, pp. 31 and 32 , pl. 268). The exhibited *Redentore* is much closer to a version from the Neave Collection that was offered at Christie's, New York, 25 January 2002, lot 78, and was on the London market in 2004 (Fig. 57.1; Constable, no. 318; Links 1998, pl. 269). It shows the same ship's prow on the right, and it alone is still accompanied by its pendant, a unique representation of the Prisons, designed by Palladio's contemporary Giovanni Antonio Rusconi (Fig. 57.2; Constable I, pl. 26; II, no. 84).

These three pairs are so uniform in style that they must have been painted at the same moment; the grey ground and light tonality indicate that this was during the artist's years in England and the translucency and delicacy of touch make a date in the late 1740s probable. No doubt they appealed not only to Canaletto's clientele for Venetian views but also to admirers of Palladian architecture, who were more fervent in England than in any other European country. Although the group is as close as the artist ever got to serial repetition, the more closely one compares the versions, the more apparent are the lengths to which the artist has gone to differentiate them.

Figure 57.1
Venice: the Churches of the Redentore and San Giacomo, probably late 1740s, oil on canvas, 18⅜ × 30⅛ in. (46.7 × 76.7 cm.). Offered at Christie's, New York, 25 January 2002, lot 78

Figure 57.2
Venice: The Prisons, probably late 1740s, oil on canvas, 18⅜ × 30⅛ in. (46.7 × 76.7 cm.). Offered at Christie's, New York, 25 January 2002, lot 78

Capriccio of a Renaissance Palace

59

Capriccio of a Renaissance Palace with a large Gateway

58

Capriccio of a Renaissance Palace

Before February 1752
Oil on canvas, shaped
45 × 39 in. (114.3 × 99 cm.)

The Lord Brabourne

Provenance:
Commissioned by Philip Dormer Stanhope, 4th Earl
 of Chesterfield (1694–1773) for his wife's 'Dressing
 or Sitting Room' at Chesterfield House, Great Stanhope
 Street, London.
By inheritance at Chesterfield House (where recorded in
 inventories of 1773 and 1815) and Bretby Hall, Bretby,
 Derbyshire, to George Cecil Arthur Stanhope, 7th Earl
 of Chesterfield (1831–1871).
His sister Evelyn (d. 1875), wife of Henry Howard
 Molyneux Herbert, 4th Earl of Carnarvon (1831–90).
Bequeathed by her to their son George Edward Stanhope
 Molyneux Herbert, Lord Porchester, later 5th Earl of
 Carnarvon (1866–1923); Bretby Heirlooms Sale,
 Christie's, London, 31 May 1918, lot 7, with the pendant
 as 'B. Canaletto – *Mansions near Venice* with fixtures –
 a pair' (130 guineas to Ancor).
Wilfred William Ashley, 1st Baron Mount Temple
 (1867–1938).
His daughter Edwina Cynthia Annette, wife of Louis
 Francis Albert Victor Nicholas Mountbatten, 1st Earl
 Mountbatten of Burma (1900–79), and by descent to
 the present owner.

Selected Literature:
Russell 1988, pp. 627–9, fig. 61.
Constable / Links 1989, I, pp. lxxvii–lxxviii, pl. 237;
 II, p. 740, no. 514*.
Links 1998, p. 45, pl. 237.

59

Capriccio of a Renaissance Palace with a large Gateway

Before February 1752
Oil on canvas, shaped
45 × 39 in. (114.3 × 99 cm.)

The Lord Brabourne

Provenance:
As for Cat. no. 58.

Selected Literature:
Russell 1988, pp. 627–9, fig. 62.
Constable / Links 1989, I, p. lxxvii, pl. 237; II, p. 740,
 no. 504*.
Links 1998, p. 45, pl. 237.

The *Capriccio of a Renaissance Palace* (Cat. no. 58) is a unique composition, distinct in type from any other by Canaletto in this genre. Demonstrating the unexpected manner in which the artist's imagination could adapt motifs for his works of fantasy, it takes as its starting point a drawing of the early 1740s of *A Farm on the outskirts of Padua* (Fig. 58.1; Constable I, pl. 126; II, no. 694); now at Windsor, that drawing was among the works sold by Joseph Smith to King George III in the early 1760s. Bellotto also used the farm as a prominent element in an imaginary composition known in two versions (Kozakiewicz 1972, II, pp. 189–90, nos 245–6, both illustrated, where dated to after 1747). While, however, Bellotto's borrowing is fairly literal, here it is limited to the basic form of the rustic building – its plan with a five-arched portico between projecting wings, their upper floors with small square windows, most of the right-hand wall with the projection supported by arches and two large chimneys above, and part of the hipped roof in the centre. That structure has been embellished, to the point of becoming almost unrecognizable, with classical ornament, an extra storey, a grand staircase and a bell tower, the latter recalling that of the Palazzo del Capitano in Padua. Beyond to the right is a small church in the classical style, not unlike the Gesuati in Venice. The composition of the pendant *Capriccio of a Renaissance Palace with a large Gateway* (Cat.

no. 59) stems ultimately from the right half of one of Canaletto's early Roman *capricci* (Constable / Links 1976, I, pl. 212; II, no. 501***). A drawing in a horizontal format in the Cleveland Museum of Art (Constable I, pl. 154; II, no. 819) was probably used for this painting, for a horizontal variant in a Scottish private collection (Constable I, pl. 92; II, no. 502) and for the upright variant which formed part of the important decorative scheme for the 5th Lord King (Fig. 14; Constable I, pl. 92; II, no. 504). The large gateway – and to an extent its setting – resembles that of the Palazzo Tasca a San Giuliano on the Rio della Guerra in Venice, as Corboz has pointed out (Corboz 1985, I, p. 119, fig. 127).

These two paintings were unknown before their publication by Francis Russell, as recently as 1988. Russell has ascertained, with the help of inventories of 1773 and 1815, that they come from Chesterfield House in Great Stanhope Street, London, the great mansion of the eminent politician, wit and man of letters Philip Dormer Stanhope, 4th Earl of Chesterfield. The foundations of the house, designed by Isaac Ware, were well under way by the summer of 1747, and the Earl's Boudoir and the Library, on the ground floor, are known to have been finished by the end of March 1749, when the earl moved in. The house, 'a monument to the taste and learning of its owner', was opened in February 1752, and survived until it was demolished in 1937. The shape of these canvases, unique in Canaletto's work, derives from their function as overdoors in the Countess of Chesterfield's 'Dressing or Sitting Room' upstairs, where they are recorded in the inventory of 1815. The interior decoration of the house was unusual in that the 'feminine' rooms were in the Rococo style, in contrast with the classicism of the main reception rooms (Worsley 1995, p. 208). As at Norfolk House, for which Canaletto received his other supremely prestigious commission to contribute to the decoration of one of the most fashionable new London houses (see Cat. nos 60–2), three paintings were supplied, although here one of them was of different shape and hung in a different room. That, showing *A Renaissance Pavilion flanked by two ruined classical Arches over a Waterway by the Venetian Lagoon* (Fig. 58.2; Constable II, no. 511(a); pl. 212 in the 1976 and 1989 editions) was first identified by Russell as from Chesterfield House, although it was published by Constable as long ago as 1923. It also hung in a 'feminine' room upstairs, the Music Room, where it was the only painting and was fitted 'in a compartment of the chimney glass'. Like Cat. no. 59 it is one of several variants, of which probably the earliest painting, possibly dating from slightly before the artist's transfer to England, is that in the Baltimore Museum of Art (Constable II, no. 511(c)). Both that and another English period version, sold from the estate of Sir Michael Sobell at Christie's, London, 8 December 1995, lot 76 (Constable I, pl. 511; II, no. 511), are square. The latter corresponds, with minor variations, with a drawing sold at Christie's, London, 4 July 1984, lot 82 (Links 1998, p. 53, no. 825*, pl. 240), which was probably preceded by another drawing, last seen at auction in 1971, which has the character of a preparatory study (Constable I, pl. 155; II, no. 823). Chesterfield was no doubt encouraged to employ Canaletto by friends such as George Garnier (for whom see pp. 12–14 and Cat. nos 23 and 54), although the decoration of Chesterfield House also included five paintings of Venetian and Roman views by Antonio Joli, Canaletto's rival in London until the former's departure for Madrid in 1749/50. Also of irregular shape, Joli's served as overdoors in the lavishly Rococo drawing-room, known as the 'French Room', on the ground floor, of which they were the only pictorial decoration.

Russell's reconstitution of the Chesterfield House commission, along with the similar use of inventories to establish that the Norfolk House paintings are unquestionably of the English period, shows that Canaletto was involved in both of the foremost schemes of interior decoration for private London houses carried out during his years there. This does much to dispel the idea that the painter was neglected by patrons during his time in England.

Figure 58.1
A Farm on the Outskirts of Padua, probably 1742,
pen and brown ink over pencil, 12⅜ × 15¼ in. (31.5 × 40 cm.).
The Royal Collection

Figure 58.2
Capriccio of a Renaissance Pavilion flanked by two ruined classical Arches over a Waterway by the Venetian Lagoon, before February 1752, oil on canvas, 53½ × 49½ in. (135.9 × 125.8 cm.). Private Collection, England

60

Capriccio of a round Church with an elaborate Gothic Portico in a Piazza,
a Palladian Palazzo and a Gothic Church beyond

61

Capriccio of a Renaissance Triumphal Arch seen from the Portico of a Palace

62

Capriccio of a Renaissance Palazzo with a monumental Staircase,
a Clock Tower and the Arch of Titus beyond

*Capriccio of a round Church with an elaborate
Gothic Portico in a Piazza, a Palladian Palazzo
and a Gothic Church beyond*

c. 1753–5
Oil on canvas
39½ × 57⅝ in. (100.3 × 146.4 cm.)

His Grace The Duke of Norfolk, Arundel Castle

Provenance:
Commissioned by Edward Howard, 9th Duke of Norfolk
(1685–1777) for Norfolk House, St James's Square,
London; recorded in the Norfolk House Inventory of 1756
as one of '3 pictures of Architecture – gilt frames' in the
Large Drawing Room on the ground floor (Arundel Castle
Archives: In. 5); also shown in James Bonus's plan of the
picture hang at Norfolk House, dated 11 November 1777
(Arundel Castle Archives); thence by inheritance to the
present owner (removed from Norfolk House on its
demolition in 1938).

Selected Literature:
Constable I, pp. 148, note 1, and 150, pl. 92; II, no. 507.
Puppi 1968, no. 272, illustrated.
Links 1981, no. 259, illustrated.
Corboz 1985, I, pp. 304 and 347, figs 367 and 421–2
    (colour detail); II, p. 713, no. P 395, illustrated.

61

*Capriccio of a Renaissance Triumphal Arch
seen from the Portico of a Palace*

c. 1753–5
Oil on canvas
39¾ × 50½ in. (101 × 128.3 cm.)

His Grace The Duke of Norfolk, Arundel Castle

Provenance:
As for Cat. no. 58.

Selected Literature:
Constable I, pp. 148, note 1, 150 and 167, pl. 92; II, no. 506.
Puppi 1968, no. 271, illustrated.
Links 1981, no. 260, illustrated.
Corboz 1985, I, pp. 298 and 364, figs 442–3 (colour detail);
    II, p. 713, no. P 394, illustrated.

62

*Capriccio of a Renaissance Palazzo with a
monumental Staircase, a Clock Tower
and the Arch of Titus beyond*

c. 1753–5
Oil on canvas
39⅞ × 57⅞ in. (100.5 × 147 cm.)

His Grace The Duke of Norfolk, Arundel Castle

Provenance:
As for Cat. no. 58.

Selected Literature:
Constable I, pp. 148, note 1, and 150, pl. 92; II, no. 505.
Puppi 1968, no. 270, illustrated.
Links 1981, no. 258, illustrated.
Corboz 1985, I, pp. 283, 286 and 320, fig. 386; II, p. 712,
    no. P 393, illustrated.

Nowhere else in Canaletto's work in England is the fertility
of his imagination more evident than in these three *capricci*.
The artist's assembly of architectural elements in widely
divergent styles – all of them Italian, without even a hint of
Englishness – is all the more remarkable given his distance
from home, and demonstrates what copious folios of drawings and prints he must have brought with him to London.
Moreover, while most of Canaletto's English period *capricci*
are of types known in more than one variant, all of the
Norfolk House compositions are unique. Cat. no. 60 is
dominated by a round church, whose slight resemblance to
the Rotunda at Ranelagh makes it the only motif of possibly
English derivation. The fresco of the apotheosis of a saint on
the upper part of the façade immediately tells us, however,
that the imaginary setting is a southern one, and the elaborate
portico is composed of elements inspired by parts of the
façade of the Basilica of San Marco. To the right, behind
a wall, are a two-storey palazzo in Palladian style, vaguely
reminiscent of the Palazzo Chiericati in Vicenza (shown
on the left in Fig. 54.3), and a gothic church. In Cat. no. 61
the foreground is occupied by a portico, the view beyond
being seen through its two arches, very much as in a drawing
in the Albertina, Vienna (Constable I, pl. 156; II, no. 828).

The triumphal arch is a kind of Renaissance version of the Arch of Septimius Severus in the Roman Forum, while to its left is a building strikingly similar to the Libreria Marciana. Reminiscences of both feature in a number of Canaletto *capricci* and are already present in his pair of very large examples of 1723 painted for the Giovanelli brothers (Constable / Links 1976, I, pl. 210; II, nos 479 ** and 479***). The pyramid beyond the triumphal arch to the right, presumably inspired by that of Caius Cestius in Rome, is also a regular feature of the painter's *capricci*, sometimes as here including the motif of a round sculpted medallion on the side, as in one of the painter's earliest paintings of imaginary compositions (Constable / Links 1976, I, pl. 212; II, no. 501*) and in a drawing of the early 1740s (Constable I, pl. 154; II, no. 818). The Arch of Titus, which also appears in Canaletto's *capricci* from the outset of his career (see Constable / Links 1976, I, pl. 212; II, no. 501***), is the only readily recognisable structure in Cat. no. 62, although the clock closely resembles that on the façade of San Giacomo di Rialto, Venice (see Constable I, pls 57 and 112; II, nos 297–8 and 611). Corboz points out that a clock tower is similarly positioned in relationship to a staircase rising to the right in Vittore Carpaccio's *Presentation of the Virgin in the Temple* (Milan, Pinacoteca di Brera).

All three paintings are in exceptionally good condition, which makes all the more apparent the confidence of Canaletto's technique. There is a minimal use of incised guidelines and dark outlines, and a section of the grey ground is left bare in the lower left corner of Cat. no. 60. The artist, who was proud of his social status as a *cittadino originario* of Venice, occasionally used the coat-of-arms of the Canal family, *azure a chevron or*, as a kind of signature and, as Constable pointed out, this features in an elaborated form on the cartouche on the triumphal arch in Cat. no. 61. It is found on eleven drawings and four etchings, but rarely on paintings, although it is also seen on a hitherto unpublished *Capriccio with the Rialto Bridge* (Fig. 54.2).

The three paintings were commissioned by Edward Howard, 9th Duke of Norfolk (1685–1777) – who had succeeded his brother Thomas in 1732 – for Norfolk House, which stood in the southern part of the east side of St James's Square. The house – which he had lent for several years to Frederick, Prince of Wales, and his wife, and where their son, afterwards George III, had been born on 4 June 1738 – was replaced in 1748–52 by a double-width

residence designed by Matthew Brettingham. The sumptuous decoration of the interior was to take several years and had a very international flavour, the Piedmontese Giovanni Battista Borra being employed to design some of the principal interiors. Its completion was celebrated in February 1756 by a series of soirées on three consecutive Tuesdays. 'You never saw such a scene of magnificence and taste' commented Horace Walpole, who was among the throngs (Walpole, *Correspondence*, vol. 37, p. 438). Also present was Captain William Farington of the Indian army, who wrote 'everyone who was there agreed that Norfolk House was infinitely superior to anything in this Kingdom … and to most things they had seen in Europe' (Fitzgerald 1973, p. 48). It was demolished in 1938, only a year after Chesterfield House (for which see Cat. nos 58–9).

All three paintings remain in the original gilt frames recorded in the 1756 inventory, which are documented as the work of John Cuenot (active 1744–62), who was paid more than £2,643 for carving and gilding at Norfolk House between 1752 and 1756. Of French origin, he lived in Warwick Street, west of Golden Square, and was thus a neighbour of Canaletto. He is now remembered above all for the carving and gilding of the Norfolk House Music Room, which was saved on the demolition of the house and re-erected in the Victoria and Albert Museum. The three paintings originally hung in the Large Drawing Room on the ground floor, along with seven full-length portraits and twelve 'heads' (information from John Martin Robinson). There was a pier glass over the chimneypiece and the over-doors were probably portraits, so they must have always hung mid-wall, an arrangement also shown in Bonus's plan of the picture hang of 1777. John Martin Robinson has suggested (private communication) that they were on the south and west walls, and it may be noted that one (Cat. no. 60) is lit from the right and the other two from the left.

The 1777 plan of the picture hang shows that the decoration of the house also incorporated paintings by a number of Canaletto's fellow countrymen and contemporaries, including landscapes by Francesco Zuccarelli and Giovanni Battista Cimaroli and an 'Inside of a Church' by Giovanni Paolo Panini.

63

Capriccio of a domed circular Church

c. 1752–5
Oil on canvas
17¼ × 28⅛ in. (43.8 × 71.4 cm.)

Worcester Art Museum, Worcester,
Massachusetts museum purchase
Exhibited at Yale only

Provenance:
'A private lady's collection at Pulborough, Sussex'
   (according to Max Rothschild in 1923).
With Max Rothschild, London, from whom purchased
   by the present owner in December 1923
   (Acc. no. 1923.211).

Selected Exhibitions:
Canada 1964–5, no. 29.

Selected Literature:
Constable I, pl. 93; II, no. 508.
Puppi 1968, no. 298, illustrated.
Links 1981, no. 264, illustrated.
Corboz 1985, I, pp. 36, 182, 286 and 291, figs 170–1
   (colour detail); II, p. 661, no. P 355, illustrated.

While Constable offers no comment about the dating of this painting and Corboz places it before Canaletto's departure from Venice in 1746, the date of 1752–6 tentatively proposed by Puppi, followed by Links, is surely correct. It should be refined, however, to exclude 1756, since the grey ground, the brushwork and the colouration, in distinctive hues of grey, brown and green with a light blue sky and clouds tinged with pink, clearly indicate a work of the painter's English years. In the light of this, it is particularly surprising that the composition corresponds, even to a large extent in the figures, with a drawing by Bellotto in the Hessisches Landesmuseum, Darmstadt (Kozakiewicz 1972, II, p. 94, no. 123, illustrated). The only significant differences in the painting are the extension of the composition on the right side, the inclusion of more foliage, and the substitution of a cross for an urn over the doorway on the right (there is evidence that this last change was made during execution). Canaletto cannot have brought his nephew's drawing to England, since it has an unbroken provenance from Bellotto's family to Darmstadt, so, if one excludes the possibilities either that the painting is also by Bellotto – which has been suggested in the past, entirely without foundation – or that it was painted by Canaletto before he and his nephew parted company in 1746, only two options remain open. That the composition was Canaletto's invention, and copied by his nephew, is not impossible but

seems unlikely, since Bellotto used his drawing as the basis for an etching, signed in the plate and with variations in the figures (Kozakiewicz 1972, II, p. 94, no. 124, illustrated). The most plausible explanation is, therefore, that Canaletto brought with him to London a copy of his nephew's drawing, and that on this occasion, in striking contrast to his work for Norfolk House and elsewhere, he was content to let his imagination take a rest.

A 'finished' drawing by Canaletto in the Fogg Art Museum, Cambridge, Massachusetts, is of fundamentally the same composition but varies from it extensively in details, suggesting that it is a later elaboration of the theme (Fig. 63.1; Constable I, pl. 157; II, no. 830). It was engraved in Venice by Jacopo Monaco (born 1730), but it has been regarded, with good reason, as also dating from the artist's English period.

A round church with a large classical portico also occupies the centre of another imaginary composition datable to Canaletto's years in England and is known in two surprisingly similar versions, both of them signed; one, first recorded in 1955 on the London art market, is in an Italian private collection (Constable I, pl. 88; II, no. 479), the other, formerly in the Albertini Collection, Rome, is now owned by the Banca Nazionale del Lavoro (Constable II, under no. 479).

Figure 63.1
Capriccio of a domed circular Church, c. 1752–5, pen and brown ink with grey wash, 7¾ × 13 in. (19.7 × 32.9 cm.). The Fogg Art Museum, Harvard University, Bequest of Charles E. Loeser

64

A domed Church seen through a ruined Arch

c. 1753–5
Oil on canvas
27 × 41½ in. (68.5 × 105.5 cm.)

Private Collection, England

Provenance:
In the present collection by 1874.

Selected Literature:
Constable II, no. 499.

This painting has hitherto remained unknown but for a brief description provided by Constable, along with incorrect measurements and with the location given as 'Private collection, England'. In notes made at the time (now in the care of the present writer), he recorded that it was 'hung too high to measure'. Had Constable been able to examine it more closely, no doubt he would not have concluded that it was 'of typical late broad and mechanical *capriccio* type'. In its striking composition, delicacy of handling and general charm the painting ranks among the most successful *capricci* of the artist's English years. Its effect derives from the contrast between the rustic and dilapidated foreground, handled fairly broadly (but hardly mechanically), and the polished finish of the immaculate Renaissance church beyond. This church is strongly Palladian in style, in its central plan with axial porticoes and in the shape of its dome and lantern recalling Mereworth Castle in Kent; built to the designs of Colen Campbell, Mereworth was roofed in 1723 and is one of the most celebrated masterpieces of English Palladianism.

The painting is first recorded in a manuscript catalogue compiled by a nineteenth-century forebear of the present owner, as 'Cannaletti – A sopro porta shaped picture. Subject a large ruined arch in centre, a church & some buildings & a bridge are seen thro' the arch beyond it, in the foreground is a man in a boat. Spiritedly painted'. The date of purchase is not recorded, but the mid-nineteenth century frame makes it probable that it was acquired at that date.

65

Capriccio with Reminiscences of Richmond House

Probably *c.* 1751–5
Pen and ink with grey wash over black chalk
9⅜ × 15⅛ in. (23.8 × 38.3 cm.)

The Victoria and Albert Museum, London
Exhibited at Dulwich only

Provenance:
John Barnard (inscribed on the *verso* in his hand '493').
Charles Parr Burney, successively Archdeacon of
    St Albans and Colchester.
His daughter Rosetta d'Arblay Wood ('R.D.W. 18'
    inscribed on the *verso*).
Her daughter Edith Mary Burke Wood, who married
    Sir Richard Douglas Powell, Bt. (1842–1925) and
    bequeathed the drawing with 31 others in 1934
    (Acc. no. E.3791-1934).

Selected Exhibitions:
Canada 1964–5, no. 123.

Selected Literature:
Constable I, pp. 148, note 1, and 149, pl. 148; II, no. 786(a).
Corboz 1985, I, p. 352, fig. 427; II, p. 756, no. D 158,
    illustrated.
Baetjer 2002, p. 220, fig. 11.

Although the drawing of Richmond House Terrace which Canaletto made on the spot and annotated so carefully (Cat. no. 22), may never have been used as the basis of a painting, it did bear fruit in the form of three finished drawings, 'each departing further from the facts in the interest of a more pleasing, less chaotic, and increasingly Italianate effect' (Baetjer 2002). The most developed of those is this sheet, in which the character of the subject is transformed by the removal of any trace of Westminster Bridge and its replacement by a stretch of water reminiscent of the Venetian Lagoon. The trees towards the left are also omitted, while there is a tree further to the right in place of the roof and three dormer windows of the wing of the tall central building. That has two shuttered windows under the eaves of its facing wall in an Italianate manner. A coat-of-arms replaces the window in the gable of the nearer of the two projecting wings of Richmond House. Other imaginary features are already present in two intermediary drawings, of which the finer and earlier is that in the Städel Museum, Frankfurt am Main (Fig. 65.1; Constable I, pl. 148; II, no. 786), which is signed on the reverse (Constable / Links 1976, I, pl. 231). There a prominent portico is first introduced in the facing wall, in place of the pyramidal roof, and a statue on a pedestal marks the near end of the railings bordering the terrace on the river side. The other

intermediate version, in the British Museum, was doubted by Constable but accepted by Baetjer (Constable II, no. 786(c); Baetjer 2002, Fig. 10). That differs in the figures, in the form of the portico and in all the windows of the building to the left being given shutters. The doorway within the portico is shown for the first time.

Two other versions attest to the popularity of the design. One, last recorded in the collection of Lord Howard de Walden, was accepted by Constable (Constable II, no. 786(b)), but corresponds exactly with the exhibited drawing and would seem to be copied from it. The other is unpublished but for an illustration in *Christie's Magazine* for May–June 2005 (p. 106); it was scheduled for sale at Christie's, London, on 5 July 2005, but was withdrawn before cataloguing due to doubts about its authenticity. It corresponds closely with the British Museum drawing, even in size, except that the bridge, having been sketched in with black chalk, is replaced in pen with a lagoon view.

While Constable suggested that 'since the handling is very calligraphic, Canaletto probably made the drawing after his return to Venice from England' (Canada 1964–5), all the variants except for that in Frankfurt have English provenances, and they may all equally date from the painter's English years, as Baetjer has pointed out.

Figure 65.1
Capriccio with Reminiscences of Richmond House and Westminster Bridge,
probably *c.* 1752/5, signed on the reverse, pen and brown ink
with grey wash, 9¼ × 14⅞ in. (23.5 × 37.7 cm.).
Städel Museum, Frankfurt am Main

66

Capriccio with the Arch of the Sergi at Pula

67

Capriccio with a ruined Roman Arch and a Gothic Chapel by the Venetian Lagoon

68

Capriccio with the Church of San Giorgio Maggiore and an English Gothic Bell Tower

66

Capriccio with the Arch of the Sergi at Pula

c. 1751–5
With inscription 'Canaletto' (lower left)
Pen and brown ink with grey wash over traces of pencil
15 × 21¼ in. (38.1 × 54 cm.)

The Metropolitan Museum of Art, New York,
Harris Brisbane Dick Fund, 1946
Exhibited at Yale only

Provenance:
Dominique Vivant, Baron Denon (1747–1825;
    his collector's mark).
George Guy Greville, 4th Earl of Warwick of the fourth
    creation (1818–93; his collector's mark, twice).
With Schaeffer Galleries, New York, from whom
    purchased in 1946, Harris Brisbane Dick Fund
    (Acc. no. 1946.161).

Selected Exhibitions:
Canada 1964–5, no. 98.
New York, 1989–90, no. 119.

Selected Literature:
Constable I, pl. 152; II, no. 807.
Corboz 1985, I, p. 116, fig. 120; II, p. 738, no. D 143,
    illustrated.

67

*Capriccio with a ruined Roman Arch
and a Gothic Chapel by the Venetian Lagoon*

c. 1751–5
Pen and brown ink and grey wash, with traces of white
heightening, over pencil
10 × 15⅛ in. (25.6 × 38.4 cm.)

The Detroit Institute of Arts,
Bequest of John S. Newberry
Exhibited at Yale only

Provenance:
Henry Petty-Fitzmaurice, 5th Marquess of Lansdowne
    (1845–1927); sale, Sotheby's, London, 25 March 1920,
    lot 13 (£250 to Colnaghi).
With P. & D. Colnaghi, London.
With Agnew's, London.
Philip Hofer, Cambridge, Massachusetts.
With Durlacher Brothers, New York, 1951.
John S. Newberry, New York, by whom bequeathed
    in 1965
    (Acc. no. 1965.177).

Selected Exhibitions:
Canada 1964–5, no. 124.

Selected Literature:
Constable I, p. 149, pl. 149; II, no. 790.
Corboz 1985, II, p. 736, no. D 126, illustrated.

68

*Capriccio with the Church of San Giorgio
Maggiore and an English Gothic Bell Tower*

c. 1751–5
Pen and brown ink with grey wash
12¼ × 18⅝ in. (31 × 47.3 cm.)

Lent by the Trustees of the British Museum

Provenance:
John Henderson, by whom bequeathed in 1878
    (Acc. no. 1878.12.28.4).

Selected Exhibitions:
Canada 1964–5, no. 29.
Venice 1982, no. 58.

Selected Literature:
Constable I, pl. 145; II, no. 770.
Corboz 1985, I, pp. 283 and 355, fig. 433; II, p. 755,
    no. D 150, illustrated.

Engraved:
Josef (Giuseppe) Wagner (1706–80), as plate 1 of the
Prospetti sei di altretanti Templi di Venezia (date unknown,
but presumably after 1755; one of the plates is by Wagner's
disciple Fabio Berardi (1728–88)).

These three drawings are excellent examples of 'finished'
capricci that incorporate English elements and thus cannot
have been made before 1746, but that may, on the other
hand, date from after the artist's return to Venice in 1755.
In the foreground of Cat. no. 66 is the Roman triumphal
arch, which survives today, at Pola (now Pula), a port on
the Istrian Peninsular in modern Croatia. Although that
lay for centuries within Venetian territory, it may safely be
presumed that Canaletto only knew it from a graphic
source. The depiction of the Roman amphitheatre at Pola
in another finished *capriccio* drawing (Constable / Links
1976, I, pl. 223; II, no. 848*) is taken from an etching by
Giovanni Battista Piranesi published in 1748 in *Antichità
romane fuori di Roma*, of which Joseph Smith owned a copy;
this representation of the arch, however, differs from the
corresponding print by Piranesi and its source is yet to be

identified. Rising above other Roman ruins beyond is an English gothic church tower.

Cat. no. 67 also features a Roman arch with a building in the English Perpendicular style in the background, in this case a chapel loosely reminiscent of King's College Chapel, Cambridge, the interior of which Canaletto is thought to have painted (see the entry for Cat. no. 20). Onto that has been appended a classical portico not dissimilar from that shown in Cat. no. 63. A probable source for the main feature of Cat. no. 68 is rather more easily identified, a drawing of San Giorgio Maggiore with similar lighting (Windsor; Constable I, pl. 112; II, no. 612). Its campanile has been omitted, along with its right transept, to make way for an English Gothic bell tower. To the right is a dome with minaret-like pinnacles possibly inspired by the Basilica of the Santo at Padua. In a drawing, also once in the Henderson Collection, which Constable considered a copy of a lost original (Constable I, pl. 157; II, no. 832), the bell tower and the small building to the left of the church recur, combined with features from another drawing, a *Capriccio with San Simeone Piccolo* in the Detroit Institute of Arts (Constable I, pl. 146; II, no. 777), which was engraved by Wagner as plate 2 in the *Prospetti sei di altretanti Templi di Venezia*.

The character of all three drawings suggests that they were made for sale as works of art in their own right. Cat. no. 67 is the only one of which a related painting is known, and that work, which almost certainly dates from after 1755, varies considerably in detail (Constable I, pl. 89; II, no. 484). A possibly autograph version of Cat. no. 68, formerly in the Heseltine and Oppenheimer collections, is in a private collection.

69

Capriccio of a ruined Gothic Chapel by a Sluice Gate

1754
Signed and dated 'A.C. / 1754'
  (on the keystone of the arch)
Oil on canvas
33 × 46⅜ in. (83.8 × 117.8 cm.)

The Museum of Fine Arts, Boston,
Bequest of William A. Coolidge
Exhibited at Yale only

Provenance:
Probably commissioned by Thomas, 5th Baron King
  (1712–79), and by descent at Ockham Park, near
  Guildford, Surrey, through William, 8th Baron King
  (1805–93), created Earl of Lovelace in 1838, to Peter
  Malcolm King, 4th Earl of Lovelace (1905–64), by
  whom transferred to Whitwell Hatch, Haslemere,
  Surrey, by 1926; his sale, Sotheby's, London, 13 July
  1937, lot 130.
Purchased at the sale for £1,400 by Borenius for HRH
  The Princess Royal (1897–1965), wife of Henry Charles
  George Lascelles, 6th Earl of Harewood, Harewood
  House, Yorkshire.
Her son George Henry Hubert Lascelles, 7th Earl of
  Harewood, Harewood House, Yorkshire; sale, Christie's,
  London, 2 July 1965, lot 79 (14,500 guineas to the
  Hallsborough Gallery).
With the Hallsborough Gallery, London.
William Appleton Coolidge, Cambridge, Massachusetts,
  by whom purchased from the above in 1967 and
  bequeathed to the present owner in 1993
  (Acc. no. 1993.33).

Selected Exhibitions:
New York 1989–90, no. 77.

Selected Literature:
Finberg 1938, pp. 69–70, pl. IB.
Constable I, pp. 41, 96, 146-7, 149 and 165, pl. 87;
　II, no. 475.
Puppi 1968, no. 305, illustrated.
Links 1981, no. 243, illustrated.
Corboz 1985, I, pp. 294 and 299; II, p. 461, fig. 510, and
　p. 703, no. P 365, illustrated.
Constable / Links 1989, I, pp. lxxvi–lxxvii, 41, 96,
　146–7, 149 and 165, pl. 87; II, no. 475.
Sutton 1995, pp. 14 and 60–3, no. 10, illustrated in colour.

Near a sluice in the foreground is a ruined English Gothic chapel, which the 1937 sale catalogue and Finberg both describe as 'slightly reminiscent of Eton College Chapel'. Although that comment has been repeated in almost every mention of the painting since then, the building in fact bears little resemblance to Eton College Chapel. It is, as Christopher Wright kindly pointed out some years ago, rather more similar to St Catherine's Chapel, which stands by the Godalming Road about three quarters of a mile south of the centre of Guildford (Fig. 69.1), a setting high above the River Wey that is very different. It is of three rather than five bays; it has no gable on the east wall; built in 1317, its arches are all pointed. It is of far more appropriate scale, however, and its proximity to Ockham Park makes it a likely candidate for Canaletto's source if one accepts that two of its companions, Cat. nos 70, 71, deliberately recall the Surrey landscape in the vicinity. Furthermore, the loss of the tracery in its east window might explain why Canaletto, who never shows an understanding of English Gothic architecture, has depicted what appears to be a fresco rather than the stained glass which would have been more appro-priate to the English setting. Finberg also suggests, more plausibly, that 'the water recalls the Thames … and some of the buildings resemble Thames-side houses'. If so, the domed, circular building near the centre might be seen as a reminiscence of the Rotunda at Ranelagh (see Fig. 34.1), although it also recalls the building shown in the *capriccio* at Worcester (Cat. no. 63). There is no London parallel for the buildings to the right, the one with pinnacles somewhat resembling that in the distance in a later *capriccio* which also shows a lock in the foreground (Constable I, pl. 90; II, no. 493).

Figure 69.1
St Catherine's Chapel, Guildford

A drawing in the Städel Museum, Frankfurt am Main, shows the composition in reverse (Fig. 69.2; Constable I, pl. 157; II, no. 831). Of rather summary handling and differing in the shape of the keystone and in showing only two figures, in different poses, its purpose is uncertain.

The painting formed part of the largest cycle of paintings executed by Canaletto during his English years, that from the collection of the Barons King and subsequently the Earls of Lovelace which was dispersed at Sotheby's, London, in 1937. Constable repeatedly refers to six paintings and Baetjer and Links express their satisfaction at having 'reunited' the six 'Lovelace capriccios' (New York 1989–90, p. 256), but in fact the cycle comprised seven paintings (lots 129–35 in the 1937 sale), the overlooked component being the most impressive, *The Bacino di San Marco on Ascension Day* (Fig. 17; Constable I, pl. 65; II, no. 343). Hidden in private collections but for appearances at Sotheby's in 1973 and Christie's in July 2005, it is clearly not a *capriccio*, and another painting from the group shows *The Island of San Michele in the Venetian Lagoon* with little divergence from reality (Private Collection, U.S.A.; Constable I, pl. 67; II, no. 367). The other components were indeed *capricci*, Cat. nos 70–1 and a pair showing *Roman Ruins with a Classical Church and the Colleoni Monument* (Fig. 13; Constable I, pl. 88; II, no. 478) and *A Renaissance Palace with a large Gateway* (Fig. 14; Constable I, pl. 92; II, no. 504).

The date of 1754 on this painting probably represents not just the date of its completion but that of the whole cycle, and suggests that the other components of the group may be dated to 1753/4. Such precise dating is rare among Canaletto's English works in this genre, and is of particular interest since it demonstrates to what extent the artist's approach could be influenced by the intended purpose of the work at hand. While the relatively small 'cabinet' paintings of views executed for Thomas Hollis in the same year are characterised by quite intricate handling and sombre tone, with strong localised highlights (see Cat. nos 4, 15, 33 and 37; Figs 10, 28.1), the King paintings, all large and with a predominantly decorative function, are bright, colourful and broadly handled. As Finberg points out, there are striations clearly visible on the surface of this painting 'due to the priming of the canvas having been applied with an unusually coarse brush'.

The date does little, however, to help ascertain the patron who commissioned the paintings, the candidates being three brothers, Peter, 3rd Baron King (1709–1754), William, 4th Baron King (1711–1767) or Thomas, 5th Baron King (1712–1779). Finberg, followed by Baetjer and Links, favoured the 3rd or 4th Barons, but the family tradition, recorded by Constable, that it was the 5th Baron who was responsible seems much the most probable. He alone married (in 1734) an heiress, Catherine Troye (known as 'the Dutch heiress'), is known to have sent his son on the Grand Tour (see Ingamells 1997, p. 577), and is recorded as a patron of contemporary artists, commissioning a pair of paintings from Claude-Joseph Vernet in 1767–8 (sold from the estate of Manon, Countess of Lovelace, at Christie's, London, 10 December 1993, lot 55). In the absence of documentation, it remains uncertain whether the paintings were intended for Ockham Park, which had been remodelled by Hawksmoor in 1725–9 and was largely demolished in 1949 after a fire, or (more probably, if the 5th Baron was indeed the patron) for a London house.

Figure 69.2
Capriccio of a ruined Gothic Chapel by a Sluice Gate, probably 1754, pen and brown ink with grey wash, 7¾ × 13 in. (19.7 × 33 cm.). Städel Museum, Frankfurt am Main

70

An Imaginary Landscape with a Palace

71

An Imaginary Landscape with a Column

70

An Imaginary Landscape with a Palace

Probably 1754
Oil on canvas
52¾ × 42⅞ in. (134 × 108.8 cm.)

The National Gallery of Art, Washington, D.C.,
Paul Mellon Collection

Provenance:
As for Cat. no. 69 until 1937; 1937 sale, lot 134
   (£1,800 to Knoedler).
With M. Knoedler & Co., London.
Philip Hill (d. 1944), a merchant banker and landowner,
   by whom purchased from the above in 1937.
Mrs Philip Hill, subsequently Mrs Warwick Bryant,
   South Africa.
With Arthur Tooth & Sons, London, by whom purchased
   from the above in 1959 and sold in May of that year to
   Dr Nathan, Zürich.
With Rosenberg & Stiebel, New York.
Paul Mellon, by whom purchased in December 1960 and
   given to the present owner in 1964
   (Acc. no. 1964.2.2).

Selected Exhibitions:
New York 1989–90, no. 75.
Birmingham 1993–4, no. 37.

Selected Literature:
Finberg 1938, pp. 69–70, pl. II A.
Constable I, p. 146, pl. 87; II, no. 473.
Puppi 1968, no. 307, illustrated.
Links 1981, no. 241, illustrated.
Links 1982, p. 192, pl. 185.
Corboz 1985, I, p. 294; II, p. 704, no. P 367, illustrated.
Links 1994, pp. 211 and 214, pls 175 (colour detail) and
   185 (colour).
Bowron 1996, pp. 35 and 38–9, illustrated in colour.

71

An Imaginary Landscape with a Column

Probably 1754
Oil on canvas
52¾ × 41⅞ in. (134 × 106.4 cm.)

The National Gallery of Art, Washington, D.C.,
Paul Mellon Collection

Provenance:
As for Cat. no. 70; 1937 sale, lot 133 (£1,250 to Knoedler).
   (Acc. no. 1964.2.1).

Selected Exhibitions:
New York 1989–90, no. 76.
Birmingham 1993–4, no. 38.

Selected Literature:
Finberg 1938, pp. 69–70, pl. II B.
Constable I, p. 146, pl. 87; II, no. 474.
Puppi 1968, no. 308, illustrated.
Links 1981, no. 242, illustrated.
Links 1982, p. 192, pl. 186.
Corboz 1985, I, pp. 294 and 299, figs 357–8
   (colour details); II, p. 704, no. P 368, illustrated.
Links 1994, pp. 211 and 214, pl. 186 (colour).
Bowron 1996, pp. 35 and 38–9, illustrated in colour.

Publishing for the first time four of the seven paintings from
the collection of the Barons King, subsequently Earls of
Lovelace (see Cat. no. 69), Finberg points out that these
two paintings

> *contain unmistakable impressions of the Surrey landscape in the*
> *neighbourhood of Ockham Park, the seat of Lord Lovelace's*
> *ancestors ... In the first,* Capriccio, with Palace, *the*
> *background is filled by a wooded hill with ascending chalk paths,*
> *a vivid reminiscence of Box Hill, which is not far from Ockham.*
> *On the hill are various buildings: a church with pointed slate*
> *steeple, similar to that at Great Bookham in Surrey; a farm; and,*
> *somewhat incongruously, a Roman arch ... our countryside so*
> *influenced [Canaletto] that in these 'Surrey' Capricci we may*
> *find the beginnings of the English school of landscape painting.*

Finberg's enthusiasm has been shared by all subsequent
writers, Baetjer and Links describing the two paintings as
'among the most exceptionally improbable, and successful,
pictures of this type that Canaletto ever painted' (New York
1989–90).

What makes these paintings unique among Canaletto's
works of the imagination is, indeed, his capture of the
character of the English landscape. This is a surprising
achievement in the absence of any drawings by him of the
English countryside, as Baetjer and Links, followed by
Bowron, point out, and is made all the more remarkable by
most of the buildings and other architectural elements
depicted being strongly Italianate in flavour. The English
gothic church on the left in Cat. no. 70 is dwarfed by the
ruined fragment of an Ionic arcade, and that on the distant
hill is dominated by the triumphal arch on the summit. The
palace in classical style on the right has been said to look like
Ockham Park, but it bears little resemblance to what we
know of the then appearance of the house (which is not near
a river and stands in open countryside). The most prominent
feature in Cat. no. 71 is a column supporting the statue of a
male saint. Beyond are a triumphal arch and a particularly
un-English fortress on a hill, while the town on the horizon
more closely resembles Padua than anywhere in England.
As Links has observed, 'both give the impression that the
artist was invited to show the neighbourhood of Box Hill
as it might have looked had some Italian architects been
building there'.

In the right foreground of Cat. no. 70 is an exotic type
of gondola carrying figures in oriental costume, one of whom
holds a parasol. A 'Chinaman' holding a parasol sits in a
similarly exotic boat at the lower left in the ex-Sobell
Capriccio of a Renaissance Pavilion flanked by two ruined classical
Arches over a Waterway by the Venetian Lagoon (Constable I,
pl. 93; II, no. 511), and a similarly attired figure is one of the
gondoliers in the right foreground of *The Bacino di San Marco*
on Ascension Day also from the King group (Fig. 17). Such
figures are not found in Canaletto's work done in Italy and it
is highly tempting to connect them with the 'Chinese barge,
and the rowers in Chinese habits', a favoured means of
transport of the Prince of Wales in 1749 (see pp. 24–6). It has
also been suggested that, like the presence of views of Venice
in English collections – and above all those of the Bacino di
San Marco on Ascension Day – the inclusion of 'Chinamen' may have been intended to convey a political message.

Exhibitions

Birmingham 1993–4 — Birmingham, Museums and Art Gallery, *Canaletto & England*, 14 October 1993 – 9 January 1994. Catalogue ed. by M. Liversidge and J. Farrington

Bergamo 1969 — Bergamo, Galleria Lorenzelli, September–October 1969, *Venezia '700: Francesco Guardi e il suo temp nelle raccolte private bergamasche*

Canada 1964–5 — Toronto, Art Gallery of Toronto, 17 October – 15 November 1964; Ottawa, National Gallery of Canada, 4 December 1964 – 10 January 1965, and Montreal, Museum of Fine Arts, 29 January – 28 February 1965, *Canaletto*. Catalogue by W.G. Constable

London 1977 — London, Somerset House, *London and The Thames: Paintings of Three Centuries*, 6 July – 9 October 1977. Catalogue by H. Preston

London 1980–1 — London, The Queen's Gallery, *Canaletto. Paintings & Drawings*, 1980–1. Catalogue by O. Millar

London 2003 — London, British Museum, *London 1753*, 23 May – 23 November 2003. Catalogue by S. O'Connell

London 2005 — Johnny Van Haeften, *Dutch and Flemish Old Master Paintings*, 15 December 2005

New York 1983 — Colnaghi, New York, *Views from the Grand Tour*, 25 May – 30 June 1983.

New York 1989–90 — New York, Metropolitan Museum of Art, *Canaletto*, 30 October 1989 – 21 January 1990. Catalogue by K. Baetjer and J.G. Links

Rome 2005 — Rome, Palazzo Giustiniani, *Canaletto: Il trionfo della veduta*, 12 March – 19 June 2005. Catalogue by B.A. Kowalczyk

Turin, Montreal, Washington & Marseille 1999–2000 — Turin, Palazzina di Caccia di Stupinigi, July–November 1999, Montreal Museum of Fine Arts, December 1999–April 2000, Washington, National Gallery of Art, May–October 2000, and Marseille, Musée des Beaux-Arts, February–May 2001, *The Triumph of the Baroque: Architecture in Europe 1600–1750*

Venice 1982 — Venice, Fondazione Giorgio Cini, *Canaletto: Disegni – Dipinti – Incisioni*, 1982. Catalogue ed. A. Bettagno

Vicenza 1973 — Vicenza, Basilica Palladiana, *Palladio*, 1973

Literature

Baetjer 2002 — K. Baetjer, 'A Drawing by Canaletto of Richmond House Terrace', *Metropolitan Museum Journal*, vol. 37, 2002, pp. 213–22

Beddington 2004 — C. Beddington, 'Bernardo Bellotto and his circle in Italy. Part 1: not Canaletto but Bellotto', *The Burlington Magazine*, CXLVI, No. 1219, October 2004, pp. 665–74

Bold 2000 — J. Bold, *Greenwich: An Architectural History of the Royal Hospital for Seamen and the Queen's House*, New Haven and London, 2000

Bowron 1996 — E.P. Bowron in D. De Grazia, E. Garberson *et al.*, *The Collections of the National Gallery of Art Systematic Catalogue: Italian Paintings of the Seventeenth and Eighteenth Centuries*, Washington, 1996

Buttery 1987 — D. Buttery, 'Canaletto at Warwick', *The Burlington Magazine*, CXXIX, No. 1012, July 1987, pp. 437–45

Buttery 1992 — D. Buttery, *Canaletto and Warwick Castle*, Chichester, 1992

Conisbee 1976 — P. Conisbee, catalogue of the exhibition *Claude-Joseph Vernet 1714–1789*, Kenwood, London, 4 June – 19 September 1976, and Musée de la Marine, Palais de Chaillot, Paris, 14 October 1976 – 9 January 1977

Constable 1923 — W.G. Constable, 'Some unpublished Canalettos', *The Burlington Magazine*, XLII, No. 243, June 1923, pp. 278–88

Constable 1927 — W.G. Constable, 'Canaletto in England: Some Further Works, *The Burlington Magazine*, I, No. 286, January 1927, pp. 17–23

Constable 1929 — W.G. Constable, 'Canaletto at the Magnasco Society', *The Burlington Magazine*, LV, No. 316, July 1929, pp. 46–50

Constable — W.G. Constable, *Canaletto*, London, 1962 (unless otherwise stated the 1976 and 1989 editions repeat the same information without alteration)

Constable/Links 1976 — W.G. Constable, *Canaletto*, 2nd ed. revised by J.G. Links, Oxford, 1976

Constable/Links 1989 — W.G. Constable, *Canaletto*, 2nd ed. revised by J.G. Links reissued with supplement and additional plates, Oxford, 1989

Corboz 1985 — A. Corboz, *Canaletto. Una Venezia immaginaria*, Milan, 1985

Dacey 1981 — J. Dacey, 'A note on Canaletto's views of Greenwich', *The Burlington Magazine*, CXIII, No. 941, August 1981, pp. 485–7

Defoe 1724–27 — D. Defoe, *A Tour thro' the whole island of Great Britain*, London, 1724–27

Delany 1861–62 — M. Delany, *The Autobiography and Correspondence of Mary Granville, Mrs. Delany...*, ed. Lady Llanover, London, 1861–62

Eglin 1999 — J. Eglin, 'Venice on the Thames: Venetian Vedutisti and the London View in the Eighteenth Century', in *Italian Culture in Northern Europe in the Eighteenth Century*, ed. S. West, Cambridge, 1999, pp. 101–15

Eglin 2001   J. Eglin, *Venice Transfigured: The Myth of Venice in British Culture, 1660–1797*, New York, 2001

Einberg 1992   E. Einberg, *Canaletto: 'The Old Horse Guards from St James's Park'*, London, 1992

Finberg 1921   H.F. Finberg, 'Canaletto in England', *The Walpole Society*, IX, 1921, pp. 21–76

Finberg 1922   H.F. Finberg, 'Canaletto in England: additional illustrations and notes', *The Walpole Society*, X, 1922, pp. 75–8

Finberg 1938   H.F. Finberg, 'The Lovelace Canalettos', *The Burlington Magazine*, LXXII, No. 419, February 1938, pp. 69–70

Fitzgerald 1973   D. Fitzgerald, *The Norfolk Music Room*, London, 1973

Haskell 1980   F. Haskell, *Patrons and Painters*, New Haven and London, 1980

Hayes 1958   J. Hayes, 'Parliament Street and Canaletto's Views of Whitehall', *The Burlington Magazine*, October 1958, pp. 341–9

Ingamells 1997   J. Ingamells, *A Dictionary of British and Irish Travellers in Italy 1701–1800 compiled from the Brinsley Ford Archive*, New Haven and London, 1997

Kerslake 1977   J. Kerslake, *National Portrait Gallery: Early Georgian Portraits*, London, 1977

Kingzett 1982   R. Kingzett, 'A Catalogue of the Works of Samuel Scott', *The Walpole Society*, XLVIII, 1982, pp. 1–134

Kozakiewicz 1972   S. Kozakiewicz, *Bernardo Bellotto*, London, 1972

Labelye 1751   C. Labelye, *A description of Westminster Bridge*, London, 1751

Levey 1971   M. Levey, *National Gallery Catalogues: The Seventeenth and Eighteenth Century Italian Schools*, London, 1971

Links 1981   J.G. Links, *Canaletto. The Complete Paintings*, London, 1981

Links 1982   J.G. Links, *Canaletto*, Oxford, 1982

Links 1994   J.G. Links, *Canaletto*, 2nd ed., London, 1994

Links 1998   J.G. Links, *A Supplement to W. G. Constable's Canaletto*, London, 1998

Lugt 1921   F. Lugt, *Marques de Collections*, Amsterdam, 1921

Parker 1948   K.T. Parker, *The Drawings of Antonio Canaletto in the Collection of His Majesty the King at Windsor Castle*, Oxford and London, 1948

Pevsner and Cherry 1973   N. Pevsner and B. Cherry, *London I: The Cities of London and Westminster, The Buildings of England*, Harmondsworth 1973

Phillips 1951   H. Phillips, *The Thames about 1750*, London, 1951

Picard 2000   L. Picard, *Dr Johnson's London*, London, 2000

Puppi 1968   L. Puppi, *L'opera completa del Canaletto*, Milan, 1968

Redford 1996   B. Redford, *Venice & the Grand Tour*, New Haven and London, 1996

Reveley 1820   *Notices Illustrative of the Drawings and Sketches of some of the most Distinguished Masters in all the Principal Schools of Design by the late Henry Reveley, Esq.*, London, 1820

Russell 1988   F. Russell, 'Canaletto and Joli at Chesterfield House', *The Burlington Magazine*, CXXX, No. 1025, August 1988, pp. 627–30

Russell 1999   F. Russell, Review of Links 1998, *The Burlington Magazine*, CXLI, No. 1152, March 1999, pp. 180–1

Sewter 1949   A.C. Sewter, 'Another English Canaletto', *The Burlington Magazine*, March 1949, pp. 82–3

Sutton 1995   P.C. Sutton, *The William Appleton Coolidge Collection*, Boston, 1995

Verey and Brooks 2000   *Gloucestershire I: The Cotswolds, The Buildings of England*, London, 2000

Vertue *Note Books*   G. Vertue, *Note Books*, in *Walpole Society*, 6 vols, London, 1930–47

Walker 1979   R.J.B. Walker, *Old Westminster Bridge: The Bridge of Fools*, London, 1979

Walpole *Correspondence*   H. Walpole, *The Yale edition of Horace Walpole's Correspondence*, New Haven 1937–83

Watson 1949   F.J.B. Watson, *Canaletto*, London/New York, 1949

Watson 1950   F.J.B. Watson, 'Some Unpublished Canaletto Drawings of London', *The Burlington Magazine*, XCII, No. 572, November 1950, pp. 315–19

Worsley 1995   G. Worsley, *Classical Architecture in Britain: The Heroic Age*, New Haven and London, 1995

Photo Credits

All illustrations are courtesy of the Canaletto Archive with the exception of the following illustrations. Every effort has been made to credit the photographers and the sources; if there are errors or omissions, please contact Yale University Press so that correction can be made in any subsequent edition.

The Sir Andrew Lloyd Webber Art Foundation, Cat. 17

Beinecke Rare Book and Manuscript Library, Yale University, Fig. 7

Birmingham Museums & Art Gallery, Cat. nos 21, 45, 46

The Lord Brabourne, Photo by Prudence Cuming Associates Ltd., Cat. nos 58, 59

© Copyright the Trustees of The British Museum, Cat. nos 3, 18, 28, 36, 49, 68

By kind permission of His Grace the Duke of Buccleuch & Queensberry, KT, Photo by Penny Davies Photography, Fig. 8

Compton Verney, Photo by Prudence Cuming Associates Ltd., Cat. nos 31, 32

© Coram Family in the care of the Foundling Museum, London / The Bridgeman Art Library, Figs 20, 21

© Samuel Courtauld Trust, Courtauld Institute of Art Gallery / The Bridgeman Art Library, Fig. 7.1

Photograph © 1991 The Detroit Institute of Arts, Cat. 67

Courtesy of Simon C. Dickinson Ltd., Fig. 13.2, Cat. nos 11, 27, 57

By permission of the Trustees of Dulwich Picture Gallery, Frontispiece, Cat. 37

The J. Paul Getty Museum, Los Angeles, Cat. nos 48, 51

The Trustees of the Goodwood Collection, Figs 25, 26

© 2006 Presidents and Fellows of Harvard College, Fig. 63.1

© Lobkowicz Collections, Nelahozeves Castle, Czech Republic/ The Bridgeman Art Library, Figs 5, 6, 27

Photograph © 1982 The Metropolitan Museum of Art, Cat. 47

Photograph © 1989 The Metropolitan Museum of Art, Cat. 66

By Permission of the Ministero per i Beni e le Attività Culturali, Venice, Figs 4.1, 16.1, 16.2

The Minneapolis Institute of Arts, Cat. 14

Moor Park, Hertfordshire, UK, John Bethell/ The Bridgeman Art Library, Fig. 22

Photograph © 2006 Museum of Fine Arts, Boston, Cat. 69

© Museum of London, UK/ The Bridgeman Art Library, Fig. 20.1

© National Gallery, London, Cat. nos 33, 40

Image © Board of Trustees, National Gallery of Art, Washington, Cat. nos 70, 71

National Gallery of Victoria, Melbourne, Australia, Cat. 55

© National Maritime Museum, London, Cat. 1, Fig. 2.1

© National Portrait Gallery, London, Fig. 2

National Trust, Cat. 34, Fig. 34.1

Reproduced by kind permission of His Grace The Duke of Norfolk, Arundel Castle, Cat. nos 60, 61, 62

Collection of the Duke of Northumberland, Figs 12, 14.1

Collection of the Duke of Northumberland, Photo by John Hammond, Fig. 29, Cat. nos 24, 25, 35, 41

The Philadelphia Museum of Art, Photo by Graydon Wood, Cat. 54

Private Collection, Fig. 28, Cat. nos 42, 43

The Royal Collection © 2006, Her Majesty Queen Elizabeth II, Fig. 54.1, Cat. nos 7, 8, 9, 10, 26, 29, 30

Courtesy of the Trustees of Sir John Soane's Museum, London / The Bridgeman Art Library, Fig. 1

Sotheby's Picture Library, Cat. 20

Städel Museum, Frankfurt am Main, Photo by Ursula Edelmann, Fig. 65.1

© Tate, London 2006, Cat. 2

Thyssen-Bornemisza Collection, Madrid, Spain / The Bridgeman Art Library, Fig. 44.2

© Tokyo Fuji Art Museum, Tokyo, Japan / The Bridgeman Art Library, Cat. nos 52, 53

V&A Images / Victoria and Albert Museum, Cat. 65

Copyright: Dean and Chapter of Westminster, Cat. 19

Worcester Art Museum, Worcester, Massachusetts, Cat. 63

Richard Caspole, Yale Center for British Art, Cover, Figs 18, 19, 23, 6.1, Cat. nos 4, 5, 6, 12, 13, 23, 38, 39, 44

Index

References to catalogue entries are followed by page numbers (in brackets).
Numbers in *italic* refer to pages on which there are figures.